Biology and violence

Biology and violence

From birth to adulthood

DEBORAH W. DENNO
University of Pennsylvania

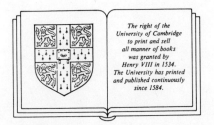

The right of the
University of Cambridge
to print and sell
all manner of books
was granted by
Henry VIII in 1534.
The University has printed
and published continuously
since 1584.

CAMBRIDGE UNIVERSITY PRESS

Cambridge
New York   Port Chester   Melbourne   Sydney

Published by the Press Syndicate of the University of Cambridge
The Pitt Building, Trumpington Street, Cambridge CB2 1RP
40 West 20th Street, New York, NY 10011, USA
10 Stamford Road, Oakleigh, Melbourne 3166, Australia

First published 1990

Library of Congress Cataloging-in-Publication Data
Denno, Deborah W.
Biology and violence : from birth to adulthood / Deborah W. Denno.
  p. cm.
Includes bibliographical references.
ISBN 0–521–36219–9
1. Criminal behavior – Pennsylvania – Philadelphia – Longitudinal
studies. I. Title.
HV6795.P5D46 1989
364.2'09748'11–dc20   89–70781
                                      CIP

British Library Cataloguing in Publication Data
Denno, Deborah W.
Biology and violence : from birth to adulthood.
1. Man. Criminal behaviour. Biological factors.
I. Title
364.2'4

ISBN 0–521–36219–9 hardback

Typeset in Times 10/12.5 pt by Graphicraft Typesetters Ltd., Hong Kong
Printed in the United States of America

To my parents

Contents

Foreword

The Collaborative Perinatal Project (CPP), launched in 1959, was one of the most ambitious and costly medical projects undertaken until then. Designed to obtain base-line data on birth defects, the project has yielded hundreds of ancillary books and articles in the medical literature. This remarkable study covered twelve cities, including Philadelphia, and when the data collection process ended the original records were put into storage. Upon learning of the project, and having engaged in an earlier birth cohort study, I sought permission to access the files and had significant physiological, psychological, and psychiatric data converted to computer tape for future use.

When the National Institute of Justice learned of our data bank, we were encouraged to submit a proposal that would link the CPP data with school records and files from the Juvenile Aid Division of the Philadelphia Police Department in order to determine how many of the children born each year of the project had a record of delinquency. Our previous experience with a 1945 birth cohort informed us about how to analyze delinquency through the span of years from age 10 to age 18. Because most of the staff of the Sellin Center for Studies in Criminology was involved in yet another birth cohort – those born in 1958 – it was necessary for me, as director of the Center, to select someone capable of learning the medical literature in order to make the proper analytical linkages with the known sociological variables and forms of delinquent behaviors. That someone, I knew from the beginning, was Deborah Denno.

The author of this volume has mastered the language of medical science, quantitative analysis, and sociological concepts to such an extent that in her person there is an interdisciplinarity that many of us have called for in criminology over the years. This young scholar has both the medical term *anomia* and the sociological term *anomie* under her commanding understanding. This volume represents years of devoted scholarship and intensive research, a grand product for the author and our Center. Colleagues in different disciplines should find this volume a mine of information in the review of relevant literature and in insightful analysis of new data.

Marvin E. Wolfgang
Philadelphia, Pennslyvania

Preface

Twelve years ago when I was a graduate student following the typical rites of passage for getting my Ph.D. at the Sellin Center for Studies in Criminology and Criminal Law, University of Pennsylvania, Marvin Wolfgang asked me if I wanted to analyze the criminal records of a sample of subjects who had participated in one of the largest medical studies in this country. When he described the study's data, I knew that I would want to be part of any effort to examine possible links that could exist between biology and crime. What I did not know was that the results of the ensuing "Biosocial Project" would form my dissertation and that the Project would dominate the next ten years of my professional life.

Those ten years were immensely enriching, but also frustrating. The Biosocial Project seemed always to be shrouded in politics. From the start, I was continually concerned that the Project might be discontinued because some influential social scientists at the time thought that any studies involving biological data were oppressive or fascist. A number of my colleagues told me that they could not understand why the Criminology Center had agreed to take on the Project because it wasn't "mainstream sociology." In the isolated apprehension that one often acquires as a graduate student, I feared that as time went on I might not be able to finish my dissertation and that my professional goals would be tainted as a result of my association with the Project. I did not attempt to write or publish anything from the Project the first year it was funded. Even after I got my Ph.D., I was aware that I might never be able to complete the additional data collection efforts and analyses necessary for this book because grant reviewers so strictly favor mainstream topics.

As both an attorney and a social scientist now, and thus with perhaps a somewhat broader perspective on my past experiences, it seems even more disturbing that such fears existed, although they have hardly ceased for others; biosocial studies of crime are still regarded skeptically and biosocial criminologists are still academically detached. Regardless, there has been a relatively greater acceptance of multidisciplinary research within the last decade and an optimistic harbinger might suppose that a number of disciplines will begin to see the lights that shine from other fields.

The purpose of this book is to analyze, from a variety of disciplines and methodologies, the lives of a select group of nearly 1,000 subjects and their families who were studied from the time of the subjects' births through their young adult years. Although this book focuses on the links between biology and violence, it also provides new information on other areas, such as intelligence, achievement, and the family. The depth of this information is enhanced because the subjects are analyzed with two different methodologies: statistically, as a group, and individually, through a study of detailed home interviews. As the home interviews show, many of the subjects in the Biosocial Project were victims of physical or sexual abuse, regardless of whether or not they became violent offenders. One value of a multidisciplinary approach, however, is the recognition that, in an attempt to eliminate precursors of crime, we can also try to remedy those factors associated with a number of different types of social pain that may not be represented through an official police record.

Over the life span of the Biosocial Project, I have become indebted to numerous individuals and agencies. Foremost is my gratitude to my mentor, Marvin Wolfgang, who has been a constant source of intellectual inspiration and support ever since I met him. It was Marvin's eminent contributions to theory and research in criminology that first drew me to the field; it is his personal integrity, erudition, and deep concern for his students that have made the Biosocial Project work so rewarding. The Project never would have started or survived without his care and academic courage. I cannot express strongly enough my thanks to him.

The Biosocial Project's research funding was provided entirely by the National Institute of Justice, the U.S. Department of Justice. Funding for this book in particular was provided by Grant No. 85–IJ–CX–0034. Points of view expressed in this book are my own and do not necessarily represent the views of the U.S. Department of Justice. I am most grateful for the research support from the National Institute of Justice and for the informed supervision of the Biosocial Project's primary grant monitors, Helen Erskine and Winifred Reed.

Frank Elliott has been an exceptional instructor in the areas of biology and crime. I owe a great debt for the time, care, and attention to detail that he has given to my work, and for his advice and continuous encouragement.

I thank Steven Aurand for his excellent data preparation, computer programming, technical assistance, and analytical commentary throughout the Project. I am also most appreciative of Neil Weiner's generosity and unfailing support and friendship.

Much credit is due to the many individuals whose work or advice contributed to the Biosocial Project: Paul Allison, Richard Clelland, Erica Ginsburg, Ruben Gur, Solomon Katz, Mark Keintz, Esther Lafair, Sarnoff Mednick, Ben Meijs, Terrie Moffitt, Israel Nachshon, and Selma Pastor. I am also grateful for Katharita Lamoza's careful copyediting. Finally, the Biosocial Project could never have been conducted without the contributions of the following organizations and their members: the graduate students and research assistants at the Criminology Center; members of the Philadelphia police and the Philadelphia School Board; and researchers at the Institute for the Continuous Study of Man.

Introduction

In recent years, rapid growth in the biological sciences has greatly increased knowledge about the complexity and diversity of human development. Such advancements have propelled the study of a variety of social disorders, ranging from alcoholism to depression and psychiatric disturbance. Relatively few studies, however, have examined biological links to criminal behavior – a topic that sparks both controversy and criticism in an area of study that has depended, for the most part, on sociological and environmental explanations of even extreme violence.

Research on biological features of criminal behavior, and its accompanying controversy, is not new. Over a century ago Cesare Lombroso, an Italian physician, suggested that some individuals were "born" criminals with distinct physical features that he thought characterized primitive men, such as sloping foreheads, long arms, and flat feet (Lombroso, 1968; see Wolfgang, 1955, for a review of Lombroso's work). Lombroso's research was severely and justifiably criticized in both substance and methodology (Wolfgang, 1955). His major formulations, however, portrayed an originality apart from nineteenth-century thought and influence and, appropriately or not, they have had a large impact on modern criminological theory and studies of crime.

As in history, current interest in biological correlates of behavior has often been perceived synonymously with radical reductionism, the philosophy that all behavior can be explained in biological terms. Edward O. Wilson's introduction of "sociobiology," for example (Wilson, 1975, 1977; Lumsden and Wilson, 1981), has generated concerns by some that all individual differences will be biologically interpreted, thereby fueling prejudices among the different sexes, races, and social classes (Kitcher, 1985; Montagu, 1980). In turn, a minority of scholars view biological explanations of behavior as enlightening, not endangering (Caplan, 1978; Mednick Pollock, Volavka, and Gabrielli, 1982). Even Wilson acknowledges the limits of absolute reductionism (Wilson, 1977: 37–38).

1

The current examination of biological differences in crime confronts a similar type of dilemma, namely, the longstanding controversy between environmental (nurture) and biological (nature) orientations in science. Are we "blank slates" ultimately defined by social and cultural forces or are we genetically predetermined organisms with prescribed roles to play? Is our behavior malleable and perfectable or is it constrained and resistant to change? Are we inherently gentle and altruistic or are we aggressive, even violent beings, barely civilized by our culture? More specifically, are the "criminals" in our society "born" or "made," a product of their biology or their environment?

Questions that probe the origins of criminal behavior are no less difficult to answer than those that concern the evolution of our humanness and our identity, the many mirrors of our selves in a culture that we learned to create either through instinct or through one another. Increasingly, research evidence suggests that a variety of both biological and environmental factors influence criminal behavior. (For reviews see Denno, 1982, 1985, 1988; Elliott, 1988; Mednick et al., 1982; Mednick, Moffitt, and Stack, 1987; Moffitt, in press; Moyer, 1987; Siann, 1985; Wilson and Herrnstein, 1985.) As yet, it is unknown, however, how these factors interact or which factors are the predominant predictors of crime.

The examination of many facets of behavior is one of the most necessary goals in the study of crime and, at the same time, one of the most ignored in actual research. The seeming indifference in the field of criminology to contributions in the biological sciences is not accidental. In part it reflects a concern that the acceptance of biological theories of crime reduces the importance of environmental factors. It also demonstrates the tendency for the different biological and environmental sciences to work in isolation, each using its own language and technique, each ultimately discouraging interdisciplinary mergence and exchange (Denno and Schwarz, 1985).

Such differences pit one research bias against the other, with neither approach singly able to discern the more complex components of behavior. Previous attempts to develop criminological theories have often failed to acknowledge variations in the physiological and psychological capabilities of individuals for learning socially approved behavior. In turn, many efforts to study biological factors in crime have ignored even the most obvious environmental and sociological influences (Denno, 1982, 1985).

One method of unraveling biological and environmental predictors of criminal behavior is to examine a sample of individuals *longitudinally* – that is, from birth through childhood, adolescence, and early adulthood.

An assessment of multiple kinds of variables collected at key developmental points over time would provide information on the possible importance of maturational changes, a factor frequently bypassed in crime research. It would also be important to study the interrelation among these factors in a group of individuals who are demographically and environmentally at a high risk for criminal behavior – for example, black and lower socioeconomic children – as most studies of crime have focused on relatively low-risk subjects (Raspberry, 1980).

In their recent review of research on crime, Wilson and Herrnstein (1985: 512, 513) emphasize the lack of longitudinal information available in the social sciences on the complex interactions among biology, environment, and crime, particularly among high-risk samples. They suggest the need for longitudinal research on black children in particular to determine the contributions of select social and environmental influences, including family structure and socioeconomic status (1985: 478).

This book describes the results of the "Biosocial Project," one of the largest research studies in this country on the relationship between crime and the biological and environmental influences on "high-risk" individuals. The Biosocial Project examined in detail numerous biological, psychological, and environmental variables collected on nearly 1,000 individuals followed from birth through early adulthood in Philadelphia. These individuals were selected from a total sample of nearly 10,000 families who participated in the Philadelphia Collaborative Perinatal Project at Pennsylvania Hospital between 1959 and 1966. Pennsylvania Hospital was one of twelve medical centers included by the National Institute of Neurological Diseases and Stroke in a nationwide study of genetic, biological, and environmental influences upon child development (Niswander and Gordon, 1972).

The Biosocial Project is unique in this country. Although numerous longitudinal studies of crime and behavioral disorders exist (Mednick, Harway, Mednick, and Moffitt, 1981), none has been able to examine so intensively, with multiple measures of key variables, a large sample of children both before and after the start of their criminal careers. Clinical records describing home visits with the most violent of these children provide additional insight into early biological, social, and behavioral characteristics during infancy and early childhood, and they supplement statistical analyses performed for the entire sample.

Two primary questions spurred the Biosocial Project's approach: Given a sample of individuals who have high-risk characteristics, which factors distinguish those individuals who become criminal from those who do not? More importantly, which factors distinguish persistently violent or serious offenders from nonviolent offenders or those individuals who never have official contact with the law?

Overall, the results of the Biosocial Project described in this book, discount one-dimensional theories of behavior. Crime and violence appear to stem from such a tightknit weave of both biological and environmental influences on behavior that the dominance of any single discipline in explaining crime cannot be justified. For example, results in this book show that what may appear to be a strictly biological trait, such as hyperactivity or severe learning difficulty, may be the product of exclusively environmental origins. The effects of lead poisoning on behavior illustrate how such biological and environmental interassociations occur. Key sources of lead poisoning are lead-based paint in old homes and lead-laden dust (Amitai, Graef, Brown, Gerstle, Kahn, and Cochrane, 1987: 758). Although these sources can be removed from a child's environment, what cannot be removed are the debilitating consequences of lead ingestion, which include, in addition to behavioral and learning problems, irreversible retardation, convulsions, or even death (Boffey, 1988). Moreover, the problems relating to lead poisoning are not restricted to the urban ghetto of the 1960s; they have persisted to the present time (Fitzgerald, 1986; Landrigan and Graef, 1987) with continuing, crippling effects.

This book does not pretend to offer a "new" bioenvironmental theory of behavior; rather, it emphasizes a social policy perspective based upon a probability framework for describing certain predictors of crime. The framework focuses on the degree of risk involved in committing a crime by analyzing the numbers and types of different biological and environmental influences during youth and young adulthood. Past proposals (e.g., Report of the Interdisciplinary Group in Criminology, 1978) have suggested that the likelihood of criminal behavior can be explained according to three different types of predictors: (1) predisposing variables (which increase the likelihood of criminal behavior); (2) facilitating variables (which, in combination with predisposing variables, further heighten the likelihood of crime); and (3) inhibiting variables (which counteract predisposing variables and thus decrease the probability of criminal behavior).

Viewed across a lifespan, combinations of these three types of predictors can explain the beginning or end of criminal behavior at different ages or show why some factors have relatively greater significance at particular points in time. For example, a predisposing variable may be premature birth, a facilitating variable may be lead poisoning, and an inhibiting variable may be stable family structure or high socioeconomic status. Depending on when these variables become most significant in an individual's life, crime or violent behavior may or may not occur. Developing fetuses and children below age 7 are most vulnerable to lead poisoning (Boffey, 1988). Should lead poisoning occur early in life, during either prenatal development (through ingestion by the mother) or early childhood, a child may develop problems in learning and behavior, particularly in the presence of other crime-facilitating factors, such as an unstable family environment or low socioeconomic status. The probability of criminal behavior would be relatively great for this child. Alternatively, if lead poisoning began later in life and a concerned family made efforts to avoid further poisoning, the likelihood of criminal behavior would be inhibited.

From a social policy perspective, society can break the chain of links among crime-causing factors by implementing relatively inexpensive procedures to "clean up" the crime-causing environment, such as deleading homes and encouraging early medical care for young children. From a socially moral perspective, it is evident that economic expenditures instituted early in the lives of high-risk individuals would decrease the chances of later criminal behavior as well as the considerably greater expense and social pain of punishment. An emphasis on both the biological and environmental contributions to criminal behavior can help to detect those factors that may lead to, and ultimately prevent, person-to-person violence in particular.

In this book the terms "biological" and "environmental" are loosely defined because of their close association with other related terms and with one another. Generally, "biological" factors are considered as "nonsocial, nonbehavioral measures of . . . constitution and functioning" (Mednick, Pollock, Volavka, and Gabrielli, 1982: 22), such as physical growth and development; "environmental" factors generally include those without a biological base, such as family income. Factors comprising "behaviorally defined characteristics," such as cognitive or intellectual ability and achievement, may have a partially biological base (Mednick et al., 1985: 22) that, presumably, can be environmentally perpetuated or altered.

The limitations of the Biosocial Project described in this book warrant emphasis. First, the Project examined only black individuals who were predominantly from the lower socioeconomic classes; thus, the results are generalizable only to those individuals with similar characteristics. Second, the Project's measures were applied in the 1960s and thus do not include the many new and sophisticated techniques for revealing biological differences that now exist. Measures of socioeconomic and environmental influences, however, are comparable to those techniques used today and the measures of official arrest data and crime seriousness are among the best currently available. For these reasons, biological effects may well be underemphasized. Third, the sample reflects the considerable attrition that often exists in longitudinal research although comparisons between "leavers" and "stayers" show negligible differences on key variables. Thus, although attrition exists, there is no strong evidence that those who were excluded from the Project by default differed markedly from those who were included.

Chapter 1 of this book discusses some biological, sociological, and environmental theories and research in order to provide a background for the theoretical framework of the Biosocial Project and the selection of variables for analysis. Chapter 2 describes the sample, the major variables of study, and the extent of crime and its seriousness among both males and females as children and as adults. Chapter 3 examines intelligence and achievement test score differences among offender groups in addition to placement in school programs for children who are mentally retarded or who have disciplinary problems. Chapter 4 presents statistical models incorporating numerous biological and environmental predictors of crime and violence that past research has found to be important. These models also include factors shown to be associated with intellectual or behavioral disorders that have never before been examined with criminal or violent individuals. Chapter 5 details clinical assessments based on home visits throughout the lives of 30 of the most violent and seriously criminal individuals in this sample. Home visits recorded information on mother–child interactions and the child's social responsiveness, illnessses or injuries, and unusual habits or behaviors. Chapter 6 discusses the future policy implications of the Biosocial Project in terms of perspectives on biology and responsibility, in particular, what role, if any, biological differences should have in criminal law defenses or in our notions of intent and free will.

1

Biological and environmental influences on crime

The domination of sociological explanations of crime and violence is attributable, in part, to a strong environmentalist approach in criminological research and theory. To this date, criminology textbooks provide either no discussion of biological research whatsoever or only a scattered page or two of the more explosive theories (Elliott, 1988).

The review that follows discusses some selected findings in both biological and environmental research on crime, giving a perspective and a description of those variables examined in this study and providing some background for a discussion of the study's results. More extensive reviews of the relationship of crime to genetic, biological, and psychological variables as well as of the various biosocial theories of crime proposed over the years have been provided in a number of recent books and articles (see, e.g., Denno, 1984, 1985, 1988; Elliott, 1988; Mednick et al., 1982, 1987; Moffitt, in press; Moyer, 1987; Shah and Roth, 1974; Siann, 1985; Wilson and Herrnstein, 1985). The following discussion does provide greater detail regarding certain biological and psychological variables, however, because of the dominance of existing reviews of sociological and environmental correlates of delinquency and crime in criminological journals and textbooks (see, e.g., Hirschi, 1969; Kornhauser, 1978). The discussion concludes with a model that integrates links among the variables and disciplines to present a probability theory of behavior for explaining serious, repeat delinquency.

Selected biological and psychological influences

Early biological theories

The evolution of biological theories of crime reads like a Ping-Pong match between the early biological researchers and the avid critics who denounced them each time a new theory or research study was introduced.

7

Historically, biological explanations of crime are perhaps tied most readily to Lombroso's doctrine of evolutionary atavism published originally in 1876 in *L'uomo delinquente (Criminal man)*. Lombroso's belief that criminals possess an innate, primitive predisposition to crime, however, was refuted 40 years later by Goring. In the United States, Dugdale's genealogical study of the Jukes family suggested a hereditary component to crime, although a stronger biological argument was raised in Goddard's 1913 genealogical investigation of feeblemindedness in the Kalikak family. One of the most extreme biological positions was Hooten's 1939 comparative study of several thousand prisoners, which concluded that the primary cause of crime was biological inferiority. This position was quickly rebutted. During the 1940s and 1950s, research by Sheldon and the Gluecks focused on the relationship between different body types (endomorphic, ectomorphic, mesomorphic) and delinquency. (Reviews of early biological theories may be found in Jefferey, 1955; Schafer, 1969; Wilson and Herrnstein, 1985; Wolfgang, 1955.)

All of these studies have been criticized severely on both conceptual and methodological grounds (Shah & Roth, 1974). Unfortunately, such justifiable critiques have inhibited recent attempts to examine biological correlates and their interaction with the environment. There exists, however, accumulating evidence that violence and some types of criminality are associated with disorders and trauma of the central nervous system (CNS) (see, e.g., Cowie, Cowie, and Slater, 1968; Elliott, 1978, 1988; Lewis Shanok, and Balla, 1979; Moffitt, in press; Shanok and Lewis, 1981). Such forms of cerebral insult appear to vary in importance depending upon their severity, their time of occurrence, and, perhaps most importantly, the environment. The chain of events initiating and perpetuating CNS disorder thus can potentially start very early in life – at birth or even before.

Prenatal and perinatal events

The term "prenatal" refers to the period between conception and birth. The term "perinatal" refers to the period near the time of birth (*Steadman's Medical Dictionary*, 1976). Considerable research points to associations among prenatal and perinatal complications and CNS dysfunction. Generally, early brain damage, primarily due to hypoxia (a severe lack of oxygen), may be related to later neuropsychiatric disturbances such as schizophrenia (Campion and Tucker, 1973; Handford, 1975), impaired intelligence or achievement (Broman, Nichols, and Kennedy, 1975; Friedman, Sactleben, and Bresky, 1977; Graham, Ernhart, Thurston, and

Craft, 1962), attention-deficit disorder (minimal brain dysfunction) (Benton, 1973; Bernstein, Page, and Janicki, 1974; Nichols and Chen, 1981; Rie and Rie, 1980; Wender, 1971), pathological cerebral dominance (Bernstein et al., 1974; Nachshon and Denno, 1987b; Vandenberg, 1973), and reading failure (Denhoff, Hainsworth, and Hainsworth, et al., 1972; Kawi and Pasamanick, 1958). Directly or indirectly through these disturbances, pregnancy complications may also lead to general physical or behavioral disorders (Cott, 1978; McNeil, Wiegerink, and Dozier, 1970; Rogers, Lilienfeld, and Pasamanick, 1955) and delinquency (Kleinpeter, 1976; Lewis and Balla, 1976; Rosenberg, 1978; Shanok and Lewis, 1981; Stott and Latchford, 1976; Stott and Wilson, 1977).

The extreme vulnerability of the fetus-neonate to brain damage explains why brain lesions early in infancy may be more severe than comparable lesions in adulthood (Towbin, 1978). Thus, children or adolescents with learning disorders or other indicators of attention-deficit disorder may demonstrate "soft" (minor and often undetectable) neurological signs of latent cerebral injury originating from some kind of perinatal stress (Benton, 1973).

In contrast, other studies show no correlation or weak links between pregnancy complications and intellectual deficits (Broman et al., 1975; Denno, 1982, 1984, 1985; Henderson et al., 1971; Nachshon and Denno, 1987a), behavioral disorders (Colligan, 1974; Minde et al., 1968; Werner et al., 1968), or delinquency (Denno, 1982, 1984, 1985; Lewis and Shanok, 1977; Litt, 1972, 1974; Pasamanick and Knobloch, 1966; Robins, 1966; Schulsinger, 1977; Shah and Roth, 1974). These discrepancies among results may be attributable, in part, to numerous conceptual and methodological differences in research approaches (for a discussion, see Chipman, Lilienfeld, Greenberg, and Donnelly, 1966).

For example few attempts have been made to categorize or more precisely define birth stress measures. In their articles on the relationship between birth stress and delinquency, Lewis et al. (1979: 419) define "perinatal difficulties" only in terms of any problem ranging from "maternal syphillis to postnatal apnea requiring incubation." In *Deviant Children Grown Up*, Robins (1966) uses "forceps delivery" as the sole indicator of perinatal injury relative to delinquency, a poor choice for several reasons. Not only is a single variable insufficient for measuring birth-related effects, but "forceps delivery" in particular has been shown in recent research to produce misleading results if not accompanied by other controls (e.g., maternal age) or related factors (e.g., birth weight) (Broman et al., 1975; Friedman et al., 1977). In his book *Studies of Troublesome Children*, Stott (1966) fails to provide any identification whatsoever of the factors that constitute the variable "pregnancy complications," although later articles are somewhat more precise (Stott and Latchford, 1976). Additional factors may confound or influence associations with birth-related events, such as the defintion and categories of delinquency and violence.

The relationship between birth events and delinquency or its correlates also appears to be environmentally dependent, not genetic or heritable (Lewis and Balla, 1976: 66–67). Accordingly, sociological and environmental effects, such as family makeup and income, should be included in analyses. However, nearly all the research cited as relating birth events to delinquency and its correlates ignores environmental factors.

Such an important omission may also explain, in part, inconsistencies in research findings on intellectual functioning. Just as early CNS damage may recur at adolescence, it may also disappear, particularly in good environments. Thus, studies measuring intelligence with young or disadvantaged subjects may find a link to birth complications relative to studies with older or more advantaged samples where this link is not made.

Such compensatory environmental influences are most detectable in longitudinal research (Werner, Bierman, French, Simonian, Connor, Smith, and Campbell, 1968, present an exemplary study). According to Sameroff (1975: 274), "the data from . . . various longitudinal studies of prenatal and perinatal complications have yet to produce a single predictive variable more potent than the familial and socio-economic characteristics of the caretaking environment." Thus, in advantaged families, prenatal and perinatal complications had negligent or nonexistent longterm effects, whereas in disadvanged families they predicted "significant retardations in later functioning" and intellectual deficits (Sameroff, 1975: 275).

Overall, then, the link between prenatal and perinatal complications and intellectual and behavioral deficits is potentially strong in poor environments. The strength of the link between intellectual deficit and delinquency or crime in particular is the topic of the next section.

Intellectual functioning and achievement

A conflicting litcrature exists concerning the extent to which delinquents or criminals differ from nondelinquents in intellectual functioning (Bach-y-Rita, Lion, Climent, and Ervin, 1971; Hirschi and Hindelang, 1977; Lewis and Balla, 1976; Offer, Marohn, and Ostrov, 1979; Spellacy, 1978; Wilson and Herrnstein, 1985; Wolfgang, Figlio, and Sellin, 1972) or school achievement (Blanchard and Mannarino, 1978; Elliott, 1966; Marshall, Hess, and Lair, 1978; Wolfgang et al., 1972) or whether any definite difference exists at all (Lewis, Shanok, Pincus, and Glasen, 1979; Murray, 1976; Prentice and Kelly, 1963). Early studies reporting lower intelligence scores among delinquents (Vold, 1979) frequently lacked nondelinquent comparisons, or controls for race, socioeconomic status, and involvement in the criminal justice system. Recent studies in which many of these factors are controlled, however, do show associations between low intelligence scores and delinquency (Hirschi and Hindelang, 1977; Moffitt, Gabrielli, and Mednick, 1981; West and Farrington, 1973; Wolfgang et al., 1972; for a thorough review of the recent literature on this topic, see Moffitt, in press).

According to Hirschi and Hindelang's review of the research (1977: 571), the relationship between intelligence and delinquency is "at least as strong as the relation of either class or race to official delinquency." They suggest that school factors may be important. Using WISC and WAIS tests, Kirkegaard-Sorenson and Mednick (1977) confirm in their Danish sample that adolescents who later become delinquent have lower tested intelligence than nondelinquents, and eventually perform more poorly in school. Subsequent analyses on Danish samples indicate similar relationships with intelligence while controlling for socioeconomic factors (Moffitt et al., 1981).

In their longitudinal study of a Philadelphia birth cohort, Wolfgang and his associates (1972) report a consistent link between delinquency, intelligence, and achievement not only within different socioeconomic classes, but also within different races. In turn, West and Farrington (1973) demonstrate the delinquency–intelligence relationship while controlling for the effects of income, family size, and parental criminality.

The nature and source of specific differences in intellectual functioning are not clear, however. Evidence of lower scores in general aptitude among delinquents or criminals has been attributed to a diffuse or global intellectual deficit (Virkkunen and Luukkonen, 1977). Other researchers suggest an intellectual balance evidenced by considerably lower verbal relative to spatial intelligence among delinquents (Andrew, 1974; McCord and McCord, 1964). Wechsler (1939) suggested some time ago that this imbalance may be related to sociopathic personality. Results of other studies have varied, or have shown evidence of an opposite pattern of verbal and spatial performance (Lewis and Balla, 1976; Mayers, Townes, and Reitan, 1974).

Such discrepancies may be due to confounding effects. For example, in one report a verbal–spatial imbalance was found among white but not among black delinquents (Henning and Levy, 1967). Delinquency may also be linked to an intellectual imbalance not related to a particular direction or discrepancy in verbal or spatial skills (Andrew, 1979). The substantial literature citing evidence of reading or learning disabilities among delinquent and violent offenders suggests the importance of investigating verbal and language processes in general (Andrew, 1979; Fogel, 1966; for a review, discussion, and critique of theories and research, see Moffitt, in press).

Consideration of the direct and indirect correlates of learning or reading disabilities may provide further explanations for the intelligence–delinquency relationship. For example, poor reading ability has been found to be associated with pregnancy complications (Kawi and Pasamanick, 1958), large family size (Zajonc and Markus, 1975), and visual defects (Allen, 1977; Barnes and O'Gorman, 1978), as well as to cerebral dysfunction and lateralization (Carter-Saltzman, 1979). A relationship between cerebral dysfunction and poor reading has also been found among both black and white delinquents (Andrew, 1981a).

The nature of the link between cerebral lateralization and intellectual and behavioral problems is still unclear. A background in some authors' explanations for the interassociation gives guidance in assessing some recent findings of ties between left hemisphere dysfunction and violence (for a further review of the literature, see Denno, 1984; Moffitt, in press; Nachshon and Denno, 1987).

Cerebral lateralization

Evidence of anatomic and functional differences in the lateralization of the two (left and right) hemispheres of the brain provides one explanation for intellectual variation in the general population. "Lateralization" refers to the "localization of a psychological function in a single hemisphere" (Burstein, Bank, and Jarvik, 1980: 204). Individuals who are more lateralized tend to show greater hemispheric specialization in processing information relative to less lateralized individuals.

For most (right-handed) individuals, the left cerebral hemisphere specializes in processing verbal stimuli – notably language functions – in a sequential, analytic, and propositional mode, whereas the right hemisphere specializes in processing nonverbal stimuli – particularly spatial functions – in a nonlinguistic, holistic, and synthetic manner (Bogen, 1969; Dimond and Beaumont, 1974). WISC Verbal IQ and other verbal measures are widely used indicators of left hemispheric abilities; WISC

Performance IQ and other spatial measures are indicators of right hemispheric abilities (Reitan and Davison, 1974).

Additional factors have also been found to be associated with cerebral lateralization, most notably hand preference (Carter-Saltzman, 1979) and, to a lesser extent, eye and foot preference (Coren, Porac, and Duncan, 1979; McBurney and Dunn, 1976). Some evidence suggests that left-handed individuals, who constitute about 8 to 10 percent of the population (Witelson, 1980), have more heterogeneous patterns of hemispheric functioning than right-handed individuals. In particular, a disproportionate percentage (about one third) of left-handers appear to show right hemispheric or bilateral language functions, in contrast to the left-hemispheric language processing of nearly all right-handers (Levy and Reid, 1976).

Generally, handedness, gender, and intellectual abilities show three basic interrelationships reported in the literature (Carter-Saltzman, 1979: 97–98): (1) a disproportionately higher incidence of males and left- or mixed-handers among children with language, reading, or learning disorders (Allen and Wellman, 1980; Keller, Croake, and Riesenman, 1973; Kinsbourne and Warrington, 1966; Reitan and Davison, 1974); (2) evidence that the different patterns of hemispheric specialization in males and females may be related to handedness (Levy and Reid, 1976); and (3) a higher incidence of left-handedness in males relative to females (Carter-Saltzman, 1979: 98; Hoyenga and Hoyenga, 1979: 258).

Some research suggests that pubertal and postpubertal sex hormone level (which affects rate of physical maturation) may influence cerebral lateralization and, among children, the development of handedness (Waber, 1976, 1977). This research is not entirely conclusive, however (Hoyenga and Hoyenga, 1979), and alternative findings and interpretations exist. Evidence that hemispheric capacity or lateralization may be genetically established at birth (Bryden, 1979: 207 Nottebohm, 1979) or result from early physical asymmetry, influenced by such factors as birth weight and perinatal maturation rate (Bever, 1980), could confound proposed associations between adolescent development and hemisphericity. As Waber (1980: 24) notes, "it may be that patterns of neuropsychological functioning related to hormonal status are laid down in the central nervous system early in life, but it is only at puberty that they can clearly be observed."

Alternatively, early CNS insult resulting from prenatal or perinatal trauma could contribute to differences in brain asymmetry, possibly in interaction with physical or developmental factors. According to Bakan,

Dibb, and Reed (1973), the greater vulnerability of the left cerebral hemisphere to the hypoxic effects of some birth stress may influence early hemispheric organization, resulting in a "switch" from right- to left-handedness. Some support exists for this argument (Coren and Porac, 1980), in addition to evidence that maternal factors may also influence birth events directly (Mednick, 1970; Mednick, Mura, Schulsinger, and Mednick, 1971) and, more indirectly, hemisphericity (Coren and Porac, 1980). Birth events may also have a more differential effect on males than on females given evidence that anatomical asymmetry is "not as marked for males as for females within the first few days of life" (Witelson and Pallie, 1973: 644).

The first documentation of evidence of an imbalance of the cerebral hemispheres and facial asymmetry among criminals was perhaps that of Lombroso (1876). He also reported a disproportionate number of left-handers among criminal populations (Lombroso, 1903). Because of serious methodological problems with other early studies of brain abnormalities among criminals (Vold, 1979), possible differences in hemispheric organization among criminal populations were not investigated again until recently, in studies by Flor-Henry (1973) and Flor-Henry and Yeudall (1973). They, and other researchers since that time, reported that psychopathy and other personality and behavioral disorders are associated with dysfunction of the left cerebral hemisphere (for a review see Denno, 1982; Nachshon and Denno, 1987a). In studies that include indicators of lateral preferences, a higher incidence of left-handedness and left-footedness has also been reported (Andrew, 1978; Fitzhugh, 1973; Gabrielli and Mednick, 1980).

Evidence that some left-handers tend to rely on the "less analytic, more emotional, more impulsive response modes" associated with the right hemisphere has been used to explain their greater involvement in delinquency and violence (Gabrielli and Mednick, 1980). This tendency may also explain why left-handers and delinquents experience greater deficits in left hemisphere tasks such as reading and language (Carter-Saltzman, 1979; see Moffitt, in press, for further discussion and review).

Some investigators suggest a greater left hemisphere deficit among both delinquents and poor readers irrespective of their lateral preference (Andrew, 1981a). Andrew (1980) has also reported disproportionately fewer left-handers among violent offenders. This result suggests that the laterality–delinquency relationship may vary according to sample composition or offender type. Other research points to a right hemisphere deficit among delinquents (Yeudall, 1980) or evidence of other symptoms of cerebral disorder, such as attention deficit disorder or what the earlier literature labeled as minimal brain dysfunction (Shan and Roth, 1974).

Attention-deficit disorder and hyperactivity

Attention-deficit disorder (ADD), or what much of the earlier literature termed minimal brain dysfunction, and hyperactivity are noted correlates of school failure and delinquency (American Psychiatric Association, 1987; Curman and Nylander, 1976; Denhoff, 1973; and Menkes, Rowe, and Menkes, 1967; Satterfield, 1987). The term hyperactivity, in particular, describes the heterogeneous behaviors of children who show one or more of the following: overactivity, perceptual–motor impairments, impulsivity, emotional lability, attention deficits, minor disturbances of speech, intellectual defects (e.g., learning disabilities), clumsiness, and antisocial responses (Elliott, 1988; Firestone, Peters, and Rivier, 1977; Loney, Langhorne, and Paternite, 1978). By definition, children with below normal intelligence or very severe neurological problems are excluded (Clements, 1966). Explanations for the causes of ADD include prenatal or birth trauma (Nichols and Chen, 1981; Towbin, 1971); neurodevelopmental lag, psychogenic factors (Kagan and Moss, 1962), minor physical anomalies (Firestone et al., 1977), genetic transmission (Morrison and Stewart, 1973), and poor living environment (MacFarlane, Allen, and Honzik, 1962).

Generally, children with ADD indicate certain learning or behavioral deficiences associated with CNS dysfunctioning (Moffitt, in press; Shah and Roth, 1974). For example, ADD children have been found to score lower on the Bender Gestalt and Goodenough–Harris drawing tests, both measures of fine motor ability and attention span (Stamm and Kreder, 1979). Two of the four major symptoms of what was earlier called minimal brain dysfunction, which were factor analyzed from numerous medical and psychological variables in the nationwide Collaborative Perinatal Project, constitute measures of cognition and learning: (1) a *cognitive and perceptual motor factor*, including Bender Gestalt, Goodenough–Harris drawing test, WISC verbal and performance subtests, and (2) an *academic factor*, including the Wide Range Achievement Test for Spelling, Reading, and Arithmetic (Nichols, Chen, and Pomeroy, 1976).

Problem behaviors among ADD children appear to correspond with age. For example, young children (ages 2 to 6 years) may exhibit lack of discipline and hyperactivity; older children (during elementary school and adolescence) may demonstrate reading and learning disorders, academic underachievement, and delinquent or aggressive behaviors (Wender 1971). Whereas CNS dysfunction may underlie some childhood disorders (Lewis and Balla, 1976: 65) evidence suggests that behavioral deviations can result from developmental or maturational lags many children eventually outgrow. Longitudinal follow-up studies indicate that children who do not outgrow behavioral disorders may retain antisocial conduct into adulthood (for a review of the literature, see Denno, 1988; Elliott, 1988; Moffitt, in press).

Associations between physical growth and development at early ages and ADD have not been examined extensively. However, physical growth variables (such as height and weight) have shown direct relationships with crime as well as indirect effects with its major correlates (e.g., learning and academic disorders).

Physical growth and development

Physical growth, even at an early age, is one of several indicators of subsequent health and development (Prahl-Andersen, Kowalski, and Heydendael, 1979) and physical maturation during adolescence (Frisch and Revelle, 1971; Katz et al., 1980). According to Great Britain's National Child Development Study, height at age 7 within a sample of nearly 15,000 children was negatively associated with low socioeconomic status, large family size, young maternal age, and late birth order, controlling for other important variables (Davie, Butler, and Goldstein, 1972).

Relationships among indicators of physical development and CNS and behavioral disorders, however, are inconsistent. In a national, prospective study, Nichols and Chen (1981) reported a higher incidence of short stature among children who, at age 7, showed certain ADD symptoms. Evidence of a considerable lag in the maturational development of psychiatrically disturbed adolescents demonstrated in one study (Littlemore, Metcalfe, and Johnsen, 1974), however, has not been replicated elsewhere, either among disturbed or delinquent samples (Henderson, 1969). Indeed, one study examining stature notes a higher frequency of tall males among samples with psychiatric and character disorders, as well as criminality (Nielsen and Tsuboi, 1970). A review of the literature on this topic confirms that both delinquent boys and delinquent girls are usually found to be above population averages for height and weight (Cowie et al., 1968). Similarly, Cortés and Gatti (1972) conclude that delinquents and criminals appear to be "physically superior" thereby providing some support for earlier studies by Sheldon and the Gluecks that reported a disproportionate number of mesomorphs among delinquent samples (see Wilson and Herrnstein, 1985, for a review).

Studies of young children suggest that physique may be related to temperament, exculsive of environmental influences (Cortés and Gatti, 1972: 347). Research on associations among physical characteristics, temperament, and behavior is flawed, however, by both measurement and methodological difficulties (Shah and Roth, 1974). Furthermore, considerable evidence points to early environmental influences that could strongly affect temperament (Cameron, 1978). Unfortunately, because multiple factors are seldom analyzed simultaneously, their separate and cumulative impact is unknown.

As the following section indicates, for example, of the few studies of female crime conducted, most have lacked a control group or a male sample for comparison. Research results do indicate, however, that there may be different biosocial influences in female crime.

Gender

At birth, a child's sex is one of the most accurate discriminators of later criminal behavior (Andrew, 1981a; Moyer, 1974). Although both official and self-report data indicate that crime among females is increasing (Adler, 1975; Cavan and Ferdinand, 1981; Datesman and Scarpitti, 1980; Kratcoski and Kratcoski, 1975; Simon, 1975), violent crime, in particular, remains dominated by males (Bowker, 1978; Cavan and Ferdinand, 1981; Ward, Jackson, and Ward, 1980; Wolfgang, 1958; Wolfgang and Ferracuti, 1982).

Explanations of gender differences in crime pinpoint both biological and sociological factors. Evidence that males are considerably more aggressive than females during preschool years (Maccoby and Jacklin, 1974) and throughout development (Hamburg, 1974; Moyer, 1974) suggests that biological factors, particularly sex hormones, may be important. However, sociological explanations for gender differences predominate, especially in light of offense rate fluctuations between males and females over time and across cultures (Jensen and Eve, 1976). In general, it appears that males and females differ both in terms of biological development and in response to variations in the social structure and environment. For example, males are relatively more vulnerable to environmental stress and developmental difficulty. They experience a higher incidence of prenatal and perinatal mortality and complications, reading and learning disorders, and mental retardation (Reinish, Gandelman, and

Spiegel, 1979), as well as left hemisphere deficits (Carter-Salzman, 1979). Historically, however, criminality among females has been attributec mostly to biological determinants (Klein, 1980; Smart, 1976). Accordin to Lombroso (1920), the female offender was inherently atavistic anc amoral. Thomas (1923) described female criminality as primarily sex ual and a result of poor socialization. Postwar views of crime perpetuatec the biological approach. In *The Criminality of Women*, for example, Pollak (1950) argued that females were inherently and physiologicall deceitful, characteristics derived from their passive roles during sexual intercourse.

Pollak's and earlier theories of female crime have been justifiably criticized (Smart, 1976). However, the biological approach still persists in some more recent research that has viewed crime among females as a product of sexual frustration, an inability to adjust to feminine roles (Vedder and Somerville, 1970), chromosomal and physiological devia-tions (Cowie et al., 1968), and premenstrual and menstrual syndromes (Denno, 1988). These studies on biological factors have been criticized extensively on methodological grounds (Bowker, 1978; Parlee, 1973; Smart, 1976) and their results remain inconclusive.

In general, most research has focused on minor female offenders such as prostitutes or drug addicts. Studies that incorporate violent and habi-tual female offenders have shown considerably stronger differences be-tween offenders and nonoffenders, and among different offender groups. Violence among females has been linked to a history of homosexuality, drinking problems, psychiatric disturbances (Ward et al., 1980), neurolo-gical abnormalities, problems with impulse control (Climent, Ervin, Rol-lins, Plutchik, and Batinelli, 1977), and poor medical histories (Shanok and Lewis, 1981). Speech and reading disorders have not been strongly evident in the few studies that have examined them among females (see, for example, Climent, Rollins, Ervin, and Plutchik, 1973).

Similar to research on the correlates of male delinquency, results with females may vary according to different samples and methodological techniques. Findings do highlight two major points: (1) With some excep-tions, those factors found to be influential in delinquency among males are also influential in delinquency among females; and (2) in light of the greater social and cultural controls on female behavior, females who do become delinquent or violent evidence relatively more biological or phy-siological deviations than their male counterparts (Cloninger, Christian-sen, Reich, and Crottesman, 1978; Cloninger, Reich, and Guze, 1975; Cowie et al., 1968; Denno, 1982).

Interactions among biological and environmental factors

Substantial evidence indicates that biological and psychological influences on behavior and development are significantly associated with socioeconomic, environmental, and racial factors. For example, black and lower socioeconomic status (SES) mothers have a higher incidence of pregnancy and delivery complications, premature births, and infants with low birth weights relative to mothers in other race and socioeconomic groups (National Center for Health Statistics, 1980a; Niswander and Gordon, 1972). Unmarried and young mothers (who are disproportionately from black and lower SES groups) also have a higher incidence of birth complications (National Center for Health Statistics, 1980b). In turn, the relationship between low birth weight (as one example) and a higher risk of infant mortality, mental retardation, CNS malformation, minimal brain dysfunction, and other physical and neurological disorders is well substantiated both in the United States and crossculturally (National Center for Health Statistics, 1980a; see also Broman et al., 1975; Hardy, Drage, and Jackson, 1979; Harlap, Davies, Grover, and Prywes, 1977; The Ontario Department of Health, 1967).

In light of this chain of relationships, biological and psychological studies of delinquency and crime should include sociological and environmental effects. Unfortunately, they rarely do. The following sections provide a review of selected social and environmental factors to give perspective on the importance of their impact.

Sociological and environmental influences

Strain and subculture

Strain theories suggest that delinquency among lower class youth is the result of a discrepancy (or strain) between culturally induced goals for success and the socially structured means of achieving those goals legitimately. The early strain theories of Merton (1957) and Cloward and Ohlin (1961) emphasize that the social structure provides very different opportunities for individuals to attain success by such acceptable, legitimate means as education and employment (Nettler, 1984). Opportunity barriers to lower class youth in particular encourage a process of alienation in which youth experience failure, consequently withdrawing from conventional norms and becoming hostile toward the larger social order. Cohen (1955) differs from other strain theorists in arguing that much of the resultant crime is malicious and has no utilitarian value or function to the delinquent.

Although strain and subcultural theories share common perspectives, subcultural theories emphasize that, some groups, while possessing many of the values and goals of the larger society, retain different cultural values and norms that may come into conflict with those of the majority. Sellin (1938) described crime as a consequence of the conflict that occurs when different groups (particularly groups of varying ethnicity) have discrepant standards of appropriate behavior. Wolfgang and Ferracuti (1982) have provided a broader examination of worldwide subcultural differences, explaining variations in violent behavior that are transmitted across generations among different ethnic groups. In turn, Miller (1958) depicts delinquency as a kind of class conflict in which the "subculture" of lower class citizens holds certain values or "focal concerns" that run counter to the values of the majority.

Socioeconomic status and community

Social class theories recognize the more generic association between lower socioeconomic status and criminality regardless of a subcultural effect. Excluding arguments that delinquency is foremost a product of labeling (Schur, 1971), most criminological research demonstrates a disproportionate involvement of the lower socioeconomic classes in crime and violence (for a review, see Brownfield, 1986). However, researchers still maintain conflicting conclusions in their assessment of the SES–crime interrelationship (see, for example, Brownfield, 1986; Tittle, Villeme, and Smith, 1978). Generally, findings vary according to the types of data analyzed, study times and locations, measures of social class and delinquency, research methodology, and different sample sizes and composition (Luchterhand and Weller, 1976; Tittle and Villemez, 1977; Tittle et al., 1978; Van Dusen, Mednick, Gabrielli, Hutchings, 1983). Particularly notable are the comparisons between self-report and official measures of delinquency, which reflect discrepant results relative to demographic and socioeconomic influences in some studies (e.g., Elliott and Ageton, 1980; Gold and Reimer, 1975; Hood and Sparks, 1970; Williams and Gold, 1972) and consistent results in others (Hindelang, Hirshi, and Weiss, 1979).

Kvaraceus and Miller (1975) note that not all lower class youths become delinquent; other social or environmental pressures exist. For example, Clark and Wenniger (1972) reported that SES becomes a significant variable in the total incidence of criminality only when an urban area reaches a certain size or composition, although lower class youths self-report a disproportionate involvement in serious offenses. Danziger's (1976) economic model of crime rates in 222 urban areas also shows a general increase in crime relative to increasing urban growth. Even so, unemployment, low income, low education, and race maintain significant associations with crime, regardless of fluctuations in density. The importance of race is not surprising considering the marked social economic discrepancies between blacks and whites, particularly twenty years ago (Wolfgang and Cohen, 1970).

Evidence that crime is associated with community and urban factors was first investigated on a large scale by Shaw and McKay (1942) in Chicago and other metropolitan areas. Some related research since that time has confirmed their conclusion that high rates of delinquency are concentrated in socioeconomically deprived areas (Chilton, 1964; Gordon, 1976). Others, however, contend that social instability, and not socioeconomic deprivation, accounts for the association between community characteristics and delinquency (Block, 1979; Bordua, 1958; Lander, 1954). Regardless of conflicting perspectives on the importance of socioeconomic disadvantage, studies converge in their conclusions that the normative structures in a community strongly influence the criminal behavior of youths (for a review, see Wilson and Herrnstein, 1985).

Within the last decade research has investigated additional community factors shown to relate to delinquency, including weak attachment to the neighborhood (as evidenced by a short length of residence, frequent moves, and so forth) number of multifamily dwellings, population density, and dangerous physical environment (Wilson and Herrnstein, 1985; Wolfgang et al., 1972). Other theories of crime emphasize the social–psychological characteristics of delinquency in terms of the "controls" or social bonds that create and perpetuate acceptable behavioral standards. These controls are learned and reinforced in interaction with others.

Social control and social bonds

According to differential association learning theories, delinquency is imitated, facilitated, and internalized with social reinforcements and modeling within small, intimate groups (Sutherland and Cressey, 1978). In turn, Hirschi's (1969) theory of social control proposes that there are four interrelated bonds that ensure normative conduct and "control" the potential for delinquent behavior: attachment, commitment, involvement, and belief. *Attachment* refers to an individual's sensitivity to the opinions and judgments of others, expressed, for example, as empathy or obligation in personal relationships. *Commitment* is the rational side of bonding determined by the assessment of potential gains and losses that may result from conforming or nonconforming behavior. *Involvement* is the degree of time and energy devoted to conventional activities, which can then displace energy available for deviant behavior. *Belief* is the moral component of the bond, reflecting the degree to which individuals agree with legal rules.

According to Hirschi, the stronger a youth's attachments, commitments, involvements, and beliefs within institutions of social control – such as the family and schools – the lower the likelihood of delinquent behavior. Irrespective of Hirschi's theory, however, some family factors have also shown consistently strong associations with both crime and violence.

Family

The variety of familial and parental variables linked to delinquency and its correlates includes broken homes (Gabrielli, 1981; Gannon, 1970; Monahan, 1957; see Wilson and Herrnstein, 1985, for a review) and absence of the father (Virkkunen, 1976), with differential effects according to the sex and race of the delinquent (Austin, 1978; Datesman and Scarpitti, 1980). A 1955 longitudinal study (McCord and McCord, 1975) of the effects of parental role models on crime has also demonstrated that children are most apt to imitate their criminal fathers under unstable home conditions (e.g., homes characterized by rejection, maternal dominance, and inconsistent discipline).

Other studies, however, have reported no relationship between broken homes and delinquency (Andrew, 1981b), or a considerably more negative relationship for delinquent girls as compared to delinquent boys (Bartol, 1980). Additional family-related variables may confound these associations. For example, large families (e.g., those comprising four or more children) appear to have a higher incidence of delinquency among males than do smaller families (Andrew, 1976). In one study, large intact families "produced the most violent male offenders" (Andrew, 1978). Barnes and O'Gorman (1978) and others (see Andrew, 1981b, for a review) reported that delinquency occurs in large families where boys far outnumber girls, presumably creating an aggressive environment.

In part, the effects of family size may be attributable to the socioeconomic, sociological, or even biological influences of birth order. According to Stott (1978; as cited in Andrew, 1981b), later-born children in a large family are more prone to social maladjustment than firstborns. Later-borns also tend to experience more prenatal and perinatal complications than earlier-born siblings (Niswander and Gordon, 1972), score lower on intelligence and achievement tests (Zajonc and Bargh, 1980; Zajonc and Markus, 1975); and possibly have fewer economic and social advantages than first borns (Steelman and Mercy, 1980; Wolfe, 1979). A recent finding of intellectually detrimental hormone depletion among closely spaced later-borns suggests that biological factors may also be influential (Maccoby, Doering, Jacklin, and Kraemer, 1979).

According to some studies, parental behavior and role modeling predict later childhood behavior disorders, although the nature of this relationship is not clear. In the Gluecks' (1970) delinquency prediction scale, three of the five elements most predictive of delinquency were related to the mother's role in childrearing: mother's affection, supervision, and family cohesiveness (see also Meade, 1973; Pilavin, Vadum, and Hardyck, 1969). Corrboration of the Gluecks' scale (Tait and Hodges, 1971) emphasizes the negative influences of poor maternal care.

Among adolescent delinquents, McTamney (1976) found that defensive and confusing parent–child communication and unsupportive parental discipline "greatly increased" the probability of delinquency; violent juveniles in particular were found to be a product of "violent, chaotic, and abusive" parents (Perry, Harburg, and Crowley, 1978; Sorrells, 1977). Further longitudinal research is needed to test these interrelationships.

Critique of the research

The research on biological and environmental influences contains numerous methodological and substantive flaws. Although a thorough critique of the literature is too lengthy to present here, notes on selected books and articles exemplify common problems.

A major difficulty is the unavailability of nondelinquent control groups when assessing the biological and sociological characteristics of different types of delinquents. Spellacy's (1978) frequently cited article on the neuropsychological characteristics of violence compares only violent with nonviolent men. Nearly all of the research by Lewis and her associates (e.g., Lewis and Balla, 1976; Lewis et al., 1979; Lewis, Shanok, Pincus, and Glazer, 1979) as well as by other researchers (e.g., Bach-y-Rita et al., 1971; Barnes and O'Gorman, 1978; Offer et al., 1979) examines only delinquent subjects.

In turn, important demographic and environmental variables are often

Biological and environmental influences on crime

never controlled. In some studies, for example, the sex, age, and race of the subjects are not clearly specified (one example is Offer et al., 1979) or never mentioned at all (e.g., Lewis, Shanok, and Balla, 1979; Lewis, Shanok, Pincus, and Glazer, 1979). The great majority of studies fails to account in any way for the influence of socioeconomic status, although the incidence of birth stress, low intelligence, and other correlates of crime are strongly related to social class differences.

In most studies, limitations in the sample sizes of subjects hinder methodological techniques and the generalizability of results. In nearly every article reviewed, data collection is retrospective and, in a considerable number of cases, data are only anecdotal (e.g., a flagrant example is Yochelson and Samenow, 1976). Additionally, in most research, the extent of delinquency is measured by self-report questionnaires or interviews; in some cases, subjects are obtained at the time of disposition or while they are incarcerated. Consequently, crime data are potentially biased by self-report estimates or processing in the juvenile justice system.

Perhaps the most consistent, and serious, weakness of biosocial research on crime in general is the wide age range among subjects. As has been shown (Wolfgang, Thornberry, and Figlio, 1987a), the nature and extent of delinquency vary considerably with age. Differences in age among small groups of delinquents may confound results, particularly if the examined correlates are also age-biased (e.g., intelligence and physical growth). Furthermore, a number of studies (e.g., Barnes and O'Gorman, 1978) examine delinquents who have neither reached the peak age of their offense-committing nor, as in most studies, yet completed their delinquent career. In only two studies (Tracy, Wolfgang, and Figlio, 1985; Wolfgang et al., 1972) has a control existed for youths who have not remained in the same area during those years of "eligibility" for delinquency (see Moffitt, in press, for a further critique of the literature).

The following section outlines the theoretical context of the present study in light of problems encountered in past biosocial research. The section emphasizes the longitudinal development and interaction of selected correlates of male and female delinquency.

Theory integration

The integration of biological and sociological theories of behavior is a crucial step toward understanding why and how crime occurs. In general, sociological and social-structural theories suggest that delinquency is an adaptation to conditions and social influences in lower class environments (Hirschi, 1969; Kornhauser, 1978). Some of these environments may be part of a "subculture of violence" that maintains norms of violence separate from the dominant culture and that may vary among different ethnic groups (Wolfgang and Ferracuti, 1982).

Recognizing that behavior has both psychological and social bases, differential association and social learning theories propose that delinquency is a consequence of social reinforcements and modeling (Sutherland and Cressey, 1978). Hirschi's (1969) social bond theory links delinquent behavior to the strength of an individual's ties with society through attachments, commitments, involvements, and beliefs.

The successful maintainance of these ties is perhaps most in jeopardy during adolescence. Although human development is continuous, some authors suggest that adolescence is a time of "moral turbulence," when a strong sense of self or behavioral control is not yet established (Zellermayer, 1976: 99). Adolescence is also the most significant period of value formation (Konopka, 1973) and when, presumably, behavior is most open to change (McMahon, 1970). School, family, and peer experiences are all influential. Given opportunities, a youth will commit a delinquent act because he or she is not yet deterred by a strong attachment to conforming values in society. Consistent with some bonding theories, those adolescents who avoid deviant influences may have greater self-esteem and self-control (Jensen, 1973). By later adolescence and early adulthood, the increased understanding of social organization that develops with age allows the individual to realize the "social and legal relations that bind him to society and constrain his behavior" (Simpson, 1976: 101). Thus, individuals outgrow those ages most susceptible to environmental influence (Schur, 1973).

Although considerable research supports the premise that social bonding and environment influence adolescent behavior, it is difficult to determine which constraints have the most impact. Moreover, bonding theories fail to explain adequately either the persistence of criminal behavior among those who have reached maturity or the start of criminal behavior among adolescents who have a favorable environment. The extent to which children and adolescents are relatively more susceptible to peer and social influences has also not been clearly gauged.

The strength of social bonding and the likelihood of a delinquent or criminal status may be dependent, in part, on early developmental, biological, and environmental factors whose cumulative and interactive in-

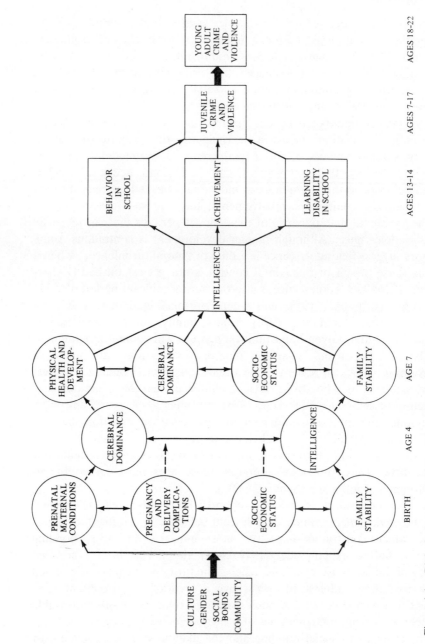

Figure 1.1. Biological and environmental predictors of violence.

fluences vary over time (see Figure 1.1). Considerable evidence indicates that many biological and developmental disorders associated with delinquency and crime (e.g., reading and learning disabilities) may be attributable, in part, to minor CNS dysfunction which is linked predominantly to complications occurring before and immediately after birth (for reviews, see Denno, 1982, 1985). The cumulative effects of indicators of CNS trauma and subsequent bonding and behavior may be theoretically analogous to the combined effects of different variables used in risk research (Garmezy, 1977; Slone et al., 1976). Infants "at risk" – those born prematurely, with low birth weights, and so on – seem to have somewhat more difficulty adjusting to poor environments than healthy, full-term infants. It appears that the relatively more immature or stressed central nervous systems of these infants are less able to become integrated in deprived circumstances (Eagle and Brazelton, 1977: 37).

At-risk infants are not only more vulnerable to their immediate environment, they are also more prone to later CNS-related disorders, including those associated with crime. These disorders include reduced intelligence or achievement, attention-deficit disorder and hyperactivity, problems associated with cerebral dominance, and learning and reading disabilities (Denno, 1982). Unfavorable environmental circumstances during childhood, such as large family size, absence of the father, late birth order, and low SES, may compound these disorders (Denhoff et al., 1972: 164–165). Likewise, CNS-related deficits accompanied by subcultural or familial deprivation may impair social bonds.

The nature and extent of relationships among at-risk factors and criminal behavior are complex and, in many ways, difficult to detect. The opportunity to identify sequential or ordering effects is an advantage of longitudinal research because biological and environmental interactions with delinquency are not always clear or consistent. Overall, specification of interrelationships of various kinds and occurrences of developmental variables may pinpoint those factors that initiate and perpetuate offense behavior.

Gender differences in behavior can also locate sociological and developmental effects. In general, developmental and biological factors are more strongly associated with female delinquency for two reasons: Females are less affected physically than males by environmental influences, and females are relatively more socialized to conform to social and cultural norms. In other words, females who become delinquent or violent generally have more biologically related difficulties than males because serious female aggression is highly abnormal conduct.

Using this framework of predisposing, facilitating, and inhibiting variables, the next chapter describes the history of the Collaborative Perinatal Project, the Biosocial Project described in this book, the children who were examined in this study, and the biological and environmental factors selected for testing. The extent and seriousness of the sample's offenses are also presented.

2

Violent criminals as children and as adults

The individuals who are the focus of this book were originally part of one of the largest medical projects over conducted in this country. In 1957, the National Institute of Neurological Diseases and Stroke launched the Collaborative Perinatal Project, a nationwide study of biological and environmental influences on pregnancy, infant and childhood mortality, and physical, neurological, and psychological development. Nearly 60,000 pregnant women participated in the study between 1959 and 1966 in 15 different medical centers. Examination of the study children from the time of their birth through age 7 continued until 1974, completing a total project cost exceeding 100 million dollars. (Further description of the Perinatal Project may be found in Chipman et al., 1966; McFalls, 1976; Niswander and Gordon, 1972.)

In 1978, the Sellin Center for Studies in Criminology and Criminal Law at the University of Pennsylvania was awarded a grant by the National Institute of Justice to examine those Perinatal Project children who were born in Philadelphia. As part of the grant, public school and police record data were collected on a total sample of about 10,000 youths. For 10 years, detailed data have been organized and analyzed on the subsample of nearly 1,000 youths who constitute the subjects for this book. These youths, who are now young adults, have grown up with the Biosocial Project. This chapter provides an in-depth look at the children who were originally selected for study, the measures analyzed on them, and their juvenile and adult crime histories.

Study subjects

The Philadelphia sample was the second largest in the Perinatal Project. It comprised the nearly 10,000 pregnant patients who delivered their children at Pennsylvania Hospital between 1959 and 1965; the children were later tested at Children's Hospital of the University of Pennsylvania.

The study included all pregnant woment who attended Pennsylvania Hospital during this time except unregistered emergency deliveries and those who were planning to deliver elsewhere.

The total sample reflects, in part, the characteristics of families who would be interested in receiving inexpensive maternity care provided by a public clinic. The sample was predominantly (88 percent) black and its socioeconomic level was slightly lower (by one decile) than that for the U.S. population at the time (Myrianthopoulos and French, 1968). Two thirds of the patients, who were disproportionately young, reported being married at the time of registration.

The racial and socioeconomic bias of this sample limits to a certain extent the generalizability of the results of this study. However, this same bias provides built-in controls for demographic and ethnic factors that have been strongly linked to crime and violence and the factors that predict them. Indeed, this study focuses upon those individuals who, in light of past research, are at a high risk of having a police contact (Wolfgang et al., 1972) but who, at the same time, are the least apt to be studied (Raspberry, 1980; Wilson and Herrnstein, 1985).

The final sample of 987 subjects analyzed in the present study was selected from the first four cohorts (1959–1962) of 2,958 black mothers who participated in the Perinatal Project. Data collection is ongoing for the latter four cohorts of subjects. A sample of white subjects was too limited in size to be included in analyses of delinquency.

The sample of 987 subjects consisted of 487 males and 500 females. These subjects were selected according to the following criteria: (1) located in a Philadelphia public school, (2) stayed in Philadelphia from ages 10 through 17, (3) received selected intelligence tests at age 7 (+/− six months) and achievement tests at ages 13 and 14, and (4) were not among sibling members excluded from the sample to prevent possible biases in multiple family membership. Comparisons between the final sample of 987 black subjects and the excluded sample of 2,158 black subjects showed no significant differences in key variables: total family income, per capita family income, the number of prenatal examinations the mother attended, the mother's age, and the distribution of males and females. In general, the final sample appeared to be representative of the sample from which it was drawn. (For a further description of these comparisons, see Denno, 1982.)

Data sources

This study analyzed three primary data sources; (1) the Perinatal Project's data set of early biological and environmental factors; (2) school records; and (3) police records for juveniles and adults. Key variables selected from these data sources, the theoretical rationale for their inclusion, and the means and standard deviations for males and females in this sample are described in depth in the Appendix of this book. The Appendix also outlines the reliability and validity of each of the variables and details on how they were coded.

Early biological and environmental factors

The Perinatal Project's data set is particularly rich for research because it contains multiple measures of variables at different ages that reflect important stages of development. Data collection for the study was prospective (looking forward). Upon registration, each mother was administered a battery of interviews and physical examinations. Data recorded for each pregnancy included information on the mother's reproductive history, recent and past medical history, prenatal examination and laboratory test results, all drugs taken during pregnancy, and labor and delivery events. Data recorded for each child included information on neurological and medical examinations at birth, throughout the hospital stay, at 4 months, and at 1 and 7 years. Psychological test batteries and behavioral data were collected at 8 months and at 4 and 7 years. Additionally, children were administered speech, language, and hearing examinations at 3 and 8 years. Socioeconomic and family data were collected during the mother's registration and at the child's 7-year examination.

Data were collected quickly and uniformly after an event occurred. Highly structured, precoded forms and manuals were used to ensure comprehensiveness and comparability among coders. All coders were either medical doctors or psychologists who were trained to record data systematically. (For further descriptions of the numerous procedures used to ensure reliability in the Project coding, see Denno, 1982; Niswander and Gordon, 1972; U.S. Department of Health, Education, and Welfare, 1966.)

School records

Philadelphia public school records contain a variety of data that are complementary to the Perinatal Project data collected during the child's first 7 years. In the present study, two types of school record data were used for analysis: academic achievement, and evidence of learning or behavioral disabilities.

Academic achievement was measured by the California Achievement

Test in grades 7 and 8, during ages 13 and 14. This test has been described as an excellent data source for both verbal and mathematical achievement (Bryan, 1978; Womer, 1978), and it has been found to correlate highly with intelligence tests measured in the Perinatal Project at age 7 (Washington and Teska, 1970). Achievement data for grades 7 and 8 were analyzed because they included measures of mathematical ability and because they were measured near to the onset of offense behavior.

Evidence of learning and behavioral problems was measured by the presence, during adolescence, of any record of involvement in special school programs for those classified as mentally retarded or disciplinary problems. Children with disciplinary problems were diagnosed as having normal intellectual ability but some record of asocial behavior in school, such as physical aggression toward teachers, firestarting, inability to adjust to school, or conduct disturbance. According to the Philadelphia School Board, recommendation of a child to a program for disciplinary problems was based solely on in-school performance and was made independently of any knowledge of a child's official, delinquent status.

Police records

Official police records were collected for all subjects for ages 7 through 22. A detailed description of the arrest data collection and coding procedure, the intercoding reliability check, major variables, and offender categories is available (Sellin Center for Studies in Criminology and Criminal Law, 1981).

In the present study, delinquency and violence from ages 7 through 17 were measured in three ways: (1) number of offenses, (2) seriousness of offenses, and (3) types of delinquency offenders according to levels of the most serious offense committed (violence, property, and nonindex). Young adult crime between ages 18 and 22 was measured according to the number of offenses, and types of criminal offenders according to levels of the most serious committed (violence, property, and nonindex).

The advantages of using official police records for indicating delinquent behavior, relative to other points of contact in the justice system such as a court trial, have been discussed elsewhere (Wolfgang et al., 1972). Most important is the relatively less biased nature of a police contact, the first event in a chain of official legal processing. In general, there is also considerable evidence that the demographic and socioeconomic distributions of offenders designated by police contacts are similar to distributions in data gathered from other sources, such as self-reports or victimization data (Hindelang et al., 1979).

It is important to note, however, that a delinquent or criminal status in this study is based on total police contacts, not just arrests. Consequently, the delinquent sample includes a portion of adolescents who may self-report participation in an illegal event but who may have only an official "remedial" status, and not a formal arrest. Thus, while only official records are examined, they include a significant proportion of police contacts that may have been ignored in other delinquency and crime research.

Study measures

Measures in this study, presented in Table 2.1, were selected according to social-structural, social bonding, developmental, and biopsychological theories of delinquency. These measures are associated with one another and thus may fall into a number of theoretical groupings.

Social structure

During the 1960s, at the time of the Perinatal Project, the majority of large metropolitan areas, including Philadelphia, experienced significant social upheaval and shifts in the distribution of nonwhite residential patterns. In general throughout the decade, there was an increase in the concentration of blacks and all nonwhites in urban areas (Glantz and Delaney, 1973). In Philadelphia, for example, the proportion of blacks rose from 23 percent in 1960 to 33 percent in 1970 (Muller, Meyer, and Cybriwsky, 1976: 14). With the exception of New York City, Philadelphia was (and perhaps still is) the most socially heterogeneous city in the United States (Muller et al., 1976: 1). Despite such diversity, however, ethnic and racial groups have a long tradition of residential segregation. Even neighborhoods that appear ethnically mixed in tabulated statistics remain firmly segregated at the block level (Muller et al., 1976: 22, 23).

In the 1960s, the majority of low income blacks in Philadelphia were concentrated in the inner city areas (Weiler, 1974: 181–182), which, as one ethnographer described, were a "world unto themselves" (Anderson, 1969: 3). Poor inner city neighborhoods were isolated socially and culturally and were marked by overcrowded, substandard housing (Clark, n.d.: 19–24). Then, as now, the social-structural constraints and conditions of these neighborhoods were recognized as "festers of crime" (Fonzi, 1960).

In the present study, the selection and characteristics of the Perinatal

Table 2.1. *Selected biological and environmental measures*

Measures at birth

1. *Prenatal maternal conditions*
   Number of prenatal examinations
   Number of prenatal conditions (a count of 8 items: mother's heavy cigarette smoking, use of sedatives, single marital status, presence of diabetes, hypertension, number of venereal conditions, number of neurological or psychiatric conditions, number of infectious diseases)
   Poor obstetrical history (number of prior abortions, stillbirths, premature siblings, or neonatal death of siblings)
   Mother's age
   Number of prior pregnancies
2. *Pregnancy and delivery conditions*
   Number of pregnancy and birth complications (a count of 17 items: placenta previa, abruptio placentae, marginal sinus rupture, uterine bleeding during the first, second, or third trimester, anesthetic shock, other anesthetic accident, cesarean or breech delivery, prolapsed cord, irregular fetal heart rate, meconium during labor, use of oxytocic during labor, loose cord around the neck, tight cord around the neck, forceps marks at delivery, mutiple birth)
   Duration of labor
   Apgar at one and five minutes
   Gestational age, birth weight
3. *Family and social structure*
   Absence of the father
   Amount of time the father is unemployed
   Mother's employment status
   Mother's marital status
   Child's birth order
4. *Socioeconomic status*
   Mother's education
   Father's education
   Total family income (adjusted to 1970 dollars)
   Total family per capita income (adjusted to 1970 dollars)

Measures at age 1

5. *Neurological factors*
   Hand preference (right, left, or variable)
   Abnormal behavioral control

Measures at age 4

6. *Intelligence*
   Stanford–Binet Intelligence Scale
7. *Cerebral dominance*
   Hand, eye, foot preference (right, left, or variable)
   Composite index of hand, eye, and foot preference

Measures at age 7

8. *Physical growth and development*
   Height and weight
   Ponderal index (height/weight^3)

Table 2.1. *(cont.)*

9. *General physical health*
   Pica
   Lead intoxication
   Iron deficiency anemia, 5 to 8 gm.
   Systolic and diastolic blood pressure
10. *Neurological factors*
   Head shape, head circumference
   Ear size, shape, and position
   Otoscopic exam
   Eye structure
   Referral needed for glasses
   Abnormal visual acuity
   Mental status (clinical impression)
   Speech (clinical impression)
   Number of neurological abnormalities
11. *Soft neurological signs*
   Nystagmus
   Abnormal movements
   Gait abnormality
   Coordination, awkwardness
   Right and left identification
   Reflexes
   Abnormal EEG
   Mixed cerebral dominance
   Position sense
   Stereognosis
12. *Cerebral dominance*
   Hand, eye, and foot preference (right, left, or variable)
   Composite index of hand, eye, and foot preference
13. *Intelligence*
   WISC Verbal IQ
   WISC Verbal subscales (information, comprehension, vocabulary, digit span)
   WISC Performance IQ
   WISC Performance subcales (picture arrangement, block design, coding)
   WISC Performance IQ–Verbal IQ difference
   Bender Gestalt Test, Koppitz scoring
   Bender Gestalt, time in seconds
   Goodenough–Harris drawing test
14. *Achievement*
   Wide Range Achievement Test (WRAT) Spelling, Reading, Arithmetic
15. *Family and social structure*
   Absence of the father
   Absence of the father at birth and at age 7
   Amount of time the father is unemployed
   Mother's religion
   Number of changes in mother's marital status (from birth to age 7)
   Mother's marital stability

Table 2.1. *(cont.)*

Number of adults, relatives in the household
Total family size
Presence of grandparents in the household
Use of childcare
Foster or adoptive parents, guardian
Number of household moves (from birth to age 7)

16. *Socioeconomic status*
   Education, occupation of household head (Census Bureau Index)
   Additional schooling of the mother since child's birth
   Number of persons supported
   Total family income (adjusted to 1970 dollars)
   Total per capita income (adjusted to 1970 dollars)

Measures at ages 13–14

17. *Achievement*
   California Achievement Tests (CAT):
   total reading (vocabulary, comprehension)
   total math (computation, concepts and problems)
   total language (mechanics, usage, and structure)
   spelling

18. *Disciplinary status*
   Enrollment in a school program for youths with disciplinary problems at any time
      during adolescence

19. *Mental retardation*
   Enrollment in a school program for youths with tested evidence of retardation at any
      time during adolescence

Measures at ages 7–17

20. *Delinquency and violence*
   Total number of officially recorded offenses (police contacts and arrests)
   Seriousness of offenses (based on weights derived from a national survey of crime
      severity)
   Classification of delinquency offenders (nonindex, property, or violent)

Measures at ages 18–22

21. *Young adult crime and violence*
   Total number of officially recorded offenses (police contacts and arrests)
   Classification of criminal offenders (nonindex, property, or violent)

Project sample serve as controls for a number of such social-structural factors. First, only black subjects were selected for analysis. In addition, all subjects were born and raised until young adulthood in the same city and received very similar medical treatment early in life. Most subjects lived in the same neighborhoods. All subjects attended Philadelphia public schools and the great majority shared a predominantly lower to lower-middle socioeconomic status. Thus, the sample represents a fairly homogeneous group with characteristics found in some past research to associate strongly with delinquency.

Aside from such homogeneity, however, previous research has demonstrated the importance of a wide range of other, or more specific, social-structural factors in predicting crime, such as familial and parental instability. In the present study, these factors include presence of the husband or father in the household, residential mobility, religion, employment, and marital status.

Social bonding

The extent to which youths are committed to normative values in society can be assessed through their degree of socially conforming ambitions and aspirations (Hirschi, 1969) as well as through their actual behavior. Academic achievement in school is often considered an indicator of commitment to conformity in terms of both current peer acceptance and the recognition of future prospects (Paternoster, Saltzman, Waldo, and Chiricos, 1983). Undisciplined or deviant school behavior is often a direct indicator of lack of normative commitment and involvement in unconventional activity.

In the present study, school achievement was measured by subjects' California Achievement Test scores for ages 13 and 14 (grades 7 and 8). Seriously problematic or undisciplined school behavior was measured by whether a subject participated in a school program for youths with disciplinary problems during adolescence.

Development and biopsychology

Developmental and biopsychological theories of delinquency emphasize the physiological and psychological capacities of individuals to adjust to their social and physical environments and to learn appropriate behavior. Individuals who experience CNS disorders, have delayed maturation, or have low intelligence test scores, for example, may be more vulnerable to negative or stressful environments. They may also have less control over their behavior. In the present study, indicators of developmental or biopsychological theories are grouped very generally into six types: (1) early CNS development, (2) intelligence and cerebral dominance, (3) physical growth, (4) neurological factors, (5) attention deficit disorder (minimal brain dysfunction) and hyperactivity, and (6) general physical health.

Early CNS development. Early CNS development is measured by a variety of prenatal and pregnancy complications (seen in the mother's obstetrical history, age, and health conditions during pregnancy and delivery) found to relate to later disorders. Measures of the child's health and physical condition include birth weight, evidence of prematurity (indicated by gestational age at birth), and Apgar score, an accepted and validated scale of health and development immediately following birth.

Intelligence and cerebral dominance. Measures of verbal and spatial ability include the Stanford–Binet, which was administered at age 4. Examinations at age 7 included the WISC and its subtests, the Bender Gestalt, and the Goodenough–Harris drawing test. School achievement, which is correlated with intelligence, was measured by the Wide Range Achievement Test at age 7 and the California Achievement Test at ages 13 and 14. All of these measures have already been used as indicators of learning disabilties and of cerebral dominance or lateralization (Reitan and Davison, 1974). Hand, eye, and foot preference at different ages represent additional measures of cerebral dominance.

Physical growth and development. Measures of height and weight selected for the present study have been found to be excellent indicators of physical growth (Davie et al., 1972). The ponderal index, as measured by height/weight^3, is an indicator of body fatness and physique that can be used to test theories by the Gluecks and by Sheldon that suggested a relationship between delinquency and physique.

Neurological factors. The presence of neurological disorders is determined in part by evidence of abnormal head shape, eye structure, and head circumference, in addition to soft neurological signs such as abnormal movements, gait, or reflexes. Some of these factors can be used to test earlier Lombrosian theories suggesting that delinquents have a disproportionate number of physical abnormalities or facial asymmetries.

Attention deficit disorder (minimal brain dysfunction) and hyperactivity. Associations among delinquency, behavior disturbance, and low school achievement have been linked frequently to health disorders such as attention deficit disorder and hyperactivity. In the present study, indicators of these dysfunctions include evidence of disciplinary problems in childhood and adolescence as well as soft neurological signs such as lack of coordination, mixed cerebral dominance, and difficulty with right–left identification.

General physical health. There is some evidence of a higher incidence of health problems among delinquents and violent offenders (see, for example, Lewis and Balla, 1976). In the present study, indicators of health or physical problems include blood pressure, pica, anemia, and lead intoxication.

Delinquency

Delinquency is measured according to different types of offenders, number of offenses, and seriousness of offenses. There are three types of offenders: violent, property, and nonindex offenders. *Violent offenders* are those individuals who have had a police contact at any time during their juvenile career for at least one violent offense: murder, assault with intent to kill, aggravated assault, simple assault, rape, robbery with injury, or any other offense that involved injury to the victim. *Property offenders* have had no history of violent offenses, but at least one police contact for property-related offenses such as vandalism, burglary, robbery without injury, or auto theft. *Nonindex offenders* are those who have had no history of violent or property-related offenses, but a police contact for at least one nonindex offense: truancy, disorderly conduct, running away, fraud, or possession of alchohol, marihuana, or hard drugs.

Offense seriousness is based upon a detailed index originally developed by Sellin and Wolfgang (1964) and then eventually expanded by the National Crime Severity Study (Wolfgang, Figlio, Tracy, and Singer, 1985). The index involves assigning numerical weights to different components of an offense, such as level of injury, amount of property theft or damage, victim intimidation, premises entered, and vehicles stolen. This score allows a more precise representation of offense seriousness not reflected in the arrest code classification and is also an excellent method of summarizing the severity of an offender's delinquency record throughout adolescence.

Criminal behavior at different ages

Few studies have examined criminal behavior over the life-span (Sellin Center, 1987; Wolfgang, Thornberry, and Figlio, 1987). Uniform Crime Report data show, however, considerable differences in the types and frequencies of arrests reported according to age. In general, juveniles (ages 10 to 18) are more likely to have a police contact for property offenses and relatively less serious crimes, and young adults (ages 19 to 25) are more likely to have a police contact for violent and serious crimes

(U.S. Dept. of Justice, 1985; Wolfgang et al., 1987a; Zimring, 1979). Moreover, juveniles who evidence relatively more aggressive childhood behavior or delinquent offenses are more likely to be adult offenders than their less delinquent or nondelinquent counterparts (Magnusson, Stattin and Duner, 1983; Spivak, 1983; West and Farrington, 1973).

Among both juveniles and adults, however, it has been found that only a small proportion of individuals is responsible for a great majority of police contacts. In a longitudinal study of a cohort of nearly 10,000 boys born in 1945 and living in Philadelphia from ages 10 to 18 (Wolfgang et al., 1972), for example, data showed that chronic offenders (those who have five or more offenses) constituted only 6 percent of the cohort and 18 percent of the offenders, but were responsible for over one-half of all the delinquent offenses committed by the cohort (Wolfgang et al., 1972: 247–248). This finding was replicated in a later study of a birth cohort of Philadelphia boys (Tracy et al., 1985) as well as in other research conducted both nationally and internationally (Farrington, 1983; Hamparian, Schuster, Dinitz, and Conrad, 1978; Shannon, 1978). Moreover, a small group of adult offenders is also responsible for most adult offenses (Farrington, 1983: 25; Sellin Center, 1987: 5, 6; Wolfgang et al., 1987: 26). In turn, "there is excellent evidence that some biological factors are especially useful in distinguishing chronic offenders" (Mednick et al., 1982: 3). Thus, the behaviors and characteristics of the chronic few are of particular importance from perspectives of both social policy and criminal reponsibility.

The following sections discuss the extent of delinquency and crime in the present sample. Delinquency distributions are first described in considerable detail and then followed with a discussion of distributions of crime during young adulthood.

Juvenile delinquency

Altogether, about 22 percent of the 987 youths had at least one police contact prior to age 18, as shown in Table 2.2. Expectedly, strong sex differences appear. Over twice as many males (31 percent) as females (14 percent) had a police contact.

The proportion of police contacts, particularly for males, is somewhat lower in comparison to the proportion found for other nonwhites raised in Philadelphia at a similar time. In a current study of a cohort of males and females who were born in 1958 and lived in Philadelphia ("Birth Cohort II") (Tracy et al., 1985), 41 percent of the nonwhite males and 18 percent of the nonwhite females experienced a police contact prior to age

Table 2.2. *Type of offender by sex*

Type of offender	Males	Females	Total
Nonoffender	336	431	767
	(69.00%)	(86.20%)	(77.71%)
Nonindex offender	64	34	98
	(13.14%)	(6.80%)	(9.93%)
Property offender	51	27	78
	(10.47%)	(5.40%)	(7.90%)
Violent offender	36	8	44
	(7.39%)	(1.60%)	(4.46%)
Total	487	500	987
	(100%)	(100%)	(100%)

18. The generally lower prevalence of offense behavior among the Perinatal Project youths may be due to several factors: (1) Perinatal Project youths participated in a medical study for the first seven years of their lives and therefore may have received certain physical and psychological benefits; (2) mothers of the Perinatal Project youths, interested enough to participate in a study for seven years, may have had a greater concern about the welfare of their offspring; (3) participation in the Perinatal Project itself may have had a positive effect on youths; and (4) the sample of nonwhites in the Birth Cohort II study may have comprised ethnic groups with higher crimes rates than blacks and thus rates for the group as a whole are inflated.

Violence and repeat offenses

Table 2.2 shows that among that 151 males who became offenders by age 18, 36 (nearly one quarter) experienced a police contact for at least one offense that involved violence or injury to at least one other person. In contrast, only 8 (12 percent) of the 69 female offenders were involved in a violent or injury-related offense. The ratio of violent male to violent female offenders is 2:1. This discrepancy is not surprising in light of the substantial literature that demonstrates higher levels of both nonviolent and violent delinquent conduct among males.

For both sexes, however, nonindex offenses predominate. More than 40 percent of the males and nearly one half of the females were nonindex offenders. Likewise, somewhat more females (39 percent) were property offenders relative to males (34 percent). Overall, then, most of the

Table 2.3. *Number of offenses by sex*

Number of offenses	Males	Females	Total
1	69	45	114
	(45.69%)	(65.22%)	(51.82%)
	[45.69%]*	[65.22%]	[51.82%]
2	35	12	47
	(23.19%)	(17.38%)	(21.36%)
	[68.88%]	[82.60%]	[73.18%]
3	10	4	14
	(6.62%)	(5.79%)	(6.36%)
	[75.50%]	[88.39%]	[79.54%]
4	12	1	13
	(7.95%)	(1.45%)	(5.92%)
	[83.45%]	[89.84%]	[85.46%]
5	5	0	5
	(3.31%)		(2.27%)
	[86.76%]		[87.73%]
6	7	1	8
	(4.64%)	(1.45%)	(3.64%)
	[91.40%]	[91.29%]	[91.37%]
7	4	0	4
	(2.65%)		(1.82%)
	[94.05%]		[93.19%]
8	1	3	4
	(0.66%)	(4.35%)	(1.82%)
	[94.71%]	[95.64%]	[95.01%]
9	2	2	4
	(1.32%)	(2.91%)	(1.82%)
	[96.03%]	[98.55%]	[96.83%]
≥ 10	6	1	7
	(3.97%)	(1.45%)	(3.17%)
	[100%]	[100%]	[100%]
Total	151	69	220
	(100%)	(100%)	(100%)
	[100%]	[100%]	[100%]

Note: Cumulative percentages are in brackets.

delinquent behavior of both males and females was nonviolent although the amount of violent behavior is sizable – especially within a subgroup of male offenders.

The number of offenses committed by these juveniles is crucial to understanding chronic, long-term delinquency. The number experienced by any one offender ranged from 1 to a maximum of 27 offenses across ages 7 to 17. Consistent with past research, Table 2.3 shows that males lominated females in the number of offenses: 45 percent of the male)ffenders but nearly two-thirds of the female offenders had only one)fficial police contact. In turn, 38 percent of the males and one quarter of he females were nonchronic repeat offenders, or those who committed 2 o 4 offenses. The relatively small percentage of chronic offenders consti- utes the major focus of this study. Their behavior is deviant not only in :omparison to nonoffenders, but also relative to their less-frequently)ffending counterparts. In total, 17 percent of the male offenders were :hronic relative to 10 percent of the females, making a male to female -atio of 1.7:1.

Incidence and seriousness

An important factor to consider in examining the different kinds of)ffenders is the amounts and the types of the offenses they commit. Altogether, the sample of 987 youths was responsible for a total of 588 offenses between the ages of 7 and 17. Males were responsible for 443 or three quarters of the total number of offenses; females were responsible for 145 offenses, making the male to female ratio 4:1.

Males committed relatively more violent offenses: 64 (14 percent) involved violence or injury; 155 (35 percent) involved property theft or damage; and 224 (51 percent) were nonindex offenses. In contrast, among females, 10 (7 percent) of the offenses involved violence; 51 (35 percent) involved property theft or damage; and 84 (58 percent) were nonindex offenses.

Sex differences were even clearer for offense seriousness. For male offenders, seriousness scores ranged from .3 to 158, with a mean score of 17. For females, they ranged from .3 to 58, with a mean score of 7. Thus, the mean level for males was nearly 2.5 times greater than for females.

Seriousness levels also differed according to groups of offenders. Among males, the mean seriousness score for one-time offenders was 3, for nonchronic repeat offenders it was 15, and for chronics offenders, 58. Among females, one-time offenders had a mean score of 2, nonchronic repeat offenders 11, and chronic offenders, 30. Clearly, chronic offenders deviated from the other groups in terms of the extent and the severity level of their offenses.

Chronic offenders

One of the most important results reported in delinquency research is the finding that chronic offenders, who constitute only a small portion of a

·total sample of youths, are responsible for a highly disproportionate share of the total number of offenses (Tracy et al., 1985; Wolfgang et al. 1972). The domination of chronic offenders in the amount of crime particularly of serious offense behavior, was also striking in the present study. The 25 male chronic offenders represented 5 percent of the total male sample and 17 percent of all male delinquents. These chronic offenders, however, accounted for 226 offenses or 51 percent of those committed by males. Chronic female offenders represented only 1 percent of the female sample and 10 percent of the female delinquents, but accounted for 60 offenses or 41 percent of those committed by females.

Chronic offenders, particularly males, also committed a highly disproportionate share of the violent crime. Among males the results were striking: chronic offenders were responsible for 61 percent of the violent offenses, 55 percent of the property offenses, and 46 percent of the nonindex offenses. Chronic females accounted for 40 percent of the violent offenses, 30 percent of the property offenses, and 48 percent of the nonindex offenses. Thus, although both male and female chronic offenders dominated the amount of offense behavior, female chronics exhibited considerably less volume and severity of crime than their male counterparts.

Age

The age at which a juvenile begins a delinquent career is strongly related to future offense behavior. In general, the earlier a juvenile commits a first offense, the more offenses will be committed throughout the juvenile career (Wolfgang et al., 1972). A juvenile's age at the onset of delinquency is also important relative to other biological and environmental circumstances.

Cumulative percentages of the age at first offense are shown in Table 2.4. The highest percentages of males and females had a police contact at ages 14 (19 percent) and 13 (17 percent); the lowest percentages occurred at both ends of the distribution, ages 11 (6 percent) and 17 (7 percent).

Some sex differences exist. The highest percentage of females became offenders at age 13 (23 percent) relative to the highest percentage of males at age 14 (20 percent). Cumulatively, nearly half of the females and the males (46 percent) became offenders before age 14. More than three quarters of the males (79 percent) and the females (81 percent) became offenders before age 16. Thus, although a higher percentage of offense behavior occurred one year earlier for females, cumulative percentages are similar for both sexes.

Table 2.4. *Age at first offense by sex*

Age at first offense	Males	Females	Total
≤ 10	18	5	23
	(11.93%)	(7.25%)	(10.45%)
	[11.93%]*	[7.25%]	[10.45%]
11	11	3	14
	(7.28%)	(4.35%)	(6.36%)
	[19.21%]	[11.60%]	[16.81%]
12	19	8	27
	(12.58%)	(11.59%)	(12.27%)
	[31.79%]	[23.19%]	[29.08%]
13	21	16	37
	(13.91%)	(23.19%)	(16.83%)
	[45.70%]	[46.38%]	[45.91%]
14	30	12	42
	(19.87%)	(17.39%)	(19.09%)
	[65.57%]	[63.77%]	[65.00%]
15	20	12	32
	(13.24%)	(17.39%)	(14.54%)
	[78.81%]	[81.16%]	[79.54%]
16	20	9	29
	(13.24%)	(13.04%)	(13.19%)
	[92.05%]	[94.20%]	[92.73%]
17	12	4	16
	(7.95%)	(5.80%)	(7.27%)
	[100%]	[100%]	[100%]
Total	151	69	220
	(100%)	(100%)	(100%)
	[100%]	[100%]	[100%]

Note: Cumulative percentages are in brackets.

An examination of the mean ages of the onset of delinquency for different offender groups confirms, in general, that the more serious offenders start younger. Mean ages for nonchronic and chronic male offenders (13.5 and 12.9 years, respectively) were significantly lower than the mean age for male one-time offenders (14.6 years) ($F[2,148] = 7.51$; $p < .001$). Likewise, mean ages for property and violent male offenders (13.6 and 13.3 years, respectively) were significantly lower than the mean age for male nonindex offenders (14.6 years) ($F[2,148] = 5.72$; $p < .005$). In turn, female offenders with two or more offenses were significantly younger (12.8 years) than female one-time offenders (14.9 years) ($F[1,67] = 24.31$; $p < .001$). No significant differences appeared among the mean ages for types of female offenders.

Table 2.5. *Juvenile and adult arrest categories by sex*

	Males	Females	Total
No juvenile or adult arrest	280	415	695
	(57.50%)	(83.00%)	(70.42%)
Juvenile arrest only	98	61	159
	(20.12%)	(12.20%)	(16.11%)
Adult arrest only	56	16	72
	(11.50%)	(3.20%)	(7.29%)
Juvenile and adult arrest	53	8	61
	(10.88%)	(1.60%)	(6.18%)
Total	487	500	987
	(100%)	(100%)	(100%)

Young adult crime

Four groups of individuals can be identified in comparing offense be-havior between the juvenile and young adult years: (1) those who never experience either a juvenile or an adult police contact; (2) those who experience at least one juvenile contact but no adult contact; (3) those who experience at least one adult contact but no juvenile contact; and (4) those who experience at least one juvenile and one adult contact. The major focus of this study is on the last two groups, who are combined in analyses of young adult crime.

Distributions for males and females according to the four groups of possible juvenile or adult arrest combinations are presented in Table 2.5. Altogether, 109 (22 percent) of the total sample of 487 male offenders experienced an adult arrest; of these, 53 (nearly one half) had previously experienced a juvenile arrest. Of the total sample of 500 female offen-ders, 24 (5 percent) experienced an adult arrest; of these, 8 (one third) had previously experienced a juvenile arrest.

Of the 109 males who had an adult arrest, 55 (one half) had one offense and only 15 (14 percent) were chronic offenders. Of the 24 adult females in this group, 15 (63 percent) had only one arrest and 2 (8 percent) were chronic offenders. Altogether then, the data show that males are considerably more likely than females both to continue crime into adulthood and to commit more than one crime. Importantly, how-ever, for both males and females, a juvenile offender has a 50 percent chance of becoming an adult offender.

The question of whether or not these juvenile and adult offenders are different from nonoffenders on intelligence test scores and selected early life factors at varying ages is discussed in the next chapter. Subsequent chapters examine whether any possible differences exist when these factors are examined simultaneously in order to predict both juvenile and adult crime.

3

Intelligence and crime

Do criminals have lower tested intelligence than noncriminals? A substantial literature suggests that they do (see chapter 1). Despite the magnitude of research on the topic, however, the nature and extent of the intelligence–crime link are not entirely clear. Indeed, most studies have not incorporated enough different measures at varying points in time to draw definite conclusions. Nor have most studies examined intelligence with other predictors of crime, such as early CNS development, socioeconomic status, or family factors.

The dearth of reliable research on intelligence, and on crime in particular, is attributable in part to the argument that intelligence is not a significant predictor of delinquency when controlling for important intervening factors, such as socioeonomic status. However, a number of the studies mentioned in chapter 1 showed that the link between intelligence and crime remains even when socioeconomic status is controlled. Conflicting conclusions about the intelligence–crime relationship are further clouded by claims that intelligence test scores, which, for the most part, have been standardized with white, middle-class children, do not adequately reflect the abilities of minorities or those from lower socioeconomic levels (see the section on intelligence tests in the Appendix). Such claims are not entirely relevant, however, in studies of children who are of the same race and socioeconomic background.

Determining exactly what intelligence tests measure is more difficult to pinpoint than determining how strongly the tests relate to other factors. In general, intelligence test scores are associated with achievement in school, which is in turn related to acceptance by peers and teachers and to later occupational success. Intelligence test scores are also linked to school conduct. Children who have problems controlling their behavior generally score more poorly on intelligence tests either because problems with testing lead to problems with behavior or, just as likely, because behavioral problems disrupt learning ability, which is then reflected in low scores (Denno, 1985; for a more thorough discussion of the meaning of psychological tests, see Moffitt, in press).

This chapter analyzes the relationship between crime and the intelligence and achievement test scores of the Biosocial Project children at ages 4, 7, and 13–14. These ages are important both for intellectual and moral development and because of their relationship to the onset of delinquency.

Moral development or moral reasoning refers to the ability to distinguish between right and wrong based upon value judgments. Generally, children of the same age share particular developmental characteristics that differ from those of children of another age, who may be at a different stage of development (Simpson, 1976). Although intellectual maturity is necessary for moral maturity, however, it is not always sufficient for adequate moral development (Shapiro and Perry, 1976). Thus, certain individuals may experience impediments in moral development and maintain a lesser stage of maturity unrelated to their age (Tomlinson-Keasey and Keasey, 1974).

The association between age and intellectual and moral development also involves the interaction of many different factors (Hogan, 1974). For example, although the acquisition of higher stages of moral development (described by Kohlberg in Kohlberg and Elfenbein, 1975) is related to intelligence, extensive longitudinal research on mental retardates indicates that developmental gains in moral reasoning, conduct, and judgment are evident throughout adolescence (Aronfreed, 1974). In turn, halts in moral development among individuals of average intelligence may be influenced by the environment. A comparison between IQ-matched normal and sociopathic children, for example, indicates that sociopathic children have a lower stage of moral development because they lack opportunities for role-taking in their families (Campagna and Harter, 1974). Other comparisons suggest that parents of delinquent children may discourage mature moral reasoning (Jurkovic and Prentice, 1974).

In addition to halts in moral development, discontinuities in both mental and physical development may exist during childhood and adolescence for a variety of reasons. For example, standard curves of both mental and physical growth tend to be nonlinear over time (Armstrong, 1980). According to Epstein (1974), spurts of mental growth generally occur during the ages of 2–4, 6, 8, 10–12, and 14–16 years. Although the link between physical and mental development is not well established, correlations, in any case, "are suggestive" (Carey and Diamond, 1980).

In this chapter intelligence, achievement test scores, and factors related to early development are examined for juvenile offender groups at different ages. The intelligence and achievement tests, described in detail in the Appendix, measure a variety of verbal and spatial abilities as well as other characteristics such as moral reasoning and impulsivity. Chapter 4 examines these variables for young adult offender groups.

Offender group differences in test scores

Distributions of intelligence and achievement test scores for the Biosocial Project children are shown in Tables 3.1 through 3.4. Scores on the WISC Full Scale IQ indicate that the means for the total sample and for each offender group fall into the lower half of the "average" intelligence range of 80 to 119 points, as specified in the WISC manual.

Offender group differences in test scores were examined using the analysis of variance (ANOVA) and the Duncan's Multiple Range test. ANOVA tests whether significant differences exist in general among offender groups. The Duncan's Multiple Range test contrasts all possible pairs of group means to determine if there are significant differences between each of the offender groups. For example, the Duncan test can show whether the mean scores for violent offenders are significantly different from the mean scores for property offenders, nonindex offenders, or nonoffenders. In turn, mean score differences between nonoffenders and property offenders can be examined, and so on.

In the tables that follow, the results of between-group differences tested with the Duncan are indicated by changes in the letters A and B (shown in the column labelled [DN]), which order groups means respectively from largest to smallest. Means with the same letter are not significantly different at the $p < .05$ level. For example, if two groups have identical letters (e.g., [A] and [A]) or share the same letter (e.g., [A] and [AB]), they are not significantly different; if two groups have discrepant letters (e.g., [A] and [B]), they are significantly different.

Violent offenders

Table 3.1 shows that some test scores for types of male offenders differed according to degrees of offense severity – particularly violence. At ages 4 and 7, violent offenders scored significantly lower than some other offender groups or nonoffenders on the following tests: Stanford–Binet, WISC Full Scale IQ, Verbal IQ and Performance IQ, WISC Digit Span, WISC Block Design, and WRAT Spelling and Reading. However, comparisons between nonoffenders and violent offenders show that the differences are not extensive (not more than three IQ points).

Similarly, when "high, medium, and low" levels of the WISC Verbal

nd Performance IQs are compared, violent offenders are dispropor-
onately ranked in the lower third of the test scores (which range from 57
> 86), but not significantly so. Relative to nonoffenders, violent offen-
ers were also not significantly represented among those youths with
orderline-or-below intelligence scores (< 80) or mentally defective in-
elligence scores (≤ 69) for either the WISC Verbal or the Performance
Q.

More striking differences existed at adolescence, however, and most
trongly for violent offenders. Compared to nonoffenders, violent offen-
ers scored 17 percentiles lower on Vocabulary, 16 percentiles lower on
'otal Reading, and between 10 and 14 percentiles lower on Total Lan-
uage, the Total Battery, Comprehension, Mechanics, and Usage and
tructure. No differences existed for the Total Math and it subtests,
idicating that violent offenders achieved more poorly in verbal and
anguage abilities.

The extent of these differences among offender groups becomes mag-
ified, particularly in adolescence, when sample test scores are grouped
ito categories of high, medium, and low. Highly significant differences
xisted in comparisons for select reading and language achievement tests.
'or example, twice as many violent offenders than nonoffenders scored in
he bottom third (ranging from 1 to 15 percentiles) of the Biosocial Project
ample for Total Reading achievement; in turn, four times more non-
•ffenders than violent offenders scored in the top third (ranging from
8 to 99 percentiles) of the sample (χ^2 [2] = 16.5; p ≤ .001). Com-
arable, highly significant disparities between nonoffenders and violent
•ffenders existed for Total Language achievement (χ^2 [2] = 11.0;
• < .01).

Test score differences for females showed that both violent and non-
ndex offenders scored significantly lower on select tests relative to
onoffenders and property offenders. Significant results with nonindex
•ffenders may be due to the relatively high frequency of their offenses
nd the fact that some misbehaviors that may be quite minor for males
e.g., truancy and disorderly conduct) are a sign of considerably more
nisbehavior when conducted by females.

As Table 3.2 shows, nonindex and violent offenders scored significantly
ower on WISC Performance IQ, violent offenders scored significantly
ower on WISC Block Design, and nonindex offenders scored significant-
y lower on the WRAT Spelling. The differences among offender groups
n these tests are greater than those found for males, although small
ample sizes limit the reliability of comparisons.

With this qualification in mind, a comparison between nonoffenders
nd violent female offenders resulted in significant differences among the

Table 3.1. *Test scores at ages 4, 7, and 13–14 years by juvenile offender type, males only*

Ages	Tests	Nonoffender			Nonindex offender			Property offender			Violent offender			F-value
		Mean	(SD)	[DN]	Mean	(SD)	[DN]	Mean	(SD)	[DN]	Mean	(SD)	[DN]	(3,483)
4	Stanford–Binet Intelligence Scale (25–175)	89.75	(12.19)	[A]	91.48	(11.00)	[A]	93.02	(12.56)	[A]	87.06	(9.82)	[B]	2.18
7	WISC Full Scale IQ (25–154)	92.67	(11.22)	[AB]	93.89	(10.97)	[A]	94.86	(8.51)	[A]	89.03	(10.90)	[B]	2.27
7	WISC Verbal IQ (45–155)	92.42	(11.35)	[AB]	94.70	(11.32)	[A]	93.10	(10.52)	[AB]	89.11	(8.97)	[B]	2.01
7	WISC Verbal Subscales													
	Information (0–20)	9.14	(2.44)	[A]	9.55	(2.38)	[A]	9.10	(2.00)	[A]	9.03	(2.12)	[A]	0.62
	Comprehension (0–20)	8.67	(2.41)	[A]	8.55	(2.75)	[A]	9.00	(2.50)	[A]	8.17	(2.25)	[A]	0.86
	Vocabulary (0–20)	8.21	(2.49)	[A]	8.50	(2.28)	[A]	8.29	(2.00)	[A]	7.72	(1.95)	[A]	0.83
	Digit span (0–20)	9.10	(2.83)	[B]	9.97	(2.75)	[A]	9.12	(2.75)	[AB]	8.08	(2.79)	[B]	3.58*
7	WISC Performance IQ (44–156)	94.27	(12.66)	[AB]	94.14	(12.84)	[AB]	97.84	(11.11)	[A]	91.03	(14.01)	[B]	2.14
7	WISC Performance Subscales													
	Block design (0–20)	9.12	(2.26)	[AB]	8.70	(2.28)	[B]	9.71	(2.12)	[A]	8.53	(2.41)	[B]	2.66*
	Coding (0–20)	9.49	(2.78)	[B]	9.73	(2.72)	[AB]	10.47	(2.96)	[A]	9.56	(3.16)	[AB]	1.81
	Picture arrangement (0–20)	8.92	(2.81)	[A]	9.05	(2.68)	[A]	8.89	(2.41)	[A]	8.03	(2.51)	[A]	1.27
	PIQ–VIQ difference	1.85	(12.61)	[A]	-0.56	(13.62)	[A]	4.74	(15.13)	[A]	1.92	(12.14)	[A]	1.58
7	Wide Range Achievement Test													
	Spelling (0–55)	22.73	(4.75)	[AB]	23.70	(3.81)	[A]	23.35	(5.37)	[A]	21.22	(3.88)	[B]	2.45
	Reading (0–84)	31.73	(7.81)	[A]	31.34	(6.79)	[A]	30.55	(6.91)	[AB]	28.22	(6.74)	[B]	2.64*
	Arithmetic (0–49)	20.20	(3.54)	[A]	20.62	(2.90)	[A]	19.43	(3.40)	[A]	19.53	(3.02)	[A]	1.58

Age	Variable	(n=336)	(n=64)	(n=51)	(n=36)	F
7	Bender Gestalt Koppitz scoring (0–30)	7.72 (3.44) [A]	7.48 (3.06) [A]	8.45 (3.06) [A]	8.83 (3.40) [A]	2.00
7	Bender Gestalt time (in seconds)	422.06 (187.67) [A]	419.67 (211.48) [A]	402.86 (169.57) [A]	393.94 (139.27) [A]	0.37
7	Goodenough–Harris drawing test (49–151)	96.79 (13.78) [A]	95.83 (12.31) [A]	98.47 (15.12) [A]	94.00 (12.03) [A]	0.85
13–14	California Achievement Test					
	Total Reading (1–99)	31.98 (25.05) [A]	30.72 (23.21) [A]	28.69 (25.47) [A]	16.50 (15.09) [B]	4.50**
	Vocabulary (1–99)	35.10 (32.34) [A]	32.59 (24.38) [A]	31.20 (25.38) [A]	18.33 (16.91) [B]	4.58**
	Comprehension (1–99)	31.06 (24.09) [A]	30.53 (23.73) [A]	27.76 (25.49) [A]	17.44 (14.18) [B]	3.74*
	Total Math (1–99)	24.01 (22.30) [A]	22.78 (20.76) [A]	19.55 (22.03) [A]	16.06 (17.47) [A]	1.88
	Computation (1–99)	24.54 (22.39) [A]	22.02 (20.30) [A]	19.96 (21.65) [A]	18.75 (17.84) [A]	1.36
	Concepts and problems (1–99)	25.97 (22.73) [A]	26.20 (21.09) [A]	22.02 (22.57) [A]	16.25 (18.27) [A]	2.44
	Total Language (1–99)	28.63 (24.24) [A]	26.27 (21.37) [A]	25.18 (22.97) [AB]	15.69 (16.29) [B]	3.51*
	Mechanics (1–99)	30.02 (24.98) [A]	27.47 (22.80) [AB]	25.25 (22.53) [AB]	17.06 (16.55) [B]	3.53*
	Usage and structure (1–99)	30.68 (22.50) [A]	30.53 (19.56) [A]	31.63 (22.48) [A]	20.47 (15.21) [B]	2.54
	Spelling (1–99)	28.69 (24.52) [A]	26.50 (21.46) [A]	23.04 (22.04) [AB]	15.36 (18.96) [B]	4.00*
	Total Battery (1–99)	25.21 (23.17) [A]	23.75 (21.00) [A]	21.24 (22.64) [AB]	12.72 (15.35) [B]	3.61*
13–14	Placements in disciplinary programs (0–9)	0.06 (0.45) [A]	0.14 (0.71) [A]	0.67 (1.64) [B]	0.50 (1.87) [B]	9.38***
13–14	Placements in programs for the retarded (0–15)	0.20 (1.23) [A]	0.14 (0.79) [A]	0.18 (0.71) [A]	0.28 (1.67) [A]	0.11
	Sample sizes	336	64	51	36	Total = 487

Notes: $*p < .05$; $**p < .01$; $***p < .001$.
Duncan [DN] significant at $p < .05$.

53

Table 3.2. *Test scores at ages 4, 7, and 13–14 years by juvenile offender type, females only*

Ages	Tests	Nonoffender			Nonindex offender			Property offender			Violent offender			F-value
		Mean	(SD)	[DN]	Mean	(SD)	[DN]	Mean	(SD)	[DN]	Mean	(SD)	[DN]	(3,496)
4	Stanford–Binet Intelligence Scale (25–175)	91.54	(13.39)	[A]	88.88	(11.76)	[A]	90.96	(11.22)	[A]	85.87	(8.15)	[A]	0.89
7	WISC Full Scale IQ (25–154)	92.45	(11.32)	[A]	89.00	(10.01)	[A]	91.18	(7.69)	[A]	85.00	(8.91)	[A]	2.20
7	WISC Verbal IQ (45–155)	91.48	(11.77)	[A]	90.00	(10.33)	[A]	91.33	(8.77)	[A]	84.50	(7.29)	[A]	1.11
7	WISC Verbal Subscales													
	Information (0–20)	9.14	(2.44)	[A]	8.91	(2.45)	[A]	8.96	(2.41)	[A]	8.00	(1.93)	[A]	0.69
	Comprehension (0–20)	8.15	(2.33)	[A]	8.00	(2.45)	[A]	8.11	(2.31)	[A]	7.87	(2.29)	[A]	0.08
	Vocabulary (0–20)	7.60	(2.36)	[A]	7.68	(1.51)	[A]	8.04	(2.24)	[A]	6.50	(1.31)	[A]	0.94
	Digit span (0–20)	9.60	(3.07)	[A]	9.00	(3.23)	[A]	9.29	(2.63)	[A]	7.62	(1.92)	[A]	1.51
7	WISC Performance IQ (44–156)	94.92	(12.08)	[A]	89.73	(11.15)	[B]	92.59	(9.30)	[AB]	88.25	(11.71)	[B]	2.93*
7	WISC Performance Subscales													
	Block design (0–20)	8.78	(2.08)	[A]	8.50	(2.27)	[A]	8.78	(1.78)	[A]	6.75	(2.37)	[B]	2.63*
	Coding (0–20)	10.64	(2.83)	[A]	9.79	(2.66)	[A]	10.07	(2.37)	[A]	9.62	(2.44)	[A]	1.55
	Picture arrangement (0–20)	8.39	(2.62)	[A]	7.32	(2.58)	[A]	7.96	(2.26)	[A]	8.62	(1.68)	[A]	2.00
	PIQ–VIQ difference	3.44	(11.98)	[A]	-0.26	(11.37)	[A]	1.26	(11.35)	[A]	3.75	(12.42)	[A]	1.24
7	Wide Range Achievement Test													
	Spelling (0–55)	23.67	(4.69)	[A]	21.44	(4.29)	[B]	23.85	(4.52)	[A]	21.62	(1.99)	[A]	2.93*
	Reading (0–84)	32.90	(8.39)	[A]	29.26	(6.75)	[A]	33.85	(8.63)	[A]	31.50	(4.34)	[A]	2.28
	Arithmetic (0–49)	20.48	(3.28)	[A]	19.56	(3.11)	[A]	20.92	(2.46)	[A]	19.75	(2.60)	[A]	1.20

	Group 1			Group 2			Group 3			Group 4			F
7 Bender Gestalt Koppitz scoring (0–30)	8.71	(3.60)	[A]	9.20	(3.37)	[A]	7.74	(3.18)	[A]	9.62	(4.40)	[A]	1.05
7 Bender Gestalt time (in seconds)	393.80	(158.86)	[A]	471.85	(339.92)	[A]	385.37	(148.81)	[A]	480.00	(116.01)	[A]	2.69*
7 Goodenough–Harris drawing test (49–151)	93.85	(11.79)	[A]	89.73	(9.74)	[A]	95.78	(13.68)	[A]	95.00	(5.95)	[A]	1.64
13–14 California Achievement Test													
Total Reading (1–99)	34.99	(26.16)	[A]	19.97	(17.00)	[B]	28.59	(24.64)	[AB]	17.62	(15.76)	[B]	5.06**
Vocabulary (1–99)	37.87	(29.45)	[A]	19.70	(15.16)	[B]	30.92	(27.39)	[AB]	21.00	(24.27)	[AB]	5.33**
Comprehension (1–99)	34.47	(24.51)	[A]	22.00	(18.90)	[B]	28.37	(21.34)	[AB]	17.50	(10.03)	[B]	4.42**
Total Math (1–99)	28.37	(22.96)	[A]	17.97	(18.70)	[B]	20.48	(17.71)	[AB]	10.25	(6.34)	[B]	4.67**
Computation (1–99)	29.82	(23.74)	[A]	19.12	(19.85)	[B]	22.33	(18.30)	[AB]	12.62	(9.05)	[B]	4.24**
Concepts and problems (1–99)	28.97	(22.36)	[A]	19.59	(19.16)	[B]	20.96	(17.75)	[AB]	10.87	(4.01)	[B]	4.51**
Total Language (1–99)	38.41	(25.97)	[A]	25.26	(17.25)	[B]	31.96	(25.08)	[AB]	15.62	(8.28)	[B]	5.15**
Mechanics (1–99)	40.73	(27.16)	[A]	26.70	(17.75)	[B]	32.89	(25.62)	[AB]	17.00	(9.18)	[B]	5.41**
Usage and structure (1–99)	36.00	(23.48)	[A]	28.15	(17.62)	[A]	34.55	(23.15)	[A]	21.37	(11.39)	[A]	2.21
Spelling (1–99)	41.12	(28.22)	[A]	25.00	(22.82)	[B]	36.04	(27.42)	[AB]	21.37	(16.11)	[B]	4.87**
Total Battery (1–99)	32.33	(25.25)	[A]	18.41	(17.52)	[B]	25.37	(22.31)	[AB]	10.87	(7.57)	[B]	5.66***
13–14 Placements in disciplinary programs (0–9)	0.002	(0.05)	[A]	0.12	(0.41)	[B]	0.04	(0.19)	[A]	0.00	(0.00)	[A]	9.67***
13–14 Placements in programs for the retarded (0–15)	0.06	(0.56)	[A]	0.38	(2.23)	[A]	0.00	(0.00)	[A]	0.13	(0.35)	[A]	1.86
Sample sizes	431			34			27			8			Total = 500

Notes: *$p < .05$; **$p < .01$; ***$p < .001$.
Duncan [DN] significant at $p < .05$.

55

three levels of the WISC Verbal IQ (χ^2 [2] = 4.7; $p < .01$): nearly twice as many violent offenders fell into the lower third of the test scores. However, no significant differences were found among the three levels for WISC Performance IQ although one of the violent female offenders was mentally defective in her Performance IQ (χ^2 [1] = 3.8; .05). There were no significant differences between nonoffenders and violent offenders in borderline or mentally defective test scores on the WISC Verbal IQ.

Great disparities were found in percentile differences at adolescence for violent and nonindex female offenders on nearly all achievement tests, including mathematics. Compared to nonoffenders, violent female offenders scored 24 percentiles lower on Mechanics, between 20 and 22 percentiles lower on Total Language, Total Battery, and Spelling, and between 17 and 19 percentiles lower on the remaining achievement tests, aside from a 15 percentile difference on Usage and Structure, which was the only test that did not demonstrate a statistically significant difference. Thus, highly significant differences appeared for tests of a number of skills, including language, reading, and mathematics.

Comparable disparities were found among levels of achievement tests. Although not statistically significant, twice as many violent offenders scored in the bottom third of Total Reading and three times as many nonoffenders scored in the top third. Whereas 44 percent of the nonoffenders scored in the top third of Total Language, no violent offenders scored in the top third and one half scored in the bottom third (χ^2 [2] = 6.5; $p < .05$).

Overall, both male and female violent offenders were discrepant from nonoffenders and less violent offenders on tests on language, reading, and spelling achievement. However, percentile differences between violent female offenders and nonoffenders were considerably greater than those for males, and they incorporated more tests, such as mathematics. Thus, female offenders appear to deviate more on tests of intellectual abilities.

Repeat offenders

Comparisons among types of repeat offenders are shown in Tables 3.3 and 3.4. Among males in Table 3.3, chronic offenders differed significantly from nonoffenders on the following tests: Stanford–Binet, WISC Full Scale IQ and Verbal IQ, WISC Vocabulary, WISC Digit Span, and WRAT Reading and Arithmetic. These differences are of a somewhat greater magnitude than those found in comparing violent offenders and nonoffenders.

Relative to nonoffenders, chronic offenders were 1.7 times more likely to be in the bottom third of the WISC Verbal IQ (χ^2 [2] = 6.0; p = .05). Although not significantly different from nonoffenders on the WISC Performance IQ in the high, medium, and low categories, chronic offenders were significantly represented among youths with borderline-or-below and mentally defective scores on the WISC Performance IQ. For example, more than twice as many chronic offenders than nonoffenders had borderline-or-below Performance IQ (χ^2 [1] = 4.4; p < .05), and over five times as many were scored as mentally defective (χ^2 [1] = 7.3; p < .01).

Again, discrepancies were strongest in adolescence. Chronic offenders scored 17 percentiles lower on the Mechanics subtest; 15 to 16 percentiles lower on Total Reading, Total Language, and Comprehension; 10 to 14 percentiles lower on Spelling and Total Battery achievement and the Vocabulary and Concepts and Problems. In general, for most tests, nonoffenders and one-time offenders scored higher than nonchronic repeat offenders, who in turn scored higher than chronic offenders.

Altogether, chronic offenders were 1.8 times more likely to be in the bottom third in Total Reading (χ^2 [2] = 10.4; p < .01) and Total Language (χ^2 [2] = 11.0; p < .01). Only one of the 25 chronic offenders scored in the top third of the Total Reading and Total Language in comparison to nonoffenders, who were 8 times more likely to score in the top third.

Test score discrepancies were even greater for females. Because females tend to commit fewer crimes, "chronic" female offenders were defined as those who had more than one offense. Table 3.4 shows that chronics scored significantly lower on the WISC Full Scale IQ and Performance IQ and the WRAT Spelling.

Chronic females also dominated the lower levels of intelligence tests. Nonoffenders were nearly four times more likely to be in the top third of the WISC Verbal IQ (χ^2 [2] = 7.0; p < .05). Although no significant differences were shown for the WISC Performance IQ, chronic females were twice as likely to have Performance IQ scores in the borderline-or-below range (χ^2 [1] = 4.4; p < .05) and were also significantly more likely to have scores in the mentally defective range (χ^2 [1] = 3.8; p < .05).

At adolescence, chronic females differed significantly from nonoffenders on all achievement tests aside from one (Usage and Structure). They scored 18 percentiles lower on the Mechanics subtest, between 16 and 17 percentiles lower on the Total Reading, Language, Spelling, Total Battery, Vocabulary, and Comprehension tests, and between 11 and 12 percentiles lower on Total Math and its subtests. They were also significantly more likely to score in the lower third percentiles of

Table 3.3. Test scores at ages 4, 7, and 13–14 years by number of juvenile offenses, males only

Ages	Tests	Nonoffender			One-time offender			Two-four-time offender			≥ Five-time offender			F-value
		Mean	(SD)	[DN]	Mean	(SD)	[DN]	Mean	(SD)	[DN]	Mean	(SD)	[DN]	(3,483)
4	Stanford–Binet Intelligence Scale (25–175)	89.75	(12.19)	[A]	92.49	(10.96)	[A]	91.35	(12.10)	[A]	85.76	(10.11)	[B]	2.34
7	WISC Full Scale IQ (25–154)	92.67	(11.22)	[AB]	94.84	(9.74)	[A]	93.05	(11.11)	[AB]	88.16	(9.03)	[B]	2.34
7	WISC Verbal IQ (45–155)	92.42	(11.35)	[AB]	95.10	(10.85)	[A]	92.58	(10.85)	[AB]	87.12	(7.62)	[B]	3.24*
7	WISC Verbal Subscales													
	Information (0–20)	9.14	(2.44)	[A]	9.55	(2.31)	[A]	9.21	(2.18)	[A]	8.64	(1.82)	[A]	1.04
	Comprehension (0–20)	8.67	(2.41)	[A]	8.91	(2.40)	[A]	8.47	(2.74)	[A]	8.08	(2.51)	[A]	0.82
	Vocabulary (0–20)	8.21	(2.49)	[A]	8.56	(2.32)	[A]	8.35	(2.00)	[A]	7.12	(1.36)	[B]	2.34
	Digit span (0–20)	9.10	(2.83)	[AB]	9.74	(2.66)	[A]	9.23	(2.87)	[AB]	7.84	(2.89)	[B]	2.86*
7	WISC Performance IQ (44–156)	94.27	(12.66)	[A]	95.54	(11.67)	[A]	94.88	(13.75)	[A]	91.68	(13.40)	[A]	0.60
7	WISC Performance Subscales													
	Block design (0–20)	9.12	(2.26)	[A]	8.96	(2.41)	[A]	9.19	(2.25)	[A]	8.68	(2.13)	[A]	0.41
	Coding (0–20)	9.49	(2.78)	[A]	9.96	(2.62)	[A]	10.00	(3.18)	[A]	9.76	(3.16)	[A]	0.91
	Picture arrangement (0–20)	8.92	(2.81)	[A]	9.17	(2.55)	[A]	8.58	(2.47)	[A]	7.96	(2.70)	[A]	1.47
	PIQ–VIQ difference	1.85	(12.19)	[A]	0.43	(13.76)	[A]	2.30	(14.20)	[A]	4.56	(13.85)	[A]	0.65
7	Wide Range Achievement Test													
	Spelling (0–55)	22.73	(4.75)	[B]	23.96	(5.21)	[A]	22.59	(3.75)	[B]	21.42	(3.22)	[B]	2.42
	Reading (0–84)	31.73	(7.81)	[A]	31.88	(7.35)	[A]	30.02	(6.23)	[AB]	28.04	(6.59)	[B]	2.61
	Arithmetic (0–49)	20.19	(3.54)	[A]	20.42	(3.28)	[A]	20.02	(2.88)	[AB]	18.56	(3.01)	[B]	2.00

Age		(n = 336)	(n = 69)	(n = 57)	(n = 25)	F
7	Bender Gestalt Koppitz scoring (0–30)	7.72 (3.44) [A]	7.67 (3.26) [A]	8.54 (3.01) [A]	8.48 (3.25) [A]	1.34
7	Bender Gestalt time (in seconds)	415.53 (186.46) [A]	369.67 (122.32) [A]	422.49 (227.29) [A]	438.60 (176.37) [A]	1.49
7	Goodenough–Harris drawing test (49–151)	96.79 (13.78) [A]	96.79 (15.06) [A]	96.70 (11.28) [A]	93.92 (12.52) [A]	0.35
13–14	California Achievement Test					
	Total Reading (1–99)	31.98 (25.05) [A]	32.77 (23.69) [A]	23.81 (23.33) [AB]	16.20 (14.33) [B]	4.96**
	Vocabulary (1–99)	35.09 (27.34) [A]	34.68 (24.78) [A]	25.00 (22.84) [B]	20.76 (19.39) [B]	4.41**
	Comprehension (1–99)	31.06 (24.08) [A]	32.65 (23.82) [A]	23.77 (23.09) [B]	15.60 (13.87) [B]	4.93**
	Total Math (1–99)	24.01 (22.29) [A]	24.46 (21.79) [A]	16.58 (20.23) [A]	16.00 (15.15) [B]	2.86*
	Computation (1–99)	24.54 (22.38) [A]	23.35 (21.26) [AB]	17.33 (19.48) [B]	20.12 (17.87) [AB]	1.98
	Concepts and problems (1–99)	25.98 (22.73) [A]	27.91 (22.39) [A]	19.14 (20.96) [B]	14.72 (13.82) [B]	3.74*
	Total Language (1–99)	28.63 (24.24) [A]	29.22 (21.94) [A]	20.82 (21.23) [AB]	13.08 (12.77) [B]	5.13**
	Mechanics (1–99)	30.02 (24.98) [A]	30.40 (23.54) [A]	21.74 (20.41) [AB]	12.92 (11.37) [B]	5.70***
	Usage and structure (1–99)	30.68 (22.49) [A]	32.58 (19.59) [A]	26.23 (21.75) [A]	22.44 (15.23) [A]	2.02
	Spelling (1–99)	28.69 (24.52) [A]	26.84 (22.49) [AB]	20.31 (19.59) [B]	16.56 (20.81) [B]	3.74*
	Total Battery (1–99)	25.21 (23.17) [A]	25.71 (21.34) [A]	17.29 (21.21) [B]	12.04 (13.12) [B]	4.54**
13–14	Placements in disciplinary programs (0–9)	0.06 (0.45) [A]	0.07 (0.49) [A]	0.54 (1.57) [A]	1.00 (2.29) [B]	13.92***
13–14	Placements in programs for the retarded (0–15)	0.20 (1.23) [A]	0.22 (0.91) [A]	0.18 (1.32) [A]	0.12 (0.60) [A]	0.05
	Sample sizes	336	69	57	25	Total = 487

Notes: *$p < .05$; **$p < .01$; ***$p < .001$.
Duncan [DN] significant at $p < .05$.

59

Table 3.4. *Test scores at ages 4, 7, and 13–14 years by number of juvenile offenses, females only*

Ages	Tests	Nonoffender			One-time offender			≥ Two-time offender			F-value
		Mean	(SD)	[DN]	Mean	(SD)	[DN]	Mean	(SD)	[DN]	(3,496)
4	Stanford–Binet Intelligence Scale (25–175)	91.54	(13.39)	[A]	91.07	(11.94)	[A]	86.13	(8.90)	[A]	1.95
7	WISC Full Scale IQ (25–154)	92.45	(11.31)	[A]	90.67	(8.74)	[AB]	87.00	(9.29)	[B]	3.15*
7	WISC Verbal IQ (45–155)	91.48	(11.77)	[A]	91.69	(10.19)	[A]	86.50	(7.21)	[A]	2.18
7	WISC Verbal Subscales										
	Information (0–20)	9.14	(2.44)	[A]	8.93	(2.72)	[A]	8.62	(1.55)	[A]	0.63
	Comprehension (0–20)	8.15	(2.33)	[A]	8.40	(2.30)	[A]	7.33	(2.31)	[A]	1.74
	Vocabulary (0–20)	7.60	(2.36)	[A]	7.95	(1.68)	[A]	7.17	(2.08)	[A]	0.96
	Digit span (0–20)	9.00	(3.07)	[A]	9.35	(3.02)	[AB]	8.21	(2.52)	[B]	2.45
7	WISC Performance IQ (44–156)	94.92	(12.08)	[A]	91.09	(10.01)	[B]	89.92	(11.52)	[B]	3.58*
7	WISC Performance Subscales										
	Block design (0–20)	8.78	(2.08)	[A]	8.60	(2.06)	[A]	8.04	(2.35)	[A]	1.51
	Coding (0–20)	10.64	(2.83)	[A]	9.95	(2.28)	[A]	9.75	(2.89)	[A]	2.25
	Picture arrangement (0–20)	8.39	(2.62)	[A]	7.64	(2.49)	[A]	7.87	(2.19)	[A]	2.05
	PIQ–VIQ difference	3.44	(11.98)	[A]	−0.60	(12.38)	[A]	3.42	(8.88)	[A]	2.36
7	Wide Range Achievement Test										
	Spelling (0–55)	23.67	(4.69)	[A]	23.20	(4.28)	[AB]	20.92	(4.01)	[B]	4.14*
	Reading (0–84)	32.90	(8.39)	[A]	31.80	(8.27)	[A]	30.42	(6.08)	[A]	1.30
	Arithmetic (0–49)	20.48	(3.28)	[A]	20.35	(3.08)	[A]	19.67	(2.35)	[A]	0.74

Age	Variable	Group 1 Mean	(SD)		Group 2 Mean	(SD)		Group 3 Mean	(SD)		F
7	Bender Gestalt Koppitz scoring (0–30)	8.71	(3.60)	[A]	8.20	(3.53)	[A]	9.58	(3.20)	[A]	1.17
7	Bender Gestalt time (in seconds)	393.80	(158.86)	[A]	428.29	(296.78)	[A]	458.95	(117.01)	[A]	2.19
7	Goodenough–Harris drawing test (49–151)	93.85	(11.79)	[A]	93.60	(10.92)	[A]	91.04	(12.33)	[A]	0.65
13–14	California Achievement Test										
	Total Reading (1–99)	34.99	(26.16)	[A]	25.44	(21.80)	[B]	18.62	(17.22)	[B]	7.08***
	Vocabulary (1–99)	37.87	(29.45)	[A]	25.69	(22.98)	[B]	21.54	(20.53)	[B]	6.93**
	Comprehension (1–99)	34.47	(24.51)	[A]	26.76	(21.09)	[B]	18.75	(14.37)	[B]	6.65**
	Total Math (1–99)	28.37	(22.96)	[A]	19.15	(18.73)	[B]	16.00	(14.79)	[B]	6.52**
	Computation (1–99)	29.82	(23.74)	[A]	21.04	(20.00)	[B]	16.96	(14.63)	[B]	6.04**
	Concepts and problems (1–99)	28.97	(22.36)	[A]	19.73	(17.75)	[B]	17.96	(17.61)	[B]	6.14**
	Total Language (1–99)	38.41	(25.97)	[A]	29.22	(21.63)	[B]	22.17	(17.57)	[B]	6.91**
	Mechanics (1–99)	40.73	(27.16)	[A]	31.11	(22.28)	[B]	22.17	(16.97)	[B]	7.83***
	Usage and structure (1–99)	36.00	(23.48)	[A]	30.04	(20.09)	[A]	29.54	(19.35)	[A]	2.12
	Spelling (1–99)	41.12	(28.22)	[A]	31.67	(25.89)	[B]	23.71	(21.29)	[B]	6.42**
	Total Battery (1–99)	32.22	(25.25)	[A]	22.67	(20.81)	[B]	15.75	(15.04)	[B]	7.84***
13–14	Placements in disciplinary programs (0–9)	0.002	(0.05)	[A]	0.04	(0.21)	[A]	0.13	(0.45)	[B]	13.00***
13–14	Placements in programs for the retarded (0–15)	0.06	(0.56)	[A]	0.29	(1.94)	[A]	0.04	(0.20)	[A]	1.72
	Sample sizes	431			45			24			Total = 500

Notes: *$p < .05$; **$p < .01$; ***$p < .001$.
Duncan [DN] significant at $p < .05$.

61

Total Reading (χ^2 [2] = 10.8; $p < .01$) and Total Language (χ^2 [2] = 9.5; $p > .001$).

Overall, for both males and females, violent and chronic offenders scored consistently lower than nonoffenders and, in most cases, than the less serious and nonchronic repeat offenders on achievement tests during adolescence. Moreover, the largest discrepancies existed generally for the same tests for both sexes: the Mechanics subtest and the Total Reading, Language, Spelling, and Battery tests. There were fewer offender group differences on tests at ages 4 and 7. However, violent and chronic offenders of both sexes tested significantly lower on the WISC Verbal IQ and, in some comparisons, showed disparities on the WISC Digit Span and the WRAT Reading and Spelling tests.

Special school programs

In light of the considerably lower test scores found for violent and repeat offenders, it would be expected that delinquents would be disproportionately enrolled in school programs for those children disagnosed as mentally retarded. Likewise, it would be expected that children with some official record of troublesome behavior would be more likely than nondelinquent children to demonstrate disciplinary problems in school.

The School District of Philadelphia has available Individual Education Programs that are recommended by a Child Study Evaluation Team for all exceptional students, particularly those with learning and behavioral difficulties. "Exceptional students" are broadly defined as "those who differ from the average to such a degree that they cannot benefit from their educational experience without special education program assistance" (School District of Philadelphia, 1979). A Child Study Evaluation Team consists of a varied group of school district personnel including the principal, school nurse, school psychologist, counselor, other therapists and professionals, and the student's parents. Together, the team identifies and evaluates exceptional students according to specific criteria established by State Guidelines (Department of Education, Commonwealth of Pennsylvania, 1979). Evaluations include a student's history, observations, review of school achievement and adjustment, plus psychological and medical examinations.

For the purposes of the present study, programs for subjects diagnosed as mentally retarded or in need of behavioral discipline were examined. The determination of mental retardation was based on a range of criteria, including results of a full battery of psychological tests that included the Stanford–Binet, the WISC-R, the Bender Gestalt, the Goodenough–Harris drawing test, and the Rorschach. Children were referred to disciplinary programs based upon continuous psychological and behavioral assessments. These children were diagnosed as having normal intellectual ability but a long record of asocial behavior in school that included physical aggression toward teachers, firestarting, inability to adjust in school, persistent alienation resulting in conduct disturbance, and indifference toward misconduct.

Altogether, 5 percent of the males and 2 percent of the females were placed in programs for the mentally retarded, a statistically significant gender difference (χ^2 [1] = 5.37; $p < .05$). In turn, 5 percent of the males and 1 percent of the females were placed in programs for youths with disciplinary problems, a highly significant difference (χ^2 [1] = 13.35; $p < .0001$).

As Tables 3.1 and 3.3 show no differences existed in the number of program placements for the mentally retarded either for violent or repeat (≥ 2 offenses) male offenders. Highly significant differences appeared, however, in the number of placements for disciplinary programs. Violent offenders had over 8 times more placements and property offenders had over 10 times more placements than nonoffenders. Repeat offenders had over 15 times the placements of nonoffenders.

Similar results appear for females in Tables 3.2 and 3.4, although nonindex offenders rather than violent offenders deviated when significant differences existed. As among males, no significant differences existed among female offenders in the number of program placements for the mentally retarded. Significantly more nonindex and repeat offenders, however, were placed in programs for youths with disciplinary problems. Relative to nonoffenders, for example, nonindex and repeat offenders were between 11 and 12 times more likely to be placed in disciplinary programs.

In light of test differences in both intellectual ability and program placement among offender groups, results have shown overall that violent, nonchronic repeat, and chronic offenders of both sexes have a significantly higher incidence of intellectual and learning difficulties, particularly in verbal ability, in comparison to nonviolent offenders and nonoffenders. These discrepancies in abilities among different types of offenders were generally greater for females than for males, and they were strongest at adolescence.

Unexpectedly, female offenders also showed significant differences in mathematical ability, whereas male offenders did not. However, the differences in mathematical ability were considerably smaller than the differences in other skills. In turn, for both sexes, only slight differences among offender groups were found for the Usage and Structure subtest of the Total Language achievement test. This subtest measures a student's

ability to distinguish between standard and nonstandard English, to recognize sentence transformations, and to identify total sentence structure
and type.

It is interesting to note that, for nearly all offender groups, fewer
differences in test scores existed at 4 or 7 years. This contrast between
smaller test score differences at early ages and the considerable differences found at adolescence may be attributable to one or more factors:

1. Tests at early ages may be cruder measures of intellectual or achievement abilities than tests at adolescence. As previous reviews have shown,
however, early test scores are strong predictors of later abilities (Cronbach, 1970; Wechsler, 1958). It is likely that developmental or situational events that occur after age 7 influence achievement test scores at
adolescence.

2. Schooling and school experiences can have a strong impact on intellectual development during adolescence, a time when psychological,
sociological, and biological changes enhance individual variation and
malleability.

3. Low achievement test scores may be associated with behavioral problems that occur during adolescence and impede learning ability. For
example, in the present study, different categories of offenders were not
disproportionately enrolled in programs for the mentally retarded;
however, a significantly greater number of male and female offenders
were enrolled in programs for the disciplinary disordered. It appears,
then, that the problems faced by offenders in school may be behavioral
as well as intellectual.

In their review of delinquency studies, Loeber and Dishion (1983) cited
a child's conduct problems and poor academic performance as two of
the four principal predictors of delinquency among males. However, the
great majority of the research they examined did not study these two
factors beside many other potential predictors. As yet, the relative
impact of conduct problems and achievement on delinquency is not
known. The next section analyzes key early developmental factors to
determine whether differences exist among offenders grouped according
to the total number of their police contacts as juveniles.

Early development and delinquency

Mean differences between nonoffenders and multiple or chronic offenders on 32 early developmental variables are shown for males in Table 3.5
and for females in Table 3.6. Variables were selected for theoretical

interest based upon past delinquency research. Chapter 5 examines distributions of early developmental variables within categories of adult offenders based upon a statistical screen from a pool of biological and environmental factors.

Table 3.5 shows that, among males, nonoffenders have significantly higher incomes than nonchronic repeat and chronic offenders. Chronic offenders have a significantly larger family size than one-time offenders but not than other offender groups. All three offender groups differ from one-time offenders in having significantly more persons supported in the household. Significant differences on a fourth variable, Apgar at one minute, show that one-time offenders have a lower score than other groups. However, no significant between-group differences appear for the Apgar score at five minutes. With regard to childhood health variables, one-time offenders are significantly shorter than other groups, whereas chronic offenders have the lowest ponderal index.

Altogether, then, results show significant differences among nonchronic repeat and chronic offenders for family background and socioeconomic variables. However, group differences do not always correspond in a hierarchical fashion to the number of offenses reported. Such inconsistencies are evident also for selected health and developmental variables: Apgar, height, and the ponderal index.

Concerning repeat offense behavior among females, Table 3.6 shows that significant differences exist mostly for family-related variables. Significantly more female repeat offenders come from families where the father is absent, where there is a foster or adoptive parent or institution, and where there is marital instability, lower income, and lower education of the household head. However, offenders also significantly differ on the ponderal index, with nonchronic repeat offenders having the lowest score. Nonchronic repeat offenders are also significantly lower on the Apgar score at one minute, mother's education, weight at 7 years, and per capita income.

Similar to those for males, then, results for females show significant differences on most socioeconomic and family background variables, although sizable differences also exist on biological and early developmental factors. Whether or not these differences exist when variables are examined simultaneously in order to predict both juvenile and young adult offense behavior is a different question, which is addressed in chapter 5.

Table 3.5. *Mean differences in independent variables for number of juvenile offenses, males only*

Variables	Nonoffender			One-time offender			Two-four-time offender			≥ five-time offender			F-value
	Mean	(SD)	[DN]	Mean	(SD)	[DN]	Mean	(SD)	[DN]	Mean	(SD)	[DN]	(3,496)
Number of prenatal examinations	4.53	(1.35)	[A]	4.51	(1.36)	[A]	4.56	(1.19)	[A]	4.36	(1.32)	[A]	0.15
Number of prenatal conditions	0.81	(0.87)	[A]	0.74	(0.83)	[A]	0.86	(0.72)	[A]	0.60	(0.58)	[A]	0.73
Marital status (0 = married; 1 = single, separated, divorced, or widowed)													
Poor obstetrical history	0.29	(0.46)	[A]	0.38	(0.49)	[A]	0.35	(0.48)	[A]	0.36	(0.49)	[A]	0.81
Mother's age at registration	0.58	(0.99)	[A]	0.55	(1.12)	[A]	0.60	(1.00)	[A]	0.80	(1.22)	[A]	0.40
Total number of birth complications	24.35	(6.48)	[A]	23.92	(7.41)	[A]	23.91	(6.24)	[A]	23.24	(5.17)	[A]	0.32
Duration of labor; sum of stages 1 and 2 (hours)	1.23	(1.15)	[A]	1.14	(0.90)	[A]	1.19	(0.91)	[A]	1.32	(0.94)	[A]	0.20
Apgar at one minute	7.90	(5.40)	[A]	8.18	(5.34)	[A]	7.73	(6.44)	[A]	7.07	(4.30)	[A]	0.27
Apgar at five minutes	7.79	(1.78)	[A]	7.21	(2.08)	[A]	7.47	(2.22)	[AB]	8.31	(0.75)	[A]	3.06*
Gestational age	8.87	(1.23)	[A]	8.86	(1.03)	[A]	8.81	(1.22)	[A]	9.24	(0.59)	[A]	0.87
Birth weight in pounds	38.31	(3.52)	[A]	38.38	(3.40)	[A]	38.47	(3.23)	[A]	38.04	(3.28)	[A]	0.10
Parity and birth order (number of siblings)	7.08	(1.15)	[A]	7.04	(1.41)	[A]	6.90	(1.29)	[A]	6.96	(1.07)	[A]	0.44
Income at registration, adjusted to 1970 dollars	2.18	(2.23)	[A]	1.87	(1.81)	[A]	2.29	(2.12)	[A]	2.50	(2.10)	[A]	0.71
Mother's education (number of years)	4333.98	(2012.98)	[A]	3798.78	(1902.84)	[B]	3561.36	(1519.08)	[B]	3608.53	1497.24	[B]	4.22**
Blood pressure, systolic	10.40	(1.86)	[A]	10.81	(1.91)	[A]	9.98	(2.36)	[A]	9.96	(1.97)	[A]	1.08
Blood pressure, diastolic	101.73	(9.81)	[A]	101.00	(10.65)	[A]	101.82	(8.43)	[A]	100.48	(8.93)	[A]	0.23
Weight in pounds at 7-year exam	62.13	(7.43)	[A]	60.96	(8.06)	[A]	61.70	(7.16)	[A]	59.84	(9.95)	[A]	1.04
Height in cms. at 7-year exam	55.10	(10.40)	[A]	56.00	(11.98)	[A]	53.23	(5.95)	[A]	51.07	(5.59)	[A]	2.04
Ponderal index (weight/height^3)	124.67	(5.73)	[A]	124.06	(5.42)	[A]	122.91	(5.24)	[B]	123.44	(5.63)	[AB]	1.88
Hand preference, 0 = right handed; 1 = left handed	0.000028	(0.0000033)	[AB]	0.000029	(0.0000048)	[AB]	0.000029	(0.0000025)	[AB]	0.000027	(0.0000021)	[B]	2.58
Eye preference, 0 = right eyed; 1 = left eyed	0.13	(0.34)	[A]	0.09	(0.28)	[A]	0.09	(0.28)	[A]	0.12	(0.33)	[A]	0.55
	0.40	(0.49)	[A]	0.46	(0.50)	[A]	0.46	(0.50)	[A]	0.44	(0.51)	[A]	0.40

Variable					F
Foot preference, 0 = right or variable footed; 1 = left footed	0.10 (0.31) [A]	0.07 (0.26) [A]	0.12 (0.33) [A]	0.12 (0.33) [A]	0.34
Foot preference, 0 = right footed; 1 = left or variable footed	0.15 (0.36) [A]	0.12 (0.32) [A]	0.19 (0.40) [A]	0.28 (0.46) [A]	1.40
Family size	5.88 (2.39) [AB]	5.35 (1.97) [B]	6.17 (2.58) [AB]	6.78 (2.73) [A]	2.64*
Husband or father in the household, 0 = present; 1 = absent	0.36 (0.48) [A]	0.46 (0.50) [A]	0.42 (0.50) [A]	0.44 (0.51) [A]	1.03
Foster parents 0 = absent; 1 = present	0.04 (0.16) [A]	0.02 (0.12) [A]	0.05 (0.22) [A]	0 0 [A]	0.81
Marital stability (0 = married at each exam, 1 = mother who is single or married at registration but not married at 7-year exam)	0.51 (0.50) [A]	0.65 (0.48) [A]	0.60 (2.51) [A]	0.60 (0.50) [A]	1.87
Number of persons supported in the household	5.79 (2.13) [A]	5.16 (1.80) [B]	6.32 (2.51) [A]	6.44 (1.89) [A]	3.98**
Income at 7-year exam (1970 dollars)	6692.61 (3374.90) [A]	6399.44 (3721.32) [A]	6343.50 (3409.78) [A]	6569.85 (3700.95) [A]	0.26
Per capita income (1970 dollars)	1279.11 (791.63) [A]	1314.77 (812.09) [A]	1082.06 (606.70) [A]	1108.40 (827.71) [A]	1.48
Education of head of household	40.84 (20.96) [A]	44.72 (20.17) [A]	38.05 (19.97) [A]	42.20 (23.10) [A]	1.14
Occupation of head of household	30.10 (25.63) [A]	30.56 (25.26) [A]	31.26 (26.23) [A]	30.16 (27.98) [A]	0.04
Sample sizes	336	69	57	25	Total = 487

Notes: $*p < .05$; $**p < .01$; $***p < .001$.
Duncan [DN] significant at $p < .05$.

Table 3.6. *Mean differences in independent variables for number of juvenile offenses, females only*

Variables	Nonoffender			One-time offender			≥ two-time offender			F-value
	Mean	(SD)	[DN]	Mean	(SD)	[DN]	Mean	(SD)	[DN]	(2,497)
Number of prenatal examinations	4.54	(1.29)	[A]	4.20	(1.34)	[A]	4.46	(1.41)	[A]	1.40
Number of prenatal conditions	0.70	(0.90)	[A]	0.64	(0.80)	[A]	1.04	(1.08)	[A]	1.70
Marital status (0 = married; 1 = single, separated, divorced, or widowed)	0.27	(0.44)	[A]	0.38	(0.49)	[A]	0.37	(0.49)	[A]	1.62
Poor obstetrical history	0.70	(1.27)	[A]	0.60	(1.05)	[A]	1.00	(1.81)	[A]	0.79
Mother's age at registration	24.67	(6.27)	[A]	23.82	(6.00)	[A]	24.04	(6.64)	[A]	0.46
Total number of birth complications	1.18	(1.15)	[A]	1.29	(1.12)	[A]	1.04	(0.95)	[A]	0.38
Duration of labor; sum of stages 1 and 2 (hours)	7.62	(5.76)	[A]	8.03	(6.09)	[A]	5.81	(4.67)	[A]	1.30
Apgar at one minute	7.88	(1.72)	[A]	7.68	(1.74)	[AB]	7.03	(2.56)	[B]	2.75
Apgar at five minutes	8.92	(1.10)	[A]	8.76	(1.40)	[A]	8.76	(1.39)	[A]	0.63
Gestational age	38.23	(3.61)	[A]	37.89	(4.96)	[A]	38.62	(3.17)	[A]	0.32
Birth weight in pounds	6.68	(1.12)	[A]	6.66	(1.06)	[A]	6.66	(1.05)	[A]	0.01
Parity and birth order (number of siblings)	2.40	(2.39)	[A]	2.73	(3.00)	[A]	2.61	(2.24)	[A]	0.44
Income at registration, adjusted to 1970 dollars	4050.23	(1912.47)	[A]	3622.75	(1461.08)	[A]	3637.80	(2002.25)	[A]	1.50
Mother's education (number of years)	10.46	(1.78)	[A]	10.27	(1.91)	[AB]	9.67	(2.01)	[B]	2.38
Blood pressure, systolic	100.08	(9.66)	[A]	101.56	(9.31)	[A]	97.58	(9.80)	[A]	1.33
Blood pressure, diastolic	60.48	(7.89)	[A]	62.27	(7.66)	[A]	60.08	(6.34)	[A]	1.13
Weight in pounds at 7-year exam	52.17	(9.48)	[A]	49.71	(5.88)	[AB]	47.68	(4.96)	[B]	4.02
Weight in cms. at 7-year exam	122.66	(5.65)	[A]	121.27	(4.70)	[A]	121.83	(5.43)	[A]	1.45
Ponderal index (weight/height^3)	0.000028	(0.0000032)	[A]	0.000028	(0.0000024)	[AB]	0.000026	(0.0000024)	[B]	3.48*

	Sample (n = 431)			Sample (n = 45)			Sample (n = 24)			F
Hand preference, 0 = right handed, 1 = left handed	0.11	(0.31)	[A]	0.02	(0.15)	[A]	0.12	(0.34)	[A]	1.71
Eye preference, 0 = right eyed, 1 = left eyed	0.41	(0.49)	[A]	0.42	(0.50)	[A]	0.54	(0.51)	[A]	0.74
Foot preference, 0 = right or variable footed, 1 = left footed	0.11	(0.32)	[A]	0.09	(0.29)	[A]	0	0	[A]	1.63
Foot preference, 0 = right footed, 1 = left or variable footed	0.24	(0.43)	[A]	0.18	(0.39)	[A]	0.12	(0.34)	[A]	1.25
Family size	6.06	(2.50)	[A]	6.15	(2.95)	[A]	5.62	(2.55)	[A]	0.38
Husband or father in the household, 0 = present, 1 = absent	0.41	(0.49)	[B]	0.51	(0.51)	[AB]	0.71	(0.46)	[A]	4.86**
Foster parents (0 = absent, 1 = present)	0.99	(0.12)	[A]	0.98	(0.15)	[AB]	0.92	(0.28)	[B]	3.14*
Marital stability (0 = married at each exam, 1 = mother who is single or married at registration but not married at 7-year exam)	0.52	(0.50)	[B]	0.62	(0.49)	[AB]	0.79	(0.41)	[A]	4.16*
Number of persons supported in the household	5.89	(2.02)	[A]	5.84	(2.19)	[A]	5.87	(2.19)	[A]	0.01
Income at 7-year exam (1970 dollars)	6699.01	(3248.76)	[A]	6116.05	(3525.51)	[AB]	4922.78	(2983.54)	[B]	3.83*
Per capita income (1970 dollars)	1229.05	(690.38)	[A]	1196.58	(880.60)	[AB]	890.51	(562.53)	[B]	2.64
Education of head of household	42.79	(20.35)	[A]	39.87	(18.70)	[AB]	31.87	(19.98)	[B]	3.60*
Occupation of head of household	33.12	(26.28)	[A]	27.09	(24.75)	[A]	22.71	(23.47)	[A]	2.73
Sample sizes	431			45			24			Total = 500

Notes: *p < .05; **p < .01; ***p < .001.
Duncan significant at p < .05.

69

4

Biological and environmental predictors of crime

What biological and environmental factors predict serious, chronic crime? Although numerous factors have been examined in isolation, few studies have analyzed many key predictors at the same time. The consideration of multiple factors helps to distinguish those variables that simply appear to influence delinquency from those that may have a "real" impact.

The following sections discriminate between weak and strong predictors of juvenile and young adult crime for males and females and then introduce longitudinal models of the strongest effects. Males and females are investigated separately in light of the varying impacts on their delinquent behavior.

Screening of biological and environmental predictors

Over 100 predictors of violent and chronic delinquent behavior (see Table 2.1) were screened for males and females separately using two dependent variables: number of offenses and seriousness of offenses. Variable screening was conducted with three types of regression equations: the forward selection technique, the backward elimination technique, and the stepwise regression – forward and backward.

Those variables found to be significant predictors at the $p \leq .05$ level for either sex with either of the two dependent variables are listed in Tables 4.1–4.6. Also in these tables are six variables that were not significant predictors in the regression screening but were included in analyses for theoretical reasons and because they were significant predictors in past research (Stanford–Binet, WISC Verbal and Performance IQ, pregnancy and delivery conditions, and family income at birth and at age 7). One variable, "otoscopic (hearing) exam," was eventually not included in analyses. Although it demonstrated a highly significant effect on delinquency, the statistical association was unreliably inflated because only two serious delinquents had an abnormal hearing exam.

70

Adult offender group differences in biological and environmental factors

In this chapter offender group differences in biological and environmental factors are examined in three different ways. First, mean group differences are analyzed for a total of 29 selected variables: 8 "dependent" variables, designated by the letter Y, that are predicted or explained, and 22 "independent" variables, designated by the letter X, that predict or explain the dependent variables. Second, structural equation models are constructed whereby the direct and indirect effects of the 22 independent variables are analyzed across different time periods to assess their simultaneous impact on the 8 dependent variables. Third, these structural equation models are examined in their "reduced form," which combines the total impact of indirect and direct effects. Details will be provided to explain the outcome of these analyses and models.

Mean differences among adult offender groups

Tables 4.1 and 4.2 show offender group differences in test scores for males and females respectively across three different ages (4, 7, and 13–14 years). Table 4.1 shows striking differences between adult male criminal repeat offender (Y_8) (those with two or more offenses) and the seriousness of offenses (Y_7) and number of offenses (Y_6) incurred as juveniles. Repeat adults had four times the mean level of seriousness as one-time adult offenders and more than eight times the mean level of seriousness as those who never became adult offenders. In turn, repeat offenders had over 3.5 times more offenses as juveniles than one-time adult offenders and nearly 6.5 times more offenses than those who never became adult offenders. These differences are very highly statistically significant, and strongly support prior research demonstrating the strong links between juvenile and adult crime. Furthermore, repeat offenders evidence four times the proportion of disciplinary problems (Y_3) accumulated over childhood school years (up to ages 13–14) than either one-time offenders or nonoffenders.

Examination of tests of intellectual ability and achievement demonstrates less consistency with past research. For example, no significant differences existed among offender groups in test scores on the Stanford–Binet at age 4 (X_7) or on the WISC Verbal or Performance tests at age 7 (Y_1 and Y_2). Moreover, no offender group differences existed in a physician's test of intellectual status (Y_{16}) or speech (Y_{17}) at age 7. However, both repeat and one-time offenders scored significantly lower than nonoffenders on language achievement at ages 13–14 (Y_4) and significantly

Table 4.1. *Test scores at ages 4, 7, and 13–14 years by number of adult offenses (Y_8), males only*

Ages		Variables		Nonoffender			One-time offender			≥ Two-time offender			F-value
				Mean	(SD)	[DN]	Mean	(SD)	[DN]	Mean	(SD)	[DN]	(3,483)
7	Y_1	WISC Verbal IQ (45–155)		92.52	(11.20)	[A]	93.35	(12.19)	[A]	91.93	(9.65)	[A]	.23
7	Y_2	WISC Performance IQ (44–156)		95.02	(12.64)	[A]	93.38	(13.57)	[A]	91.04	(11.56)	[A]	2.54
13–14	Y_3	Disciplinary problem (0 = absent; ≥ 1 = present)		.13	(.83)	[B]	.11	(.57)	[B]	.44	(1.36)	[A]	3.10*
13–14	Y_4	Language achievement (1–99)		29.06	(24.16)	[A]	20.64	(19.95)	[B]	19.07	(18.49)	[B]	6.73***
13–14	Y_5	Mental retardation (0 = absent; ≥ 1 = present)		.04	(.20)	[AB]	.04	(.19)	[B]	.11	(.32)	[A]	2.51
7–17	Y_6	Number of delinquent offenses		.54	(1.34)	[B]	.95	(2.33)	[B]	3.48	(5.32)	[A]	40.07***
7–17	Y_7	Seriousness of delinquent offenses		2.32	(8.28)	[B]	5.93	(16.04)	[B]	24.06	(38.30)	[A]	46.06***
Birth	X_1	Pregnancy and delivery conditions (1–17 items)		1.22	(1.06)	[A]	1.11	(1.16)	[A]	1.26	(1.08)	[A]	.33
Birth	X_2	Mother's education (number of years)		10.49	(1.83)	[A]	9.72	(2.25)	[B]	9.65	(2.10)	[B]	7.54***
Birth	X_3	Father's education (number of years)		10.35	(1.65)	[A]	10.45	(1.57)	[A]	10.87	(1.26)	[A]	2.54
Birth	X_4	Family income (1970 dollars)		4229.50	(2008.45)	[A]	3741.60	(1588.34)	[A]	3833.60	(1735.77)	[A]	2.24
Birth	X_5	Time father unemployed (number of months)		3.13	(9.02)	[AB]	1.58	(1.97)	[B]	5.76	(13.14)	[A]	3.02*
1	X_6	Hand preference (0 = right; 1 = left variable)		.90	(.29)	[A]	.96	(.19)	[A]	.94	(.23)	[A]	1.40
4	X_7	Sanford–Binet (25–175)		90.27	(12.00)	[A]	89.04	(12.02)	[A]	90.20	(11.83)	[A]	.25
4	X_8	Hand preference (0 = right; 1 = left)		.12	(.33)	[A]	.02	(.13)	[B]	.09	(.29)	[AB]	2.89*
4	X_9	Eye preference (0 = right; 1 = left)		.32	(.47)	[A]	.40	(.49)	[A]	.31	(.47)	[A]	.72
4	X_{10}	Foot preference (0 = right; 1 = left variable)		.18	(.39)	[A]	.09	(.29)	[A]	.20	(.41)	[A]	1.58
7	X_{11}	Neurological abnormalities (total number)		.11	(.31)	[A]	.11	(.31)	[A]	.07	(.26)	[A]	.34

Period	Variable		Group 1			Group 2			Group 3			F
	X_{12}	(0 = absent; 1 = present)	.01	(.11)	[A]	.55	(.23)	[A]	.02	(.14)	[A]	2.22
7	X_{13}	Abnormal vision (0 = absent; 1 = present)	.17	(.37)	[A]	.13	(.33)	[A]	.07	(.26)	[A]	1.82
7	X_{14}	Lead intoxication (0 = absent; 1 = present)	.01	(.11)	[B]	0.00	(0.00)	[B]	.06	(.23)	[A]	3.16*
7	X_{15}	Anemia (0 = absent; 1 = present)	.01	(.10)	[A]	0.00	(0.00)	[A]	.02	(.14)	[A]	.47
7	X_{16}	Intellectual status (0 = normal; 1 = abnormal)	.04	(.19)	[A]	.02	(.13)	[A]	0.00	(0.00)	[A]	1.25
7	X_{17}	Speech (0 = normal; 1 = abnormal)	.04	(.21)	[A]	.02	(.13)	[A]	.07	(.26)	[A]	.99
7	X_{18}	Foster parents (0 = absent; 1 = present)	.97	(.17)	[A]	.93	(.26)	[A]	.96	(.19)	[A]	1.36
Birth–7	X_{19}	Father in household (0 = present; 1 = absent)	.20	(.39)	[A]	.20	(.41)	[A]	.20	(.41)	[A]	.01
Birth–7	X_{20}	Household moves (total number)	1.68	(1.58)	[B]	1.65	(1.64)	[B]	2.26	(1.85)	[A]	3.12*
7	X_{21}	Persons supported (total number)	5.72	(2.14)	[A]	6.29	(2.42)	[A]	5.87	(1.81)	[A]	1.76
7	X_{22}	Family income (1970 dollars)	6612.00	(3463.77)	[A]	6904.40	(3249.01)	[A]	6240.90	(3478.45)	[A]	.51
		Sample sizes	378			55			54			Total = 487

Notes: *$p < .05$; **$p < .01$; ***$p < .001$.
Duncan significant at $p \leq .05$.

73

Table 4.2. *Test scores at ages 4, 7, and 13–14 years by number of adult offenses (Y_8), females only*

Ages	Variables	Nonoffender Mean	(SD)	[DN]	One-time offender Mean	(SD)	[DN]	≥ Two-time offender Mean	(SD)	[DN]	F-value (3,496)
7	Y_1 WISC Verbal IQ (45–155)	91.29	(11.47)	[A]	92.53	(11.61)	[A]	87.78	(13.22)	[A]	.51
7	Y_2 WISC Performance IQ (44–156)	94.54	(11.95)	[A]	91.27	(12.39)	[A]	89.44	(10.89)	[A]	1.31
13–14	Y_3 Disciplinary problem (0 = absent; ≥ 1 = present)	.01	(.12)	[B]	0.00	(0.00)	[B]	.11	(.33)	[A]	2.91*
13–14	Y_4 Language achievement (1–99)	37.22	(25.78)	[A]	29.07	(17.32)	[A]	27.00	(24.50)	[A]	1.42
13–14	Y_5 Mental retardation (0 = absent; ≥ 1 = present)	.02	(.14)	[AB]	0.00	(0.00)	[B]	.11	(.33)	[A]	1.84
7–17	Y_6 Number of delinquent offenses	.23	(.91)	[B]	.67	(2.06)	[B]	2.78	(3.56)	[A]	26.69***
7–17	Y_7 Seriousness of delinquent offenses	.60	(2.82)	[B]	3.36	(8.83)	[B]	16.72	(23.22)	[A]	64.38***
Birth	X_1 Pregnancy and delivery conditions (1–17 items)	1.17	(1.13)	[A]	1.20	(1.15)	[A]	1.78	(1.39)	[A]	1.26
Birth	X_2 Mother's education (number of years)	10.44	(1.79)	[A]	10.27	(2.42)	[AB]	9.11	(1.44)	[B]	2.44
Birth	X_3 Father's education (number of years)	10.36	(1.84)	[A]	10.06	(2.26)	[A]	9.69	(2.26)	[A]	.74
Birth	X_4 Family income (1970 dollars)	3996.40	(1876.21)	[A]	3986.60	(1406.18)	[A]	3765.50	(2942.32)	[A]	.07
Birth	X_5 Time father unemployed (number of months)	4.98	(15.81)	[A]	4.29	(13.30)	[A]	2.72	(2.04)	[A]	.11
1	X_6 Hand preference (0 = right; 1 = left variable)	.91	(.28)	[A]	.80	(.33)	[A]	.89	(.41)	[A]	1.17
4	X_7 Stanford–Binet (25–175)	91.41	(13.14)	[A]	87.87	(12.62)	[A]	87.89	(12.67)	[A]	.83
4	X_8 Hand preference (0 = right; 1 = left)	.08	(.26)	[A]	.13	(.35)	[A]	.11	(.33)	[A]	.40
4	X_9 Eye preference (0 = right; 1 = left)	.34	(.47)	[A]	.20	(.41)	[A]	.33	(.50)	[A]	.68
4	X_{10} Foot preference (0 = right; 1 = left variable)	.18	(.39)	[A]	.07	(.26)	[A]	.22	(.44)	[A]	.72
7	X_{11} Neurological abnormalities (total number)	.08	(.26)	[A]	.07	(.26)	[A]	0.00	(0.00)	[A]	.37

Age	Variable	Mean	(SD)	Duncan	Mean	(SD)	Duncan	Mean	(SD)	Duncan	F
7	(0 = absent; 1 = present)	0.00	(.04)	[B]	0.00	(.26)	[B]	.07	(0.00)	[A]	7.82***
7	X_{13} Abnormal vision (0 = absent; 1 = present)	.15	(.35)	[A]	.13	(.35)	[A]	.11	(.33)	[A]	.06
7	X_{14} Lead intoxication (0 = absent; 1 = present)	.03	(.16)	[AB]	.13	(.35)	[A]	0.00	(0.00)	[B]	2.97*
7	X_{15} Anemia, (0 = absent; 1 = present)	.01	(.09)	[A]	0.00	(0.00)	[A]	0.00	(0.00)	[A]	.10
7	X_{16} Intellectual status (0 = normal; 1 = abnormal)	.02	(.15)	[A]	.07	(0.00)	[A]	0.00	(.26)	[A]	.70
7	X_{17} Speech (0 = normal; 1 = abnormal)	.02	(.14)	[A]	0.00	(0.00)	[A]	0.00	(0.00)	[A]	.26
7	X_{18} Foster parents (0 = absent; 1 = present)	.98	(.13)	[A]	1.00	(0.00)	[A]	.89	(.33)	[B]	2.37
Birth–7	X_{19} Father in household, (0 = present; 1 = absent)	.20	(.40)	[A]	.20	(.53)	[A]	.44	(.41)	[A]	1.67
Birth–7	X_{20} Household moves (total number)	1.80	(1.77)	[A]	1.80	(2.09)	[A]	1.89	(1.66)	[A]	.01
7	X_{21} Persons supported (total number)	5.89	(2.05)	[A]	5.93	(2.09)	[A]	5.22	(1.64)	[A]	.48
7	X_{22} Family income (1970 dollars)	3996.40	(3270.86)	[A]	3986.60	(3812.60)	[A]	3765.50	(3163.92)	[A]	.29
	Sample sizes	476			15			9			Total = 500

Notes: *$p < .05$; **$p < .01$; ***$p < .001$.
Duncan significant at $p \leq .05$.

75

more repeat offenders than one-time offenders were enrolled in a pro
gram for school children assessed as mentally retarded or learning di
abled (Y_5). These results suggest that offender groups show no diffe
ences on tests, or in a physician's assessment, of intelligence at a pr
school or near-school age, but that they do have difficulties in learnir
once they are enrolled in school.

Explanations for these differences appear to be attributable to selecte
early familial effects, particularly for repeat offenders. The mothers
repeat and one-time offenders have a significantly lower educational lev
(X_2), although the difference is only by one year. However, the fathers
repeat offenders have significantly longer periods of unemployment (X
and the family experiences a higher number of household moves betwee
birth and age 7 (X_{20}). In turn, repeat offenders show significantly high
levels of lead intoxication at age 7 (X_{14}) relative to either one-tin
offenders or nonoffenders. Likewise, one-time offenders have a low
incidence of left-handedness at age 4 (X_8), thereby supporting the prop
osition that certain types of offenders have a lower, rather than a highe
incidence of left-handedness. No other significant differences were four
among groups on the other variables.

Results for females, shown in Table 4.2, are strikingly similar to th
results found for males. Repeat female adult offenders show nearly
times the level of seriousness in past juvenile offenses (Y_7) relative
one-time offenders, and 28 times the level of seriousness relative
nonoffenders. Moreover, as juveniles, they had 4 times more offens
(Y_6) than one-time offenders and 12 times more offenses than nonoffe
ders. Similar once again to male offenders, female offenders showe
significantly more evidence of disciplinary problems in school (Y_3). N
differences existed in tests of intelligence or achievement, although sigr
ficantly more two-time offenders were enrolled in a program for th
mentally or learning disabled (Y_5).

Other factors are also significant. Repeat offenders have mothers wi
significantly fewer years of education (X_2), they are more likely to liv
with foster parents, that is, to have been adopted (X_{18}), and they e
dence significantly more signs of "abnormal movements" (X_{12}) – one
several possible indicators of attention deficit disorder and minim
brain dysfunction. Contrary to male offenders, however, they show sigr
ficantly less evidence of lead intoxication (X_{14}).

These results are important for what they do not show, in addition
the significant differences that they do show. No significant mean diffe
ences existed among offender groups relative to "traditionally" importa

influences, such as family income and family size (number of persons supported), nor do other variables, such as hand preference, appear to be distinguishing factor.

It must be emphasized, however, that any impact these factors may have on adult crime is contingent on both their simultaneous influences and their indirect and direct effects on both juvenile and adult crime. If, for example, mean differences in achievement test scores are primarily attributable to the influences of disciplinary problems, then, in a regression model where all variables "control" or account for one another, the significance of test scores differences may disappear. These simultaneous effects are examined in the next section.

Direct and indirect effects on number of adult offenses

Longitudinal relationships among the 22 independent variables and 8 dependent variables in Tables 4.1 and 4.2 were examined using structural equation path models. Structural equation models, combining features of factor analysis and regression analysis, have been found to be useful in many areas of the social and behavioral sciences (Jöreskog, 1973; Jöreskog and Sorbom, 1979). The models are appropriate for analyzing longitudinal panel data because each equation represents a "causal link," in contrast to other techniques such as ordinary least squares regression where each equation represents an empirical association (Goldberger, 1972; Goldberger, 1973: 2).

In the initial models, number of offenses and seriousness of offenses were used as separate, dependent measures for delinquency. Because the final results were very similar for both measures, however, only those findings for number of offenses are reported. Likewise, only number of offenses was used as the dependent measure for young adult crime.

In general, models tested direct and indirect interrelationships among variables across five different "theoretical" points in time: birth, and ages 4, 7, 13–14, and 7–22 years. Results of model testing for males and for females for number of adult offenses, the final dependent variable, are shown in Tables 4.3 and 4.4, respectively. Coefficients can be interpreted in the same way as ordinary least squares regression. The effects of independent variables upon dependent variables are represented by X; the effects of dependent variables upon other dependent variables are represented by Y. Interrelationships among significant direct and indirect effects are illustrated in Figures 4.1 and 4.2.

Table 4.3. *Structural equation model of biological and environmental effects on juvenile and adult crime, males only*

		Dependent variables							
Variables	Ages	WISC Verbal IQ, age 7 (Y_1)	WISC Performance IQ, age 7 (Y_2)	Disciplinary problem, ages 13–14 (Y_3)	Language achievement, ages 13–14 (Y_4)	Mental retardation, ages 13–14 (Y_5)	Number of delinquent offenses, ages 7–17 (Y_6)	Seriousness of delinquent offenses, ages 7–17 (Y_7)	Number of adult offenses, ages 18–22 (Y_8)
Y_1 WISC Verbal IQ	7	–	–	–	.308*** (6.95)	–	–	–	–
Y_2 WISC Performance IQ	7	–	–	–	.253*** (5.72)	–	–	–	–
Y_3 Disciplinary problem	13–14	–	–	–	–	–	.220*** (5.04)	.170*** (3.82)	–
Y_4 Language achievement	13–14	–	–	–	–	–	–.096* (–2.22)	–.115** (–2.63)	–.081* (–1.99)
Y_5 Mental retardation	13–14	–	–	–	–	–	–	–	–
Y_6 Number of delinquent offenses	7–17	–	–	–	–	–	–	–	.244** (2.96)
Y_7 Seriousness of delinquent offenses	7–17	–	–	–	–	–	–	–	.226*** (2.73)
X_1 Pregnancy and delivery conditions	Birth	–	–	–	–	–	–	–	–
X_2 Mother's education	Birth	–	–	–	–	–	–	–	–.120** (–2.92)
X_3 Father's education	Birth	–	–	–	–	–	–	–	.083* (2.02)
X_4 Family income	Birth	–	–	–	–	–	–	–	–
X_5 Time father unemployed	Birth	–	–	–	–	–	.179*** (4.15)	.115** (2.62)	–
X_6 Hand preference	1	–	–	–	–	–	–	–	–

X_7 Stanford–Binet	4	.543*** (14.18)	.323*** (7.50)	—	—	−.153*** (−3.45)	—	—	—
X_8 Hand preference	4	—	—	.094* (2.09)	—	—	—	—	—
X_9 Eye preference	4	—	—	—	—	—	—	.059** (2.67)	—
X_{10} Foot preference	4	—	—	—	—	—	—	—	—
X_{11} Neurological abnormalities,	7	—	—	—	—	—	—	—	—
X_{12} Abnormal movements	7	—	—	—	—	—	—	—	—
X_{13} Abnormal vision	7	—	—	—	—	—	—	—	—
X_{14} Lead intoxication	7	—	—	.125** (2.77)	—	—	.149*** (3.46)	.143** (3.26)	—
X_{15} Anemia	7	—	—	.121** (2.67)	—	—	—	0.044* (1.95)	—
X_{16} Intellectual status	7	−.136*** (−3.55)	.158*** (−3.66)	—	—	.263*** (5.97)	—	—	—
X_{17} Speech	7	—	—	—	—	.092* (2.08)	.045* (2.05)	—	—
X_{18} Foster parents	7	—	.087* (2.11)	−.87* (−1.95)	—	—	—	—	—
X_{19} Father absence	Birth–7	—	—	—	—	—	—	—	—
X_{20} Household moves	Birth–7	—	—	.111* (2.48)	—	—	.092* (2.12)	.112 (2.55)	—
X_{21} Persons supported	7	—	—	—	—	—	—	.09** (2.06)	—
X_{22} Family income	7	—	—	—	—	—	—	—	—
R^2		.332	.153	.060	.222	.119	.157	.128	.247

Sample size = 487

Notes: The *t*-statistic is reported in parentheses (2-tailed test).

$*p < .05; **p < .01; ***p < .001.$

Male model χ^2 (166) = 150.28; $p = .804.$

79

Table 4.4. *Structural equation model of biological and environmental effects on juvenile and adult crime, females only*

		Dependent variables							
Variables	Ages	WISC Verbal IQ, age 7 (Y_1)	WISC Performance IQ, age 7 (Y_2)	Disciplinary problem, ages 13–14 (Y_3)	Language achievement, ages 13–14 (Y_4)	Mental retardation, ages 13–14 (Y_5)	Number of delinquent offenses, ages 7–17 (Y_6)	Seriousness of delinquent offenses, ages 7–17 (Y_7)	Number of adult offenses, ages 18–22 (Y_8)
Y_1 WISC Verbal IQ	7	–	–	–	.225*** (4.56)	–	–	–	–
Y_2 WISC Performance IQ	7	–	–	–	.206*** (4.83)	–	–	–	–
Y_3 Disciplinary problem	13–14	–	–	–	–	–	.232*** (5.40)	.110*** (2.57)	.295*** (5.95)
Y_4 Language achievement	13–14	–	–	–	–	–	–.101* (–2.39)	–.089* (–2.03)	–
Y_5 Mental retardation	13–14	–	–	–	–	–	–	.111** (2.60)	–
Y_6 Number of delinquent offenses	7–17	–	–	–	–	–	–	–	–.267** (–3.10)
Y_7 Seriousness of delinquent offenses	7–17	–	–	–	–	–	–	–	.524*** (6.36)
X_1 Pregnancy and delivery conditions	Birth	–	–	–	–	.090* (2.08)	–	–	–
X_2 Mother's education	Birth	.131*** (3.73)	.082* (1.98)	–	.093* (2.39)	–	–	–	–
X_3 Father's education	Birth	–	–	–	.095* (2.44)	–	–	–	–.112** (–2.70)
X_4 Family income	Birth	–	–	–	.095* (2.44)	–	–	–	–
X_5 Time father unemployed	Birth	–	–.082* (–2.10)	–	–	.112* (2.51)	–	–	–
X_6 Hand preference	1	–	–	–	–	–	–	–	–

80

X_7	Stanford–Binet	4	.566*** (15.82)	.367*** (8.80)	—	.138** (2.87)	—	—	—	—
X_8	Hand preference	4	—	—	—	—	—	—	—	—
X_9	Eye preference	4	—	—	—	—	—	−.080* (−1.95)	−.086* (−2.02)	—
X_{10}	Foot preference	4	—	—	—	.113** (3.07)	—	.153*** (3.74)	.101* (2.35)	—
X_{11}	Neurological abnormalities	7	−.122*** (−3.39)	−.164*** (−4.00)	—	—	—	.095*** (3.86)	—	—
X_{12}	Abnormal movements	7	—	—	.503*** (12.89)	—	—	.082*** (3.94)	—	—
X_{13}	Abnormal vision	7	.096** (2.90)	—	.105** (2.68)	—	—	—	—	—
X_{14}	Lead intoxication	7	.077* (2.33)	—	—	—	—	—	—	—
X_{15}	Anemia	7	—	—	—	—	—	—	—	—
X_{16}	Intellectual status	7	—	—	—	—	.146** (3.26)	−.052* (−2.11)	—	—
Y_{17}	Speech	7	−.104** (−3.05)	—	—	—	—	—	—	—
X_{18}	Foster parents	7	—	.113** (2.92)	—	—	—	−.207*** (−5.06)	−.257*** (−6.02)	—
X_{19}	Father absence	Birth–7	—	—	—	−.109** (−2.80)	—	.108** (2.60)	.095* (2.20)	—
X_{20}	Household moves	Birth–7	—	—	—	—	—	—	—	—
X_{21}	Persons supported	7	—	—	—	−.138*** (−3.61)	—	—	—	—
X_{22}	Family income	7	—	—	—	—	—	—	—	—
	R^2		.437	.232	.262	.348	.045	.206	.134	.188

Sample sizes = 500

Notes: The t-statistic is reported in parentheses (2-tailed test).

$*p < .05; **p .01; ***p < .001$.

Female model χ^2 (154) = 116.80; p = .989.

81

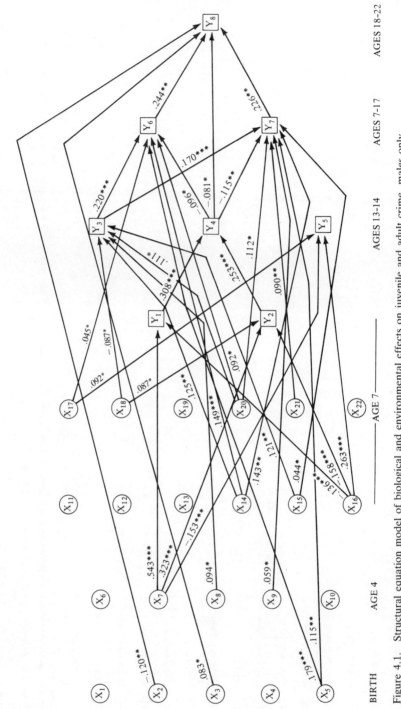

Figure 4.1. Structural equation model of biological and environmental effects on juvenile and adult crime, males only.

BIRTH   AGE 4   ——— AGE 7 ———   AGES 13-14   AGES 7-17   AGES 18-22

82

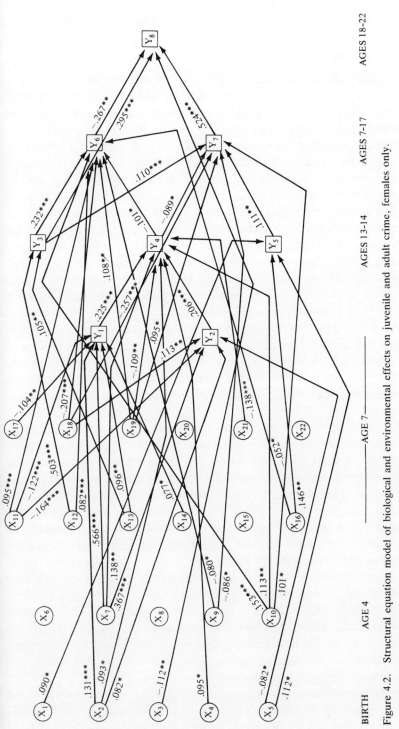

BIRTH   AGE 4   ————AGE 7————   AGE 13-14   AGES 7-17   AGES 18-22

Figure 4.2.   Structural equation model of biological and environmental effects on juvenile and adult crime, females only.

83

Effects on male offenders

Five factors showed significant effects on the number of adult offenses for males. As would be expected, number and seriousness of juvenile offenses showed the most highly significant effects, along with mother's education. The strong effect of mother's education suggests that, whatever slight variation education showed in mean score differences, its impact in predicting future adult crime is strong and direct (it had no apparent impact on predicting juvenile crime). In turn, the positive impact of father's education may simply be an artifact because it is highly related to mother's education. Language achievement significantly impacted not only on adult offense behavior, but also on the number and seriousness of juvenile offenses.

Indeed, the effects on juvenile crime are important because of their indirect effects on adult crime, and because they may have a large influence on initiating and perpetuating a youth's involvement in crime. Evidence of disciplinary problems in school shows the most highly significant association with delinquency for males. This association demonstrates that, not unexpectedly, school-related aggression and behavioral disturbance are strong predictors of future behavioral disorders. Moreover, it appears that delinquents evidence fewer attachments and commitments to conforming and normative behavior, at least in the school setting.

An examination of those factors that significantly predict disciplinary status in school suggests that behavioral problems may also reflect disorders of the central nervous system and an unstable environment, both of which are precursors of attention deficit disorder and minimal brain dysfunction. For example, placement in a disciplinary program is strongly linked to three biological effects: lead intoxication, anemia, and left-handedness. As reviewed previously, left-handedness is one indicator of dominance of the right cerebral hemisphere, and it has been associated with a number of behavioral and intellectual disorders, including impulsivity and discontrol. There is also considerable evidence of high lead levels among hyperactive and behaviorally disordered children (Boffey, 1988; Davie et al., 1972; de la Burde and Choate, 1975; Dubey, 1976) although lead intoxication has not been generally studied relative to delinquency. As Table 4.3 shows, however, toxicity had a highly significant impact on the number of official police contacts among males. The influence of iron deficiency anemia on behavioral problems has also not been thoroughly investigated in past research, although anemia was found to be related to disciplinary problems in the Perinatal Project sample. Moreover, iron deficiency anemia is one of several factors that has been shown to increase susceptibility to lead toxicity (Committee on Environmental Hazards, 1987: 460). Overall, then, these findings confirm the importance of biological factors as direct contributors to behavioral problems.

Other predictors of disciplinary problems in school reflect the importance of familial or parental instability. Having a foster parent and frequent household moves had highly significant impacts on disciplinary disorders in school. The number of household moves was also a strong predictor of an official delinquency status. In general, disciplinary disorders represent a constellation of biological and environmental factors that have either direct or indirect links to delinquency.

Surprisingly, disciplinary problems in school were not highly correlated with school achievement in language, which did show a significant direct effect on delinquency. It appears, then, that behavioral disturbance has more of a direct effect on delinquency in lieu of an indirect, or impeding, effect through school achievement.

What factors do have an impact on language achievement? Both WISC Verbal and Performance IQ have highly significant direct effects. However, contrary to some past research (Moffitt et al., 1981; West and Farrington, 1973; Wilson and Herrnstein, 1985), early intelligence scores showed no direct effect on delinquency. The link between intelligence and achievement is expected, and it does indicate that intelligence scores have an indirect effect on delinquency. In addition, the relatively more dominant effect of Verbal IQ on achievement among males confirms past evidence that poor verbal ability (one indicator of left hemisphere deficit) may be an important factor in academic underachievement (Reitan and Davison, 1974).

Early predictors of Verbal and Performance IQ point to other indirect links to delinquency. Not surprisingly, Stanford–Binet at age 4 had a strong impact on Verbal IQ, Performance IQ, and placement in a program for the mentally retarded during adolescence. The status of having foster parents directly impacted on Performance IQ, indicating that some familial factors contribute to early test scores. Clinical impressions of the intellectual status of the Perinatal Project children at age 7 also predicted Verbal IQ and Performance IQ at age 7, as well as evidence of mental retardation during adolescence. These associations validate physicians' capabilities to determine intellectual performance independent of intelligence tests and to predict intellectual capacity later in life. However, evidence of an abnormal intellectual status at age 7 or of mental retardation during adolescence did not have a significant direct effect on delinquency.

Importantly, a physician's clinical assessment of a child's speech at age

7 did have a significant effect on delinquency. The impact of speech is particularly telling in light of the finding that, of all the tests of adolescent achievement examined as predictors of delinquency at ages 13 and 14, only language ability was significantly associated. In turn, evidence of abnormal speech early in life predicted placement in a program for the mentally retarded during adolescence. In the Perinatal Project, physicians were instructed not to code as abnormal "those qualities of speech and language which are common among [a child's] peers" (U.S. Department of Health, Education, and Welfare, 1970, Part III E: 25), thereby ensuring that a rating of "abnormal speech" was not a reflection of a child's background or neighborhood.

Contrary to past research (e.g., Denno, 1985) no direct link was found between delinquency and total family income either at the time of the child's birth or at age 7. It appears, however, that previous associations between socioeconomic status and delinquency may have reflected an underlying relationship between factors that may be tied to low income but which have not been examined intensively in delinquency research (e.g., familial and parental characteristics). In the present study, the number of times the family household moved between the child's birth and seventh birthday demonstrated a significant direct effect on delinquency. The length of time a father was unemployed showed the most highly significant impact, second only to disciplinary problems in school. Thus, patterns of familial instability and disorganization appear to be more important than the dollar amount a family earns.

Overall, crime and violence among males is most strongly a product of three factors – behavioral, intellectual, and familial – all of which are influenced directly or indirectly by biological and environmental effects. In line with some past research (Loeber and Dishion, 1983), evidence of behavioral problems predicted delinquency among males most strongly. Factors that are investigated infrequently in delinquency research, such as lead intoxication and father's employment status, were also highly significant predictors. Low language achievement in school, abnormal speech at an early age, and number of household moves during early childhood followed in strength as significant predictors. Direct and indirect effects on the most highly significant predictors demonstrated that CNS disorders such as attention deficit disorder and hyperactivity may be important contributing elements in a delinquency career.

Effects on female offenders

Predictors of adult and juvenile crime were similar for males and females, although clear gender differences also appeared. Four factors showed direct significant effects on number of adult offenses among females: number and seriousness of juvenile offenses, disciplinary problems at age 13–14, and low level of father's education.

Being raised in a foster home showed the strongest effect on delinquency among females. Foster home status, in particular, has not been frequently investigated in delinquency research aside from adoption studies, which focus on the genetics of crime rather than on the influence of being a foster child (see, for example, Mednick, Gabrielli, and Hutchings, 1984). Children who were placed in foster care in the Perinatal Project were often originally from disruptive and abusive homes where one or both parents were absent. Although the children were placed in foster care at any time between infancy and age 7, it appears that their early family experiences had an effect on their later delinquency. This conclusion is confirmed by the significant association found between father absence both at birth and at age 7 and delinquency. Moreover, it appears that familial circumstances affected intellectual attainment: foster parent status negatively impacted on Performance IQ and father absence negatively impacted on language achievement.

Evidence of disciplinary problems in school was also strongly associated with delinquency among females. As with males, predictors of behavioral disturbance were linked to CNS disorders indicative of minimal brain dysfunction. In Figure 4.2, the presence of abnormal movements during an intensive neurologic examination at age 7 was a highly significant predictor of placement in a disciplinary program for females. Abnormal movements were usually assessed during standard tests of coordination or while observing the child's spontaneous activity. For example, a test child would be asked to hold out both arms horizontally for 30 seconds to ease the detection of abnormal posture, chorea (rapid involuntary jerks), and athetosis (slow, spasmodic repetitions). Many different types of abnormal movements were recorded, including fasciculation, tremors, tics, and mirror movements.

The number of disciplinary problems in school was also highly significantly associated with a physician's assessment that a child was found to be abnormal on a visual screening examination. Visual acuity was determined to be abnormal if any one of the following three conditions existed: (1) visual acuity was less than 20:30 (with or without glasses), (2) there was hyperopia test failure, and (3) there was muscle balance test failure. Abnormal visual acuity showed a direct effect on Verbal IQ as well, thereby indicating its influence on both verbal test scores and behavior.

Other factors showed highly significant effects on both Verbal IQ and Performance IQ. Negative effects on only Verbal IQ included the presence of speech abnormalities and lead intoxication. These relationships are not surprising in light of the strong association between speech and verbal ability found in past research (Reitan and Davison, 1974) and the link between lead toxicity and neuropsychological deficit (Needleman, Gunnoe, Leviton, Reed, Peresie, Maher, and Barrett, 1979). In turn, the number of neurological abnormalities a child evidenced during a medical exam was highly negatively associated with both Verbal IQ and Performance IQ. Medical examiners were asked to report as abnormalities "conditions, which may not in themselves be neurological but are often related to CNS disorders, such as abnormalities of skull size and shape, spinal anomalies, and primary muscle disease. Mental retardation would be coded here, as well as emotional and psychiatric disorders" (U.S. Department of Health, Education, and Welfare, 1970, Part III–E: 25). Not surprisingly, the Stanford–Binet at age 4 had a highly significant impact on both Verbal IQ and Performance IQ; its effect on Verbal IQ was particularly strong.

Other effects on early intelligence test scores were related to parents' characteristics. Although mother's education had no effect on ability and behavior among juvenile males, it showed significant effects on Verbal IQ and Performance IQ among females. This result is consistent with the longitudinal research findings of Bayley and Schaefer (1964), who showed that the intelligence test scores of girls were primarily correlated with the mother's own intelligence and social class. In the present study, only Performance IQ was significantly negatively affected by the length of time a father was unemployed, thereby indicating that factors associated with familial instability had a negative impact on intellectual development of spatial skills.

As with males, both Verbal IQ and Performance IQ showed direct effects on language achievement. In turn, language achievement had a significant effect on delinquency. Although no independent variables had a significant effect on language achievement among males, six variables demonstrated a significant effect on achievement among females. Positive effects were mother's education, Stanford–Binet, right footedness, and family income at birth; negative effects were father absence both at birth and at age 7 and the number of persons who were supported in the household. Thus, both biological and environmental factors influence achievement among females, and therefore indirectly influence delinquency.

The number of times a child was enrolled in a program for the mentally retarded during adolescence showed no significant direct effect on delinquency. However, evidence of retardation was associated with number of perinatal complications, a clinical impression of abnormal intellectual status, and the amount of time a father was unemployed. It appears, then, for both males and females, that delinquency and violence are associated with learning difficulties and low achievement, but not with the more debilitating types of mental impairment characteristic of retardation. This finding is consistent with the results in chapter 3, which indicated generally that the more violent and chronic delinquents had lower intelligence and achievement scores, but that they were not significantly represented in programs for the mentally retarded.

Predictors of female delinquency and violence comprised both biological and environmental effects. However, biological factors contributed a considerably greater role in the delinquency of females as compared to males. Although foster care and disciplinary problems showed the most highly significant effects on female crime, neurological disorders and factors associated with attention deficit disorder were also important. Factors associated with attention deficit disorder were: the number of neurological abnormalities a child evidenced at an exam, mixed cerebral dominance as indicated by left-footedness and right-eyedness, and abnormal movements. Many of these factors influenced language achievement, which had a direct negative impact on delinquency.

Overall, there were two significant effects on delinquency for both sexes: disciplinary problems in school – the strongest predictor for males and among the strongest predictors for females – and language achievement. This finding accords in part with research reviewed by Loeber and Dishion (1983) that found problems with conduct and academics to be among the principal predictors of delinquency. Apart from academic achievement, however, other factors showed a highly significant impact on delinquency for both sexes. Thus, although achievement is significantly associated with delinquency, it is not among the principal predictors found for either sex in this study.

Total impact of effects on number of adult offenses

An examination of the total impact of independent and dependent variables through the summation of direct and indirect effects provides another way of predicting adult and juvenile offenses, as seen in Tables 4.5 and 4.6. This approach can answer questions that relate to the combination of independent effects on intervening variables as they influence crime. For example, among males, what is the total effect of lead intoxication on adult crime, given that lead has a direct effect on delinquency as well as an indirect effect through disciplinary problems? What

Table 4.5. *Reduced form equations for achievement and juvenile and adult crime, males only*

Variables	Ages	Language achievement, ages 13–14 (Y_4)	Number of delinquent offenses, ages 7–17 (Y_6)	Seriousness of delinquent offenses, ages 7–17 (Y_7)	Number of adult offenses, ages 18–22 (Y_8)
X_1 Pregnancy and delivery conditions	Birth	–	–	–	–
X_2 Mother's education	Birth	–	–	–	-.120
X_3 Father's education	Birth	–	–	–	.083
X_4 Family income	Birth	–	–	–	–
X_5 Time father unemployed	Birth	–	.179	.115	.070
X_6 Hand preference	1	–	–	–	–
X_7 Stanford–Binet	4	.249	-.024	-.029	-.033
X_8 Hand preference	4	–	.021	.016	.009
X_9 Eye preference	4	–	–	.060	.013
X_{10} Foot preference	4	–	–	–	–
X_{11} Neurological abnormalities	7	–	–	–	–
X_{12} Abnormal movements	7	–	–	–	–
X_{13} Abnormal vision	7	–	–	–	–
X_{14} Lead intoxication	7	–	.177	.165	.080
X_{15} Anemia	7	–	.027	.065	.021
X_{16} Intellectual status	7	-.082	.008	.009	.011
X_{17} Speech	7	–	.045	–	.011
X_{18} Foster parents	7	.022	-.021	-.017	-.011
X_{19} Father absence	Birth–7	–	–	–	–
X_{20} Household moves	Birth–7	–	.116	.131	.058
X_{21} Persons supported	7	–	.078	.091	.039
X_{22} Family income	7	–	–	–	–

Sample size = 487

Table 4.6. *Reduced form equations for achievement and juvenile and adult crime, females only*

Variables	Ages	Language achievement, ages 13–14 (Y_4)	Number of delinquent offenses, ages 7–17 (Y_6)	Seriousness of delinquent offenses, ages 7–17 (Y_7)	Number adult offenses, ages 18–22 (Y_8)
X_1 Pregnancy and delivery conditions	Birth	–	–	.010	.004
X_2 Mother's education	Birth	.140	–.014	–.012	–.003
X_3 Father's education	Birth	–	–	–	–.112
X_4 Family income	Birth	.095	–.010	–.008	–.002
X_5 Time father unemployed	Birth	–.017	.009	.014	.005
X_6 Hand preference	1	–	–	–	–
X_7 Stanford–Binet	4	.340	–.034	–.030	–.007
X_8 Hand preference	4	–	–	–	–
X_9 Eye preference	4	–	–.080	–.086	–.024
X_{10} Foot preference	4	.113	.142	.091	.010
X_{11} Neurological abnormalities	7	–.061	.101	.005	–.089
X_{12} Abnormal movements	7	–	.199	.056	.039
X_{13} Abnormal vision	7	.022	.022	.010	.030
X_{14} Lead intoxication	7	.017	–.002	–.002	–
X_{15} Anemia	7	–	–	–	–
X_{16} Intellectual status	7	–	–.042	–.016	.020
X_{17} Speech	7	–.023	.002	.002	–
X_{18} Foster parents	7	.023	–.210	–.259	–.080
X_{19} Father absence	Birth–7	–.110	.119	.105	.023
X_{20} Household moves	Birth–7	–	–	–	–
X_{21} Persons supported	7	–.138	.014	.012	.003
X_{22} Family income	7	–	–	–	–
Sample size = 500					

is the total effect of hand preference, given that it has only an indirect effect on delinquency through its impact on disciplinary problems?

In both tables, the strength of the coefficients for reduced form equations is determined by comparisons with other coefficients in the equations. For males in Table 4.5, the number of adult offenses is most strongly influenced by four factors: mother's and father's education, lead intoxication, the amount of time the father was unemployed, and the number of household moves. Delinquency was most strongly associated with three factors: amount of time the father was unemployed, lead intoxication, and number of household moves.

For females in Table 4.6, the number of adult offenses is most strongly influenced by five factors: father's education, number of neurological abnormalities (in a negative direction), foster home status, abnormal movements, and abnormal vision. Delinquency was most strongly associated with foster parent status, abnormal movements, left foot preference, father absence, and number of neurological abnormalities (in a positive direction). In general, then, factors found to be important in the direct and indirect effects were also important in the reduced form models, although the relative strength of their impact shifted somewhat.

Conclusion

Overall, the results of this study showed that direct, indirect, and total influences on juvenile and adult crime demonstrated that biological and environmental factors were significant for both sexes, although biological factors appeared to have relatively more impact among females. Concerning adult crime for males and females, the number and seriousness of juvenile offenses had the strongest predictive impact. The number of disciplinary problems in school was also a very strong predictor for females, whereas low language achievement and mother's and father's low educations were strong predictors for males. The total impact of the selected variables (exclusive of the intervening delinquency and achievement variables) showed the following: Adult male offenses were most strongly influenced by relatively low levels of mother's and father's education, high levels of lead intoxication, and the number of gaps in the father's employment history. Adult female offenses were most strongly influenced by father's low education, number of neurological abnormalities (negative direction), the status of coming from a foster home, and abnormal movements and vision. Thus, father's low educational level had a significant effect on both male and female adult crime.

Two predictors showed significant effects for both male and female juvenile crime: the number of a child's disciplinary problems and low language achievement in school during ages 13–14. These results confirm past research that highlights the importance of behavior and ability in predicting delinquency (Loeber and Dishion, 1983). However, a number of variables examined in the present study had never before been included in crime research, thereby augmenting, in some respects, the list of established factors to be analyzed.

For males, delinquency was most strongly predicted by the number of a child's disciplinary problems by ages 13–14, the amount of time a father was unemployed at age 7, and the presence of lead intoxication at age 7. Evidence of abnormal speech at age 7 and language achievement at ages 13–14 were significant but showed considerably less impact. Disciplinary problems were associated with factors indicative of attention deficit disorder and hyperactivity, such as lead intoxication, anemia, and left-handedness. Foster parent status and frequent household moves were less strongly related.

For females, delinquency was most strongly predicted by foster home status at age 7, number of disciplinary problems at ages 13–14, left foot preference at age 4, and the number of neurological abnormalities at age 7. Father absence at birth and at age 7, language achievement at ages 13–14, abnormal movements at age 7, and right eye preference at age 4 followed in decreasing order of magnitude. Disciplinary problems were significantly related to two neurological disorders: abnormal movements and abnormal vision at age 7.

Results of the present study did not confirm past findings of direct relationships between delinquency and early intelligence, mental retardation, socioeconomic status, or early CNS dysfunction as measured by the number of pregnancy complications. The lack of strong, significant associations among these variables and delinquency may be due to several factors: the cultural and demographic characteristics and homogeneity of the sample; the infrequent occurrence of some of the independent variables (for example, particular types of pregnancy and delivery complications), which could underestimate true associations; or the simultaneous analyses of both biological and environmental variables, which could negate more "traditional" findings. Because much of the research analyzing biological factors and crime has not controlled adequately for social, demographic, and environmental influences, some past findings of biological links to intelligence or to crime may be artifacts of environmental effects. In turn, longstanding associations between environmental factors and crime may disguise the significance of biological effects because they are rarely incorporated in delinquency research. Other variables, such as disciplinary problems, may be an outcome of both biological and environmental precursors (e.g., neurological abnormalities and familial instability), although most delinquency research offers only sociological explanations.

Results of the present study do suggest that both biological and environmental variables contribute strong and independent effects on delinquency. Moreover, school behavior and achievement appear to be significant mediating factors. The importance of school factors in delinquency is not new, of course. What may be informative, however, is the possible chain of events that contribute to making school factors consequential in a sample of subjects who are at high risk for both learning and behavioral problems.

In examining this chain, considerable support exists for Hirschi's (1969) theory of social bonding (see chapter 1), but with some modification. This modification incorporates biological and age-related factors that may influence bonding ability. In the present study, typical bonding impediments such as neurological or CNS disorders, low achievement, and unstable social structure predicted delinquency for both sexes. Behavioral misconduct was stronger and more direct evidence of a lack of social commitment.

Other factors are possible antecedents of weak bonding. In the present study, intelligence scores demonstrated no direct effect on delinquency for either sex; however, intelligence had indirect effects on delinquency through school achievement. Moreover, violent and chronic delinquents evidenced generally lower scores on some tests of intellectual ability at early ages, as discussed in chapter 3. These associations support Hirschi and Hindelang's (1977) emphasis on the school experience as a crucial factor in crime.

Overall, however, this study suggests that delinquency is more directly related to familial instability and, most importantly, to a lack of behavioral control associated with neurological and CNS disorders. It appears that attention deficit disorder and hyperactivity could be associated with the learning and behavioral disorders evidenced in some members of the Perinatal Project sample. These problems would considerably inhibit the ability of young children to create social bonds even before the school experience. Academic failure would perpetuate misconduct and impede attempts at future bonding. Indeed, a sizable amount of research shows that children who evidence attention deficit disorder and hyperactivity are significantly more likely to retain antisocial conduct during adulthood, a time when most individuals start to show commitments to socially desirable behavior (Elliott, 1978, 1988; Shah and Roth, 1974). The studies reviewed in chapter 1 demonstrating that a relatively higher proportion of males have behavior problems may also partially explain sex differences in crime.

Chapter 5 examines more intensely the biological, familial, and environmental characteristics of the most violent and chronic delinquents in the Biosocial Project sample, in addition to their adult arrest histories. This examination focuses on possible factors that may distinguish violent from nonviolent children who, confronted with similar types of environmental and familial deprivation, react behaviorally in many different ways.

5

Case studies of violent and career criminals

In the Biosocial Project sample, nearly one quarter of the delinquent males and 12 percent of the delinquent females were violent, and frequently chronic, offenders. Relative to nonoffenders, these individuals had lower tested achievement, they evidenced more disciplinary problems in school, and their behavior was associated with certain biological and environmental disadvantages.

This chapter provides a closer look at the 28 most violent and chronic criminals in the sample and a matched control group of noncriminals in order to detail additional biological and familial factors that could contribute to differences in behavior. Criminals and their controls are compared, using information gathered during home interviews with the Biosocial Project children and their families, as well as written observations and impressions made during the children's medical and psychological examinations. Adult arrest histories are also examined to characterize those who continued to demonstrate problem behaviors after adolescence.

Interviews and observations

Much of the information on the Biosocial Project sample was gathered through extensive home interviews with the child's primary caretaker, usually the mother, and observations of the child. Interviews and observations were conducted by experienced social workers as early as four months after the child's birth and continued every four to six months until the child's eighth birthday. Home interviews provided data on the family's income, living conditions, number of family members, quality of parent–child interactions, and parents' employment status, as well as most of the Perinatal Project data on socioeconomic and household characteristics. However, other information, collected systematically on the child's behavior, health, and family interactions, was never coded.

96

Also never coded were extensive clinical impressions of the child provided by social workers during the home interviews and by trained psychologists and physicians at the Perinatal Project examinations conducted at Children's Hospital of Pennsylvania.

Home interviews were scheduled every four months during the child's first year and then every six months until the child's eighth year, providing a total of 16 scheduled interview times. On the average, the child's caretaker was interviewed 10 times during the course of participation in the Perinatal Project. Missing interviews were distributed evenly across the eight-year period. In light of the consistency found in children's behaviors during early childhood, it appears that little information was lost as a result of missed interviews. All children attended the 1-, 4-, and 7-year psychological and pediatric examinations at Children's Hospital, where clinical impressions by psychologists and physicians were recorded.

In order to examine this information, raw records for selected Biosocial Project children were coded and also summarized in written form by the author and a research analyst who has been working with the Perinatal Project data for 10 years. Coding and written summaries were performed systematically and without any knowledge of whether records belonged to criminals or to their controls.

Tables 5.1 and 5.2 list the behaviors coded for 56 children: a sample of 15 male delinquents and their controls and a sample of 13 female delinquents and their controls, respectively. A behavior was listed if it was noted in the raw records one or more times prior to age 4, between ages 4 and 8 years, or if it was noted both prior to and after age 4 (0–8 years). If the behavior was never mentioned in the raw records it was listed as "not noted."

Criminals and their controls

Each of the 15 male criminals selected as a case study had a police record that met three criteria: at least one violent offense, a total of five or more offenses, and a high seriousness score summarizing all offenses. Each of the 13 female criminals had a police record that met two criteria: a total of two or more offenses, which included all females who had at least one violent offense, and a high seriousness score summarizing all offenses.

The 28 most violent and chronic male and female criminals were each matched with a noncriminal control according to three criteria: (1) WISC Verbal IQ score at age 7, (2) language achievement score at ages 13–14, and (3) total family income at age 7. A composite score for all three criteria was created for each of the selected criminals and for each of the

98

Table 5.1. *Childhood behaviors observed at exams and home visits, males only*

Childhood behaviors	Criminals				Controls			
	< 4 Years	4–8 Years	0–8 Years	Not noted	< 4 Years	4–8 Years	0–8 Years	Not noted
Child's exam behavior								
Flattened affect	1	5	0	9	0	5	1	9
Hyperactivity	0	2	1	11	1	4	0	10
Fear of examiner/exam situation	0	4	0	11	0	4	0	11
Echolalia	1	0	0	14	0	1	0	14
Poor attention	2	4	0	9	1	4	2	8
Needs reassurance	0	4	0	11	1	3	0	11
Sleeping								
Night terrors	0	2	0	13	0	4	1	10
Bed wetting	1	3	2	9	1	6	1	7
Rocking to go to sleep	2	0	4	9	3	0	4	8
Head banging before sleep	1	0	3	11	0	1	3	11
Eating								
Pica – plaster or paint	6	0	1	8	4	0	1	10
Pica – cigarettes or ashes	3	1	1	10	3	0	0	12
Pica – other	6	0	2	7	7	1	2	5
Late weaning	0	0	0	15	1	1	0	13
Lead poisoning	3	0	0	12	0	0	0	15
Playing								
Fighting/aggressiveness	1	3	3	8	1	4	3	7
Likes rough play	3	2	8	2	3	3	7	2
Imaginary playmates	0	2	0	13	0	0	0	15
Daytime rocking	5	2	1	7	2	2	1	10
Daytime head banging	1	0	1	13	2	0	1	12
Destructiveness	1				2			

Social responsiveness								
Temper tantrums	3	1	6	5	2	1	8	4
Fears animals	1	2	1	11	0	2	1	12
Fears dark, thunder, shadows, noises	1	1	1	12	1	3	1	10
Overattachment to mother	0	0	0	14	0	2	0	13
Disobedience	4	1	0	10	1	1	0	13
School behavior problems	0	5	0	10	0	2	0	13
Verbal performance skills								
Poor articulation/stuttering/stammering	1	3	1	10	0	7	1	7
Baby talk	0	0	0	15	0	2	0	13
Health								
Auditory or visual disability	0	3	0	12	0	5	0	10
Head injury	4	4	0	7	2	1	0	12
Obesity	0	0	0	15	0	0	0	15
Family situation								
Maternal abandonment	1	0	0	14	0	1	1	13
Father absence	2	1	3	9	1	1	6	7
Family member incarcerated	2	0	0	13	1	2	0	12
Public assistance (DPA)	0	2	5	8	1	3	5	6
Poor housing conditions	0	4	3	8	1	4	3	7
Alcoholism/drug abuse by a parent	0	0	0	15	0	1	0	14
Seizures, epilepsy in family	0	3	0	12	0	0	0	15
Relative a policeman, teacher, minister	0	0	0	15	0	3	0	12
Parental characteristics								
Poor appearance	1	0	1	13	0	0	0	15
Lack of interest	0	1	0	14	2	0	0	13
Rudeness/hostility	2	0	0	13	2	0	0	13
Mention of physically disciplining child	2	4	0	9	1	4	1	9
Psychiatric treatment/distress	1	2	0	12	0	2	1	12
Uncommunicativeness	1	1	0	13	0	0	1	14

Table 5.2. *Childhood behaviors observed at exams and home visits, females only*

Childhood behaviors	Criminals				Controls			
	< 4 Years	4–8 Years	0–8 Years	Not noted	< 4 Years	4–8 Years	0–8 Years	Not noted
Child's exam behavior								
Flattened affected	0	4	0	9	0	2	0	11
Hyperactivity	1	3	0	9	1	2	0	10
Fear of examiner/exam situation	0	3	0	10	1	4	0	8
Echolalia	0	0	0	13	0	0	0	13
Poor attention	0	2	0	11	0	5	0	8
Needs reassurance	0	3	0	10	0	2	0	11
Sleeping								
Night terrors	1	1	0	11	2	0	1	10
Bed wetting	0	4	0	9	1	2	1	9
Rocking to go to sleep	0	0	0	13	4	0	0	9
Head banging before sleep	1	0	0	12	2	0	0	11
Eating								
Pica – plaster or paint	5	0	0	8	5	0	0	8
Pica – cigarettes or ashes	5	0	0	8	6	0	0	7
Pica – other	4	1	5	3	6	3	2	2
Late weaning	0	0	1	12	0	1	1	11
Lead poisoning	0	0	0	13	1	0	0	12
Playing								
Fighting/aggressiveness	3	1	4	5	2	5	1	5
Likes rough play	4	3	4	2	3	3	3	4
Imaginary playmates	0	0	0	13	0	1	1	11
Daytime rocking	2	1	0	10	3	0	1	9
Daytime head banging	1	0	0	12	2	0	0	11
Destructiveness	2	2	1	8	1	3	1	8
Clumsiness, poor coordination	0	0	1	12	1	2	0	10

100

Social responsiveness								
Temper tantrums	1	4	4	4	2	1	4	6
Fears animals	0	4	1	8	2	2	1	8
Fears dark, thunder, shadows, noises	0	1	2	10	1	1	0	11
Overattachment to mother	0	0	0	13	0	1	0	12
Disobedience	1	2	1	9	0	3	0	10
School behavior problems	0	2	0	11	0	0	0	13
Verbal performance skills								
Poor articulation/stuttering/stammering	1	0	0	12	1	3	1	8
Baby talk	0	0	0	13	0	0	0	13
Health								
Auditory or visual disability	0	2	1	10	0	1	0	12
Head injury	0	3	0	10	0	0	0	13
Obesity	0	0	0	13	0	1	1	11
Family situation								
Maternal abandonment	0	3	2	8	2	0	0	11
Father absence	1	2	6	4	2	2	6	3
Family member incarcerated	3	2	2	8	1	0	0	12
Public assistance (DPA)	2	3	5	3	2	1	3	7
Poor housing conditions	1	3	0	9	1	6	0	6
Alcoholism/drug abuse by a parent	0	1	0	12	0	0	0	13
Seizures, epilepsy in family	0	2	0	11	1	1	1	10
Relative a policeman, teacher, minister	0	0	0	13	0	1	0	12
Parental characteristics								
Poor appearance	0	0	0	13	3	0	0	10
Lack of interest	0	1	0	12	2	0	0	11
Rudeness/hostility	1	0	0	12	1	0	0	12
Mention of physically disciplining child	1	3	1	8	2	2	2	7
Psychiatric treatment/distress	0	2	1	10	1	2	0	10
Uncommunicativeness	1	1	0	11	2	1	1	9

noncriminals in the Biosocial Project sample. Squared differences between the scores for each noncriminal and each criminal were then computed. Those noncriminals with the lowest squared differences (from each criminal) in their composite scores were retained as matched controls for the criminals.

Tables 5.3 and 5.4 provide distributions of scores and offenses for each of the criminals and their controls. Mean scores for male and female offenders on Verbal IQ and language achievement were equivalent to those scores reported in chapter 3 for violent offenders. Obviously, the mean scores for matched controls are considerably lower than the scores reported previously for nonoffenders. Thus, the controls have comparable background characteristics to the criminals; however, they never attained a juvenile offense record. With one exception, none of the controls became an adult offender.

As Table 5.3 shows, all male criminals had Verbal IQ scores in the low-average to average range aside from one criminal whose score of 74 was in the borderline range. The average range of these scores confirms once again that the most violent criminals were not mentally defective or mentally retarded. Regardless, only 6 criminals tested above the tenth percentile in language achievement during adolescence. In general, then, the level of language achievement for criminals was markedly lower than the level of their Verbal IQ.

Adult offenses were collected for the Biosocial Project sample through the end of 1985. Thus, adult data are available through age 26 for those individuals born in 1959 and through age 23 for those born in 1962. Table 5.3 shows that, consistent with past research (Sellin Center, 1987), the great majority (80 percent) of the violent and chronic male criminals had at least one arrest as an adult; 40 percent became chronic adult offenders. In contrast, none of the controls had an arrest record as an adult. Clearly, a juvenile offense record is strongly predictive of offense behavior in adulthood although the concordance between number of juvenile and adult offenses is not always high.

Distributions for females, shown in Table 5.4, were similar to those reported for males on Verbal IQ and achievement, although considerable gender differences existed for the number of juvenile and adult offenses. The mean Verbal IQ scores for criminal females (86.7) were only one point lower than the mean scores for males (87.8), although three females fell in the borderline IQ score range. The mean achievement scores for females (18.2) were one percentile above the mean for males (17.1) and, like males, there were sizable differences between the level of Verbal IQ scores and the relatively lower level of achievement test scores. However,

Table 5.3. *Matching of criminals and controls on selected variables, males only*

	Criminals						Controls[a]		
Case number	Verbal IQ age 7	Language achievement ages 13–14	Family income age 7	Number of juvenile offenses	Seriousness of juvenile offenses	Number of adult offenses	Verbal IQ age 7	Language achievement ages 13–14	Family income age 7
1	94	53	2830.6	7	58.3	3	94	89	2819.7
2	99	4	6126.8	6	51.6	7	97	6	5315.7
3	89	24	5337.2	22	137.6	8	89	22	6086.3
4	97	30	3898.9	9	71.0	4	99	32	3829.8
5	91	2	6497.0	14	111.0	2	89	3	6203.4
6	104	34	6510.1	6	41.2	0	106	36	6510.1
7	89	12	5200.5	7	43.6	2	89	11	6126.8
8	97	6	17600.7	14	69.0	0	99	12	18091.0
9	80	7	5908.0	27	130.4	10	80	9	6018.2
10	85	6	6173.7	7	49.5	13	81	4	6126.8
11	81	22	5075.5	14	97.1	6	81	22	5348.0
12	74	1	6052.1	9	77.0	0	66	3	6035.1
13	80	5	3759.6	5	157.5	4	74	4	3776.9
14	82	1	6789.4	14	96.8	1	82	1	6510.1
15	87	2	16306.3	6	46.0	7	91	2	10148.9

[a] No criminal controls had an arrest record as an adult.

Table 5.4. *Matching of criminals and controls on selected variables, females only*

	Criminals						Controls[a]		
Case number	Verbal IQ age 7	Language achievement ages 13–14	Family income age 7	Number of juvenile offenses	Seriousness of juvenile offenses	Number of adult offenses	Verbal IQ age 7	Language achievement ages 13–14	Family income age 7
1	95	7	1782.7	2	19.2	0	97	8	2685.4
2	75	9	2784.9	8	11.8	0	79	8	1703.3
3	75	2	4772.6	4	30.1	5	75	2	4951.7
4	89	6	2738.1	11	20.1	0	89	7	2750.9
5	97	34	5231.4	2	10.0	0	95	36	5786.1
6	85	18	2917.9	2	14.4	0	85	22	2965.1
7	81	3	6052.1	9	36.2	0	79	7	6035.1
8	94	59	5283.8	2	17.2	0	94	61	4734.1
9	87	11	3928.7	9	58.0	3	87	12	3851.3
10	92	17	2738.1	8	31.9	1	89	16	2717.8
11	79	6	9300.8	3	12.4	13	80	2	9881.6
12	86	20	3682.1	6	4.9	0	86	22	3759.6
13	94	37	4704.5	8	49.0	4	92	34	4159.6

[a] One criminal control (case number 3) had one arrest as an adult.

the most violent and chronic female offenders engaged in far less serious offense behavior than their male counterparts. Moreover, 30 percent, or half the proportion of male criminals, had at least one arrest as an adult; only one female adult offender was chronic. In turn, although one juvenile control had an arrest record as an adult, the record was for one minor offense.

Altogether, then, the sample of 56 male and female criminals and their controls was characterized by low-average intelligence levels and comparably lower achievement levels. Although these individuals were not disproportionately mentally retarded or defective, they ranked lowest as a group in their test scores relative to the other Biosocial Project subjects. Expectedly, males had more serious and more extensive arrest records than females both as juveniles and as adults.

Behaviors observed at exams and interviews

Tables 5.1 and 5.2 list the nine categories of behaviors observed for both delinquents and their controls during the home interviews. The category *child's exam behavior* pertained to observations during the 1-, 4-, and 7-year examinations with psychologists and physicians. For example, children were coded as having flattened affect if they were described as being unusually passive or unemotional during the examination. Echolalia was coded if children demonstrated a pathological repetition of what was said during either the examination or the home interviews.

Behaviors related to *sleeping* were based upon reports by the child's caretaker during home interviews. Sleeping disorders ranged from bed wetting, which has been observed disproportionately among children with behaviorial disorders and delinquency (Denno and Schwarz, 1985), to head banging and body rocking, which have not been examined among criminals. Head banging and body rocking are part of a number of stereotypic behaviors found among autistic, mentally retarded, or environmentally deprived children, as well as among normally developing infants (Lewis, MacLean, Bryson-Brockmann, Arendt, Beck, Fidler, and Baumeister, 1984). Pathological stereotypic behaviors are defined as "immature voluntary behaviors in the repertoire for a long time and out of synchrony with 'normal' development, whose patterns tend to be unresponsive to environmental change" (Berkson, 1983: 240). Body rocking in particular is characterized by "a slow, rhythmic, backward and forward swaying of the trunk from the hips usually while in a sitting position" (Lasich and Bassa, 1985: 188). In some cases the rocking may become so violent that the child's bed is moved from one side of the room to the other during sleep.

Whether or not a stereotypic behavior is considered pathological depends in part upon the child's age. For example, certain repetitive behaviors occur among normal infants as a part of healthy play and physical exercise that promote cognitive and motor growth; however, they may be retained if children are raised in an environment deprived of the social experience and stimulation appropriate for their developmental level (Berkson, 1983). In one study, rocking, head banging, and swaying occurred in 15 to 20 percent of the children examined from an unselected pediatric clinic population; these behaviors were also observed more often in boys (Lasich and Bassa, 1985). As shown in Table 5.1, 17 (57 percent) of the male criminals and controls exhibited daytime rocking, suggesting that certain disorders among these children can be expected to be higher than average in light of the Biosocial Project sample's background and environment.

The origins and functions of stereotypic behaviors are not fully known. However, the major literature suggests that body rocking in particular is self-stimulating, that it accelerates motor development, regulates arousal level, and maintains a "perceptual or cognitive structure" (Berkson, 1983: 242). Other theories suggest that rocking is linked to maternal neglect, erotic gratification, and excessive physical restraint (Lasich and Bassa, 1985).

The primary disorders related to *eating* in Tables 5.1 and 5.2 were pica and lead intoxication. Pica refers to the eating of unnatural substances, such as lead, ashes, or paint, that often occurs in states of nutritional deficiency or mental imbalance (Smith, Delves, Lansdown, Clayton, and Graham, 1983). The numerous intellectual and behavioral disorders linked to high lead levels include learning disabilities, delayed nervous system development, deficits in visual motor function, hyperactivity, hypoactivity, and abnormal social and aggressive behavior (Committee on Environmental Hazards, 1987; Needleman et al., 1979). Moreover, adequate parental attention and stimulation are necessary to minimize the brain damage that may result from lead toxicity. For example, according to a statement by the Centers for Disease Control (1985), behavioral abnormalities attributed to lead intoxication can be greatly increased by continually abnormal mother–child relationships. At the time of the Perinatal Project, it was acknowledged that lead poisoning was occurring disproportionately in many inner city slums. One large study of Philadelphia schoolchildren examined in 1971 concluded that "black children in public schools from areas of deteriorated housing had marked elevations of dentine lead, with 20 per cent of the children having levels in the range associated with toxicity" (Needleman, Davidson, Sewell, and Shapiro, 1974). Thus, it is not surprising that a disproportionate number of the Perinatal Project subjects exhibited lead toxicity.

Direct observations or maternal reports of the child's *playing* behavior or *social responsiveness* provide some information on children's level of aggression at an early age, their quality of interaction with peers, and the display of any abnormal behaviors, such as daytime rocking and head banging. Evidence of poor *verbal performance skills* and *health* disabilities were based on mother's reports, the interviewer's observations, medical records, and clinical impressions noted at the time of the medical and psychological examinations.

During examinations and home interviews, an extensive amount of information was recorded on the child's *family situation* and *parental characteristics*. Questions were directed toward the family's financial and housing situation; possible absence, abandonment, or incarceration of the parents; and any history of psychiatric or medical problems, such as epilepsy, in the parents or immediate family members. Information on parent–child interactions and communication was based on observations during the home interviews and in the psychological and medical examinations.

Behaviors observed among criminals and controls

Frequencies of abnormal behaviors observed among criminals and their controls are shown in Tables 5.1 and 5.2. Due to small sample sizes, between-group comparisons are descriptive, not statistical. Frequencies can, however, indicate the prevalence of certain behaviors in the sample as a whole, as well as suggest whether criminals appear to show major differences from their noncriminal counterparts.

Comparisons between criminal males and their controls in Table 5.1 reinforce the need for including a control group in case studies; there is a noticeable lack of between-group differences on most of the behaviors. Indeed, controls showed a higher incidence of some disorders, such as bed wetting or father absence. When between-group differences were three or greater, however, a higher proportion of disorders appeared for criminals. Criminals evidenced more lead poisoning, daytime rocking, disobedience, head injury, and a history of epileptic seizures among themselves or their immediate family members. The prevalence of reported epilepsy and head injury among criminals is particularly important. These two categories combined accounted for 11 or nearly three-quarters (73 percent) of the criminals. In turn, controls reported more night terrors, problems with articulation, and the presence of relatives such as a policeman or minister. This last category, of course, indicates a positive and crime-preventive influence in the child's life.

In contrast, criminal females manifested fewer disorders than their controls where differences in number were three or greater, as shown in Table 5.2. Controls demonstrated a higher incidence of poor attention during the exam situation, rocking behavior prior to sleep, poor articulation, maternal abandonment, public assistance, poor housing conditions, and poor appearance. Criminals, in turn, evidenced higher frequencies of head injury and having a family member who was incarcerated. These disorders can perhaps be considered more serious and influential than the disorders mentioned for controls. In light of the considerable number of highly significant differences found among female criminals and non-offenders in chapters 3 and 4, it may simply be argued that the disorders noted during home interviews were not pertinent for distinguishing among different groups of females.

The examination of these variables gives an overall perspective on aggregate differences between criminals and their controls. In general, male criminals showed more disorders than their controls, although the opposite was apparent in comparisons between female criminals and controls. However, comparisons on factors screened for their high association with violent, chronic criminality in earlier analyses demonstrated that both male and female criminals differed significantly from their controls on both biological and environmental variables.

Despite the need for aggregate analysis, in-depth, clinical descriptions of the backgrounds and behaviors of individuals provide important details that can be missed in groups. The purpose of the following section is to apply the knowledge derived from group investigations to case studies of the early behaviors and family life of some of the more serious criminals and some of those who never had a criminal offense. Altogether, five case studies are presented along with their matched, noncriminal controls.

Perhaps most striking about the comparisons between criminals and their controls are their similarities, not their differences. Why one individual becomes a serious and chronic criminal and adult offender whereas the other individual never has an official contact with the law remains relatively unclear. Both have deprived backgrounds; slight variations in the nature and degree of the deprivation, however, appear to be the most important distinguishing element in determining future unlawful behavior.

Case studies

Criminal, Case No. 9: Male, age 23

This subject had the most extensive offense history in the sample: 27 offenses as a juvenile and 10 offenses as an adult. His first recorded offense was for truancy at age 10. From ages 12 to 22, he had at least 2 and as many as 6 police contacts every year. As a juvenile, his police contacts generally increased in number each year; they included several assaults and robberies, burglaries, disorderly conducts, and arrests for possession of marijuana. As an adult, he also engaged in a variety of offenses such as theft, robbery, possession of drugs, persistent disorderly conduct, and assault.

The subject demonstrated consistently low intelligence and achievement test levels. His score on the Stanford–Binet was borderline (74) and he failed the Porteus Maze test at age 4. His age 4 test summary specified suspect fine motor development and suspect concept formation. At age 7, his WISC Full Scale IQ (72), his WISC Performance IQ (68), and his WISC Verbal IQ (80) were all borderline. There was a 12-point discrepancy between Verbal IQ and Performance IQ test scores. The subject scored in the seventh percentile on language achievement in school.

A striking feature of this subject's record was the very severe speech problem he showed at an early age. From all accounts, he appeared to be tongue-tied, although there was no mention that any medical intervention was taken to eliminate the problem. In record after record he was described by his mother, the home interviewers, and all psychological and medical examiners as speech disordered and nearly unintelligible. Thus, at age 2, an examiner noted that "the mother is very concerned about the child's speech." At that age, the child's speech was composed primarily of vowels with an occasional use of consonants. The mother stated that the child knew about seven words that were spoken plainly; otherwise, the child's speech was described by the examiner as "unintelligible."

At the 4-year exam, the examiner noted that the child's mouth was "abnormal" and that he had a "severe articulation problem." These problems contributed to the examiner's assessment that the Stanford–Binet was "over the child's head" and that he was simply unable to verbalize his answers. At the 7-year exam he was described again as being "almost unintelligible," although he was cooperative with the examiner and "refuses to admit that he has difficulties with certain tasks." At age 8 the child was completely unable to be tested for the speech exam because of a "severe articulation problem."

Also at an early age, this subject showed cognitive and neurological disorders as well as symptoms of attention-deficit disorders. Starting at 7 months, the subject banged his head against the side of the crib and rocked before going to sleep each night. Head banging and body rocking continued through childhood. He evidenced rocking periods during play with other children and often rocked and banged his head when he was angry. At age 4 he was rated as having suspect fine motor and gross motor development. For example, he could hop on his left foot but was unable to hop on his right foot. At age 7 he demonstrated unusual muscular movements. He was unable to go down steps progressively and handwriting and pencil control were awkward. He required considerable amounts of time for visual-motor tasks. He was described as being awkward in coordination and other neurological tasks. At age $5\frac{1}{2}$ he still wet his bed nightly.

Although the subject did not appear to experience major illnesses, there was mention of a head injury due to a bad fall at 18 months. Medical records stated that the child fell out of a couch and hit his head, after which time he developed a high fever, vomited, and became groggy.

There were a considerable number of familial and environmental problems in the child's living situation. The child was fourth-born in a family of 8 children consisting of 7 boys and 1 girl. The mother separated three years after the child's birth. She had not worked since the child was born and the family lived on welfare. The family had a history of moving frequently and the child's housing situation appeared to be continually deprived. In one record his home was "in very poor condition"; in another it was in a "poor, tough, neighborhood"; in yet another the house was characterized as "one of the few on the block which is not condemned."

The child's mother demonstrated difficulty in comprehending and answering questions during interviews and during the child's examinations. In several home observations she appeared to have little control over her children's behaviors. Other comments pointed to more general physical neglect. At the 8-months exam, for example, a pediatrician described the following situation when the child appeared: "The child had on a torn polo shirt and piece of material as a diaper with no other pants. The mother did not bring any other diaper for the child. The mother appeared slow in comprehension – she placed him on his stomach when asked to place him on his back."

In an interview at 3 years, an examiner noted that the child "seemed definitely fearful of his mother. He cried when she called to him, but he quickly stopped crying and approached the visitor when she asked him to

ome to her." At the same time, the mother complained that the child
vas "hardheaded" and that she had "to beat him to make him obey." At
$4\frac{1}{2}$ years, a different examiner noted that the "mother frequently refers
o the kids getting on her nerves. She is very short tempered and, while
noisily disobedient, they seem to be fearful of her."

Consistently, examiners noted the lack of a father figure in the household. Moreover, the child had "very little contact" with his biological
father, who was incarcerated.

Despite these conditions, the child was nearly consistently rated as
friendly and pleasant during examination situations and at home interviews. At age 4, he was described as "cooperative" during the exam,
although he was frustrated because so many of the tasks were beyond his
abilities. At age $5\frac{1}{2}$ he was viewed as "not shy, attractive, friendly and
responsive." At age 7, an examiner noted that he "is not particularly
embarrassed or inhibited by his severe speech problem in the test situation." Indeed, the subject was "an eager, cooperative boy who enjoyed
all tasks and tried very hard at everything." Particularly during early
examination situations the subject appeared to be affectionate and to like
affection in return from those around him.

There are numerous factors in this subject's background that could
start and perpetuate criminal behavior. These factors include borderline
intellectual ability and low school achievement, a severe articulation
problem, neurological disorders, lack of coordination, bed wetting, serious head injury, middle birth order, large family size, large number of
male siblings, unemployed and separated mother, frequent household
moves, poor housing conditions and neighborhood, welfare status, in-
effective and intellectually dull mother, neglectful and possibly physically
abusive mother, no father figure present, and a biological father who was
criminal. However, the child's early behavior appeared to be friendly and
cooperative when observed by examiners and home interviewers. The
contrast between earlier and later behaviors suggests that behavioral
problems may have started in school. For example, the subject had an
official record of truancy starting at age 10 and was arrested for assaulting
a public school teacher at age 15.

Noncriminal control for Case No. 9

The control for this subject also evidenced physical and familial handicaps
but their number and severity were substantially less. The child's intelligence test scores were in the borderline range and from an early
age he showed difficulty in following directions and maintaining adequate

attention span. For example, at the 7-year exam he was described as "dull, slow, and minimally responsive." He experienced frequent illnesses throughout childhood, such as colds, rashes, infections, and asthma attacks. His gait and gross motor ability were poor and he was predominantly left-handed. At age 2 he started stuttering.

His mother was 15 when the child was born and she was single for the first 4 years after his birth, although the child saw his father frequently. The mother engaged in odd jobs, such as being a waitress or a nurse's aide, during which time the child and his two younger siblings were cared for by a babysitter. The family was on welfare before the mother married. By the time of the child's 4-year exam, the mother had married a man in the armed services. There was mention that when the child was age 5 the family moved to Europe to spend the summer with the stepfather. In general, despite his difficulties with school work, the child was described as pleasant and no behavioral problems were reported.

Altogether, then, there were positive influences in this child's life despite some of the disadvantages. Perhaps a major element was the mother's marriage, which provided greater stability for a relatively small sized family. Moreover, the child's physical and intellectual problems were not nearly so disabling as those described for the criminal subject. On nearly every level, the control child had a more favorable and supportive background.

Criminal, Case No. 3: Male, age 25

This subject had a record of 22 juvenile offenses and 10 adult offenses. His record started with 6 offenses at age 14; during age 16 he committed a total of 15 offenses, 5 of them purse snatchings which were just a month or days apart. His second robbery at age 16 was waived to adult court and it formalized the start of an adult arrest record that included thefts, aggravated assaults, and possession of drugs.

The intelligence and achievement test scores for this subject were low-average. His Stanford–Binet (89) at age 4 and his WISC Performance IQ (82) and WISC Verbal IQ (89) at age 7 were within the same low-average range. At age 7 he scored very poorly on the Illinois Test for Psycholinguistic Abilities and on the Bender Gestalt. His overall psychological evaluation was rated as "suspect" by the examiner. He scored in the twenty-fourth percentile in language achievement in school.

This subject demonstrated a number of physical problems starting in early childhood, although no one event or problem appeared to be an overriding influence on his development. At 8 months, the child was described by the examiner as "somber, quiet, and underactive." He had few toys and was tentative in his initial play behavior. At 1 year the child was rated as neurologically suspicious because of delayed locomotor development. At that age there were also many medical reports of accidents and illnesses – for example, the child had experienced three falls, he had spilled insect repellant on his chest, and he had been sick with three colds and two ear infections. During the speech exam at age 3, the child was described as having a short attention span and an inability to grasp any of the directions given to him. His speech was characterized as echolalic; he would repeat anything said to him without comprehending its content. By the time of the 7-year exam the child evidenced a number of different physical and neurological disorders, including a perceptual-motor problem detected by the Bender Gestalt, signs of hearing disability, and some difficulties with eye convergence.

A notable feature of this subject's background was the history of disorders reported for family members. The child's paternal grandfather had epileptic seizures and the child's father had been an in-patient at several hospitals for anxiety and nervous disorders. At the time of the child's 7-year examination the father had been an in-patient at Philadelphia Graduate Hospital for one month for feelings of anxiety that were eventually treated with tranquilizers and group therapy. During a home visit when the child was $2\frac{1}{2}$ years, an examiner noted that the child was afraid of the father and that the father "smacks the kids whenever they misbehave." A different examiner observed that at 8 years the child was very close to his mother although not to his father.

During those times when the father was hospitalized and out of work, the family received public assistance. Family housing was generally described as inadequate. At a home visit when the child was $6\frac{1}{2}$ years old, an examiner noted that the house was "sloppy," the "walls and floors were peeling," and there were "bugs everywhere." Two years later the home was described as being in "poor condition."

In general, there was no mention that the child evidenced behavioral disorders at an early age. During the 7-year examination he was characterized as "friendly and cooperative, though shy" and he appeared to enjoy playing with other children. Although his first report card in school was very poor, the examiner noted at a home visit at 7 years that the child "is doing better in school and enjoys it."

Overall, several factors appear to be problematic in this subject's background: low-average intellectual ability and low school achievement, delayed locomotor development, unusual number of accidents and illnesses, echolalia and short attention span at an early age, perceptual motor problems, hearing and visual difficulties, grandfather's epileptic seizures, father's hospitalization for anxiety and nervous disorders, distant relationship between father and child, father's periodical unemployment, and inadequate and poor housing.

Noncriminal control for Case No. 3

This subject's control evidenced a number of potentially crime-preventive factors in his background despite obvious intellectual impairments. The control's intelligence test scores were in the low-average range and his score on the Tactile Finger Recognition Test was "remarkably poor." All academic subjects were below grade level and the child was described as making "wild guesses" during examinations in an attempt to solve problems.

The child also showed signs of other disorders. From infancy until age 6 he engaged in head banging. At ages $1\frac{1}{2}$ and 2 years he was hospitalized for pneumonia with iron deficiency anemia and at age 3 he broke his hip in a bicycle accident. At age 6 it was noted that his pronunciation was not clear and that he would need speech classes.

The control child's family situation was positive, however. His brother was a police officer, his parents were married and living together, his father had regular employment, and the health of his parents and 6 siblings was good. In independent reports the house was described as "clean" or "nicely furnished." In turn, the parents, particularly the mother, appeared to be concerned about the child's welfare and behavior. One interviewer commented that the mother and father were "quite religious" and made an effort to teach their children to be religious also. At the child's 1-year exam the mother expressed ethusiasm about the Perinatal Project and was characterized as "very receptive and eager to talk about family life." Moreover, the mother commented that she "is anxious that the child get ahead but she will not push him." Overall, then, features in the child's family life and environment seemed to have a positive effect on his behavior.

Criminal, Case No. 10: Male, age 24

This subject had the highest number of offenses as an adult (13) although among the lowest number of offenses as a juvenile (7). His first offense was for burglary at age 11. However, his next recorded offense did not occur until age 14, when he evidenced three police contacts during the course of the year. His juvenile offenses included truancy, possession and selling of marijuana, and possession of a weapon. As an adult he was arrested 13 times between the ages of 18 and 20 for a variety of offenses including thefts, assaults, possession of drugs, and robberies. It is likely that he was incarcerated at age 20 for his last offense, a robbery, since there were no further offenses recorded for him.

The subject's generally low-average intelligence levels ranged from a near-average score on the Stanford–Binet at age 4 (95) to a low-average score on the WISC Verbal IQ (85) at age 7 and borderline scores on the WISC Performance IQ (76) and WISC Full Scale IQ (79). He scored in the sixth percentile on language achievement in school.

From the moment of birth this subject showed numerous physical ailments and behavioral problems. Of all the offenders he had the highest number of complications at birth. At 4 months the pediatrician's report stated that the child suffered from stomach aches, constipation, continual vomiting of bottled food, loss of breath, and a heart murmur. Also at that age his sleep was punctuated with restlessness, frequent crying, and wakefulness. Between the ages of 4 and 5 months he experienced the onset of cyanotic spells (periodic discoloration of the skin due to oxygen deficiency).

Medical reports at later ages exemplify the kinds of additional ailments this subject experienced: frequent falls at age $1\frac{1}{2}$, swollen jaws at age 2, diarrhea at age $2\frac{1}{2}$, rash and occasional vomiting at age $3\frac{1}{2}$, and recurrent, day-long headaches at age 6 for which no cause was found. At age $5\frac{1}{2}$ it was reported that the child was in an auto accident in which he experienced loss of consciousness for about one hour, in addition to vomiting, loss of appetite, and a fever. He was in the hospital for four days. A home visitor noted that at age 7 the subject still sucked his thumb and wet his bed.

This subject was rated "suspect" in general for intelligence and visual motor abilities at the 7-year exam. Moreover, in the neurological exam his gait was described as somewhat unsteady when walking heel to toe.

It is the examiners' comments about his response to testing, however, that provide considerable insight into the reasons for the subject's behavior and what appears to be a host of nervous disorders. As early as age 4, for example, the subject was described as being "rigid in his approach to tasks." During the 7-year exam he was characterized as a "passive, overly agreeable" child who required continual nurturance: "[X] was a very shy and anxious child. He was extremely cooperative and passive. [X] tried to please and responded well to approval. He needed constant reassurance and approval.... His expression was somewhat flat. He is aware of limitations and seems to be working to capacity as he functions at an average level intellectually."

Despite his passive nature in exam situations, however, home interviews and observations occasionally characterized the subject as aggressive and disobedient. Although he generally related well to peers, an observer commented that at $3\frac{1}{2}$ years the subject fought with other children (usually over toys), that he was destructive with his toys, and that he had trouble sharing. At this age he had to be threatened in order to obey. At age 5 another observer noted that the subject "gets angry if another child annoys him and [the subject] swings at him." He also had a tendency to fight if "he doesn't get his own way."

The child also demonstrated behavioral problems at school. Although he responded that he liked school, his grades were low (C's and D's) and the teacher claimed that he could perform better if he did not "talk and play so much."

These problems may be directly related to a home life that appeared to be in total chaos. Consistently the subject's home was described as "wild," "filthy," and "smelly" by different observers at different points in the child's life. The comments of one observer at the 7-year exam are representative: "This home is filthy. The smell is sickening. The mother is harried; she can't cope with the children at all. They were all naked, dirty and running wild through the house. She knew very little about the child and was not able to answer my questions well. The child was not in school and he answered most of my questions."

When asked about methods of discipline, the mother responded that she hit the subject and all other family members "with a stick to make them obey." In other home visits it was noted that the mother and her 5 children did not wear underclothes; nor did the mother have a tooth brush for the child when he was visited at age 3.

Other aspects of the family situation were relatively stabilizing. The parents were married and living together. There were generally no serious financial problems in the family and the family's income was above public assistance level.

The problems in this subject's background that could contribute to criminality are clear: birth complications, low average intellectual ability and low school achievement, numerous physical ailments and sickness, falls, head injury with loss of consciousness, bed wetting, thumb sucking, unsteady gait, early aggression and fighting, poor school performance, disorganized and chaotic home life, mother's lack of interest in the child, and possibly abusive physical discipline.

Noncriminal control for Case No. 10

As would be expected the control subject also evidenced handicaps; however, there were positive features in his life that possibly circumvented serious behavioral problems. Indeed, a striking effect noted by several home interviewers was the highly positive change in the control subject's physical and emotional condition after his mother abandoned him when he was 10 months old. At that time the child's daytime caretaker took the child into her home and, along with her husband, eventually became the foster parent. As one observer commented, "the foster mother nursed the baby back to health...." Although early records documented the foster parents' attempts to find the child's biological mother, later records indicated that the biological mother had no interest in having further contact with her child.

The control child showed physical problems at an early age that were possibly linked, according to some records, to a family history of epilepsy. His intelligence test scores were borderline and his language achievement percentile was low. At age 4 he showed a "complete inability to comprehend the task of concept formation at higher levels" and his fine motor development was suspect. At age 7 he demonstrated "great difficulty with vocabulary" and was attending summer school for additional help. In two home interviews the child was described as clumsy or falling "all the time." His 7-year neurologic exam revealed a visual abnormality due to oscular muscle imbalance and he was referred to an eye clinic.

There was some minor evidence of early aggression, although it was not emphasized. Records mentioned that the child liked to fight at age $2\frac{1}{2}$ years and fought with children over toys at age 5. Twice it was noted that the child had a bad temper.

In all records the control child's foster parents were characterized as warm, affectionate, and concerned. Interviewers commented that the parents "loved" and "adored" the child. Both parents worked, they had no financial problems, and they felt that the best punishment for the child was to prevent him from going outside. It can be considered that these factors may have provided a buffer against possible negative influences on the child's behavior.

Criminal, Case No. 9: Female, age 24

The subject had a record of 9 offenses as a juvenile and 3 offenses as an adult. Her delinquency career started at age 10 with 4 runaway offenses in one year. At age 17 she was arrested twice for assault with intent to kill. Her 3 adult offenses were aggravated assaults. This relatively large number of personal injury offenses is unusual for a female offender.

The subject generally demonstrated low-average intelligence levels on the Stanford–Binet (87) and the WISC Verbal IQ (87), although the WISC Performance IQ was borderline (72). There was a 15-point discrepancy between the Verbal IQ and the Performance IQ test scores. The subject scored in the eleventh percentile in language achievement in school. During the 7-year exam it was noted that the child was handicapped by a visual motor problem and indeterminate hand preference. Although her verbal ability was normal, she demonstrated problems with many of the performance items. During the exam she was described as "restless and fidgety."

The child evidenced several different medical problems. Starting at age 3, for example, she was diagnosed as having a hearing disability in her left ear. At 6 years she engaged in daily pica and in turn was diagnosed for lead intoxication at age 7. Also at age 6 the child was knocked down in a car accident that injured her head, although she did not lose consciousness or suffer afterwards. Another head injury occurred at age 8, although again there were no signs of serious sequelae.

Outstanding in this child's medical and home visit records were the numbers of times she demonstrated aggressive and destructive behaviors at early ages. The frequency and the extent of her aggressiveness would be considered unusual even for a boy her age. Thus, as early as age 2 it was observed that she liked rough play and "fights when angry." At ages 3 and $3\frac{1}{2}$ she was viewed as destructive with toys and when angry she "throws things" at her mother and "kicks and screams." At age $4\frac{1}{2}$ she engaged in "fights with boys" as well as other aggressive acts such as pulling hair, breaking and biting toys, and pulling out dolls' eyes. At later ages she was described by her mother as needing to be "whipped" in order to behave.

In general, her family situation was unstable. During the 8-month exam it was noted that her father was in a juvenile detention home and so was unable to provide support for the child. At the same time the mother was in the tenth grade so that the maternal grandmother cared for her when the mother was not home. Until age $3\frac{1}{2}$ the child lived with both the mother and the grandmother in what was characterized as "very poor living conditions" supported by public welfare. The mother eventually "disappeared," only to begin to visit the child yearly when the child turned 5. It was noted that the father visited the child once a month. At this time both parents were providing support for the child although they lived apart from her and from one another.

Overall, then, this child evidenced a number of disorders found to relate to delinquency: low-average intelligence and achievement levels, a visual motor problem, indeterminate hand preference, hearing disability, lead intoxication, head injuries, early aggressive and destructive behavior, father with a criminal record, abandonment by her mother, not living with either parent, and very poor living conditions.

Noncriminal control for Case No. 9

This child's control showed few signs of any disorders whatsoever. She evidenced some early body rocking, pica, and nightmares and at age 4 she started to stutter. In some home interviews she was described as having a "quick temper" and moodiness. However, her behavior was not characterized as destructive. Although her parents were separated, her family life was generally stable and she saw her father regularly.

Criminal, Case No. 11: Female, age 24

This subject had a record of 3 offenses as a juvenile and the highest number of offenses (13) as an adult relative to the other female offenders. Her juvenile record began at age 14 and consisted of two thefts and one offense for possession of marijuana. As an adult she was arrested for two robberies and two drug offenses; the remaining offenses were theft related.

The subject's intelligence scores were borderline on the Stanford–Binet (74) and WISC Verbal IQ (79) and low-average on the WISC Performance IQ (83). She was in the sixth percentile in language achievement. At age 7 the examiner noted that her abnormal score on the Bender Gestalt and her reversals in spelling indicated that the child had a perceptual motor problem. Generally she appeared to be disinterested in the exam and in schoolwork: "She performed minimally throughout the exam. She lacks motivation and needs encouragement."

The subject's infancy and childhood included some notable disorders. When she was 4 days old, she experienced Rh trouble and received two complete blood transfusions. At this time she also had a mild case of jaundice. At nearly every exam starting at one year the interviewer mentioned the child's problems with pica and temper tantrums. Thus, at 1 year it was noted that the child chewed cotton and paper every day for six months and that she also chewed wallpaper with plaster on the back. At $1\frac{1}{2}$ years the examiner commented that the child licked ashes out of the ash tray three or four times every day and that her stomach needed to be pumped after an incident in which she drank turpentine. Her stomach was pumped once again at age $2\frac{1}{2}$ after she swallowed paint thinner.

The examiners consistently mentioned that the child had temper tantrums at least once a day and at the $3\frac{1}{2}$-year exam it was highlighted that the child engaged in five or six temper tantrums a day for over one year. The mother's usual response to these tantrums was to beat the child "to make her stop."

Starting at age 4 the child evidenced signs of eye disorders and at the 7-year exam it was recorded that she was referred to an eye clinic for further evaluation. At 8 years she fell from her bicycle, hit her head, and lost consciousness for a few minutes. The neurological exam revealed that the child had nystagmus, although it was unknown if the condition had been present before the head injury. The records noted that the child never attended the appointment made for her at the eye clinic so that she could be treated for the nystagmus.

Generally, the child's family life appeared to be quite stable. The parents were married and living together and, most of the time, both worked while the aunt cared for the family's 7 children. The child was described as "partially obedient" in response to the mother's discipline.

Noncriminal control for Case No. 11

In the entire sample of comparisons between criminals and their controls, this was one of the few cases where the control child's physical condition and familial background appeared to be equivalent to or worse than the criminal subject's. A major distinction between the criminal and her control, however, was the consistent observation that the criminal evidenced behavior problems throughout her childhood (e.g., disruptive trantrums), whereas the control showed only phases of disobedience.

During infancy and throughout childhood, the control demonstrated a number of disorders that appeared to be associated in part with a nervous personality also characteristic of her mother. At 8 months it was noted in the medical exam that the child banged her head on her high chair about twice a week and that she experienced two episodes of falling out of bed. At age 5 she had pneumonia. At age 3 the child had two "accidents": in the first she "bumped against a lit cigarette" and badly burned her arm; in the second she fell out of bed and her bottom teeth cut through her lower lip. At the time of her exam this injury had still not healed. Her mother noted that when the child was spanked very hard her lips would become gray, she would perspire and throw up, and then fall to her knees.

Consistently in examination reports the child was described as very nervous and high-strung. She bit her nails and sucked her thumb all day. However, it was noted that the child "is not rough, does not get mad easily" and that "her feelings get hurt easily." Thus, it appeared that the child's emotions and deprivation were demonstrated through hyperactive and nervous behavior rather than through aggression and anger. Once again, this distinction may have been important in predicting benign behavioral or personality disorders as opposed to future juvenile or adult crime.

Overview of case studies

The five case studies described in this section provide a detailed characterization of the backgrounds of some of the more serious juvenile and adult offenders in the Biosocial Project and their matched controls. The need to examine controls in addition to criminals is crucial in light of the fact that most disordered or lower class children never become juvenile or adult offenders.

The five selected cases in this section did not necessarily represent those subjects with the "worst" backgrounds, however; a number of criminals and their controls appeared to be raised in extremely disabling circumstances. Thus, for example, the female delinquent who had 11 police contacts as a juvenile but no reocrd as an adult evidenced an array of neurological disorders and illnesses as a child. Medical records showed that the child's mother, who was alcoholic and sentenced for second degree murder, appeared to have administered an overdose of tranquilizing pills to the child on a number of different occasions. In turn, the child herself made several suicide attempts prior to age 9.

It is to be emphasized as well that children can experience abuse and deprivation without ever attaining an official arrest record. Two of the female controls who never had an offense record had obviously been subject to serious sexual abuse because both had venereal disease and enlarged vaginas in medical examinations when they were very young. Other records and home interviews chronicled episodes of physical violence that a select number of the control children witnessed or experienced.

What factors then predict crime? The results of this study suggest that the number and severity of a variety of biological, familial, behavioral, and environmental factors are important to consider in distinguishing among groups of children as well as among individuals. Certainly this study demonstrates that a bias in favor of one discipline or another is not warranted; indeed, the results of the prediction equations in chapter 4 suggest a fairly even balance between biological and environmental factors in explaining the variance in behavior. Similarly, clinical impressions and case studies point to a variety of different influences at the individual level. Overall, then, greater consideration must be given in future crime research for facets of the person and behavior that may be important but are frequently ignored.

The last chapter of this book discusses briefly the implications of the Biosocial Project's results in terms of social policy and criminal responsibility. The discussion focuses on two issues relevant to the relationship between biology and crime: crime prevention and criminal law defenses based upon our current knowledge, as well as our ignorance, of both.

6

Biology and responsibility

The results of the Biosocial Project indicate that both biological and environmental factors influence criminal behavior among both juveniles and young adults. Moreover, these influences are so interdependent that separate labels designating them as "biological" or "environmental" are not always warranted. Likewise, the Project's results support a probability theory of behavior that views crime as a product of three categories of variables: predisposing, facilitating, and inhibiting (Report of the Interdisciplinary Group, 1978).

Predisposing variables can be defined as "having a necessary but not sufficient or compelling relationship with the phenomenon being studied" (Report of the Interdisciplinary Group, 1978: 30). Their presence increases the likelihood of, and may account for, a significant portion of criminal behavior. Variables include genetic, psychophysiological, neurological, and social influences. Facilitating variables "do not by themselves explain or cause the phenomena in question but, in combination with the predisposing factors, increase the probability that the behavior will occur" (Report of the Interdisciplinary Group, 1978: 31). Such factors include the use of drugs and alcohol, victim provocation, the availability of weapons, and the environmental and social context of the situation. (For a review of the literature on situational influences, and an analysis of their effect on violent behavior in the Biosocial Project sample, see Denno, 1986.) Inhibiting variables "are those which, in the presence of predisposing factors, tend to decrease the probability of the behavior from occurring at all" (Report of the Interdisciplinary Group, 1978: 33). For example, factors that may deter crime include the internalization of social–ethical norms, fear, guilt, the desire to avoid punishment, high intelligence, and the socialization of acceptable behavior.

Some variables may belong in more than one category depending upon when and how they become significant within an individual's lifetime. For example, the Biosocial Project showed that low achievement level is a

123

predisposing variable bearing a strong relationship to future criminality; high achievement level could in turn be considered a strong inhibiting variable.

A major outcome of this study, however, is the recognition that many of the factors that strongly predicted crime and violent behavior could be prevented. Appropriate methods of prevention would not intrude upon individual freedom because, even though some of the factors may have biological consequences, they also have clear environmental origins that can be eliminated. Lead poisoning has been used as example throughout this book because it illustrates the powerful impact that a preventable toxin can have on the lives of individuals who are not always in a position, either situationally for environmentally, to control what happens to them. Recent research shows, for example, that "exposure to relatively low levels of lead during early childhood can slow and perhaps permanently stifle mental development" ("New Proof," 1988: B17). Lead poisoning leads to learning difficulties as well as hyperactivity and other behavioral disorders (Amitai, et al., 1987), which can start in childhood and culminate in juvenile and young adult crime (Satterfield, 1987). Lead poisoning can be prevented, however, through the deleading of homes and other areas frequented by children (Amitai et al., 1987) as well as through early detection (Committee on Environmental Hazards, 1987; Landrigan and Graef, 1987).

Alternative crime-prevention strategies can involve the schools and programs for the learning disabled. If children demonstrate hyperactivity before school age, it seems likely that preschool programs may prevent later academic and behavioral disorders. Past analyses of the Biosocial Project sample have shown that early nursery school attendance did show a positive effect on verbal ability at age 7, which was, in turn, positively associated with achievement during adolescence. Nursery school attendance had no significant direct effect on delinquency, however (Denno, 1985). This result may be due in part to the timing and the length of the program which was analyzed.

For example, recent studies of preschool intervention programs indicate that those programs that start earliest in childhood and last the longest generally have the most positive impact on both ability (Darlington, Royce, Snipper, Murray, and Lazar, 1980; Schweinhart and Weikart, 1980) and behavior (Schweinhart and Weikart, 1980). In one of the most extensive studies of a preschool program yet conducted, Schweinhart and Weikart (1980) use a social bonding explanation for their finding that preschool education decreased the later delinquent behavior of impoverished teenagers. They suggest that early education strengthens bonds to school, which in turn inhibit misconduct.

Likewise, a current 2-year study in Brooklyn Family Court conducted by the Foundation for Children with Learning Disabilities shows that 40 percent of the juveniles who appear have learning disabilities. The purpose of the study is to more accurately identify these learning disordered children and thus direct them to an appropriate remedial program at an early age (Morgan, 1988: B1, B3). Program sponsors argue that such treatment not only benefits juveniles and prevents crime, but is also cheaper than court costs (Morgan, 1988: B3). In turn, the strong link between school achievement and employment success found in other research (Jencks et al., 1979) affirms the economic feasibility of investing in programs that can enhance school success so as to avoid the later costs associated with punishment and institutionalization. Altogether, then, prevention efforts are not only more humane, they can be far less expensive in the long run.

Crime prevention efforts focus on the relative strength of how selected biological and environmental factors can predict juvenile and young adult crime. There is an alternative way of examining the issue of prediction, however: How well do all of these factors together predict behavior?

In the present study, complete models of biological and environmental variables predicted 25 percent of future adult criminality among males and 19 percent of future adult criminality among females. Although these percentages are statistically significant, 75 to 81 percent of behavior is left unexplained. In a previous article (Denno, 1988), it was argued that there are two ways of regarding this result: (1) the statistical model examined is either incomplete (although its level of explanation is comparable to or better than most other social science models); or (2) varying degrees of free will and determinism exist in all actions, including violent crime, depending on certain biological and environmental contingencies. A key question is, however: At what point does behavior approach the determinism end of the continuum so that it may be considered outside of an individual's control and, therefore, nonblameworthy? Where, in other words, does responsibility end and excuse begin?

Such a question is perhaps best left to philosophers (see Denno, 1988, for a review of some major arguments). In contrast, a probability theory of behavior would suggest that responsibility ends when factors contributing to the likelihood of committing criminal behavior are so strong that an "acceptable level" of determinism exists. What level can be considered acceptable is beyond the scope of this chapter. However, because strong causal linkages between biological factors and crime are so difficult to demonstrate and, in most cases, are nearly nonexistent (if they were to be tested statistically), it is difficult to warrant the acceptability of one criminal law defense over another.

Unless an adequate point of decision making can be reached, then, or unless better statistical models can be developed, it may be best to limit using biological propensity as a defense to violent behavior and concentrate on preventing violent behavior altogether. Not only can such a focus be considered "more just," because we do not know which biological defenses are feasible and which are not, it may also be more realistic. If in fact only a small proportion of our behavior will ever be open to explanation, it may be that each person's thoughts and movements are so thoroughly individualistic that they are impossible to predict. The availability of only a select number of biological defenses, then, would not be appropriate. Moore (1985) offers a further comment: If we assume that all behavior can be excused or defended by simply locating the causing factors, we thus create "the absurd conclusion that no one is responsible for anything" (Moore, 1985: 1092). Such varying perspectives on cause and responsibility converge, however, in what may be considered a more general, if not more fleeting, view: Until more information on human nature becomes available, the notion of complete freedom from responsibility is best left to utopian ideals, not to our current knowledge of human conduct.

Appendix: Selection and distribution of Biosocial Project variables

For the purposes of the present study, nearly 300 Collaborative Perinatal Project variables, as well as school and delinquency variables, were selected for preliminary screening and analyses. Criteria for selection incorporated both the theoretical issues and methodological concerns presented in chapter 1 of this book.

The following sections discuss the reliability, distributions, and inter-relationships of those variables used in the present study, as well as attempts to scale and aggregate the prenatal and perinatal indicators of early birth and CNS trauma.

Birth related variables

As was noted in chapter 1, there have been many attempts to measure or scale birth related events with the Collaborative Perinatal Project (hereafter CPP) data and other kinds of data sets. Unfortunately, few attempts have been made to assess the reliability of these measures in terms of either the relationships among the individual indicators used for scaling or the subjective weights of seriousness applied to them by experienced examiners.

For the purposes of this study, the interrelationships among 38 selected indicators of prenatal and perinatal stress were examined preliminarily for possible scale construction. The nature and extent of birth related events were assessed by trained physicians with detailed instructions provided by the CPP on how to record data. Altogether, 31 variables were treated dichotomously: 11 variables were true dichotomies and 20 variables were classified into dichotomies. Seven variables were treated as continuous. Two main techniques of aggregation were applied: a reliability check based upon the coefficient alpha and a principal components analysis.

The following section describes each of the 38 selected variables in three ways: (1) the method by which the variable was classified – normal

127

or abnormal, present or absent, and so on, (2) a brief definition of the variable and, in some cases, its incidence in past studies, and (3) the nature and severity of the variable's stress-related correlates, such as hypoxia and cerebral hemorrhage. Because the CPP began over 20 years ago, the references used to discuss and describe the variables in this section include both recent and older publications.

In general, variables are classified according to their usual time of occurrence, that is, prenatal, during pregnancy, or at delivery, although it is recognized that no such classification is entirely precise. For this reason, techniques of aggregation are applied according to variable classifications as well as to all variables simultaneously.

1. Dichotomous pregnancy and delivery variables

a. Type of delivery

i. *normal*   vertex, undifferentiated
              occiput
  abnormal breech
              version and extraction
              cesarean section
              brow, face, or chin (sinciput)

Source: U.S. Department of Health, Education, and Welfare, Part IIIA, 1966: 65–71

ii. Delivery types and their subsequent complications are characterized in part by the presentation, position, and posture of the fetus. Presentation refers to the "relation of the long axis of the fetus to the long axis of the mother" (Taylor, 1976: 188). The presentation may be longitudinal or transverse, according to whether the long axis of the fetus is parallel or angular with the long axis of the mother (Taylor, 1976: 188). Longitudinal presentations constitute over 99 percent of all full term labors (Eastman and Hellman, 1961: 325). They are either cephalic (relating to the head) or breech (relating to the buttocks or lower limbs) depending on which part of the fetus presents itself, that is, enters the mother's pelvis.

The posture or attitude of the fetus (the relationship of the fetal parts to one another) may have some influence on four possible cephalic presentations: (1) the vertex or occipital presentation, which occurs when the head is well flexed near the thorax (upper chest) and the vertex or the occiput (areas of the infant skull) is the presenting part; (2) the face presentation, when the neck is very extended and the chin or face is the leading part; (3) the sincipital presentation, when the head assumes a partially flexed position between the two extremes of the vertex and face presentation and the large fontanel or the sinciput (parts of the infant skull) is the presenting part; or (4) the brow presentation, when the head assumes a partially extended presentation and the brow becomes the presenting part. In a number of descriptions of types of presentation relevant to delivery, the vertex and occipital presentations, which are the most common, are treated nearly synonymously; the brow, face, or chin (sincipital) presentations are discussed as variations or abnormalities (Eastman and Hellman, 1961: 324–330; Greenhill, 1966: 321–345; Taylor, 1976: 188–294). The breech position occurs when the pelvis or lower limbs of the fetus are the presenting part in the delivery (Taylor, 1976: 275).

The cesarean section and version and extraction are methods of delivery rather than presentations. The caesarean section is an incision through the abdominal wall and the uterus in order to extract the fetus (Greenhill, 1966: 1159–1160). Version is a preliminary procedure whereby the fetus is moved manually by the obstetrician from one presentation to another, more normal one. Extraction of the fetus, usually by a vacuum device, occurs when the version is complete (Greenhill, 1966: 1102–1108; Taylor, 1976: 533–537).

iii. The vertex presentation represents the great majority (about 95 percent) of deliveries; the occipital presentation (without complications or unique positions) is usually not distinguished from the vertex. These presentations are the most normal for the fetus and thus the least problematic in terms of delivery complications (Rydberg, 1966: 188–294).

The breech and sincipital (brow, face, and chin) presentations, the cesarean section, and version and extraction are abnormal types of deliveries. Depending on their nature and severity, they introduce considerable risks for the fetus and infant in terms of higher rates of mortality, brain injury, and generalized trauma or damage to the CNS (Perlstein, 1966).

A breech presentation, which occurs in about 3 to 4 percent of all deliveries, is attributed to a variety of factors that may interfere with fetal adaptation, including prematurity, extension of the legs, hydramnios (surplus amniotic fluid), multiple pregnancy, placenta previa, and congenital anomalies (Hellman and Pritchard, 1971: 853–855; Taylor, 1976: 275). Little evidence exists that the breech presentation alone is associated with a prolonged delivery; in fact, the length of labor for breech and vertex presentations is very similar (Friedman and Kroll, 1972: 117–121). In general, however, the prognosis for the child in breech presentations is considerably worse than in vertex presentations. This prognosis results in part because of related complications such as prematurity but also because of mechanical factors associated with the delivery such as prolapse of the umbilical cord and intracranial hemorrhage (Fianu, 1976: 1–85) or subsequent CNS dysfunction (Drorbaugh, Moore, and Warram, 1975: 529–537).

Sincipital (brow, face, and chin) presentations can also be problematic. The brow and face presentations, which occur respectively in about .1 and .2 percent of all deliveries (Hellman and Pritchard, 1971: 863–872), have similar etiologies. More than one fifth of all brow presentations are related to prematurity or a contracted pelvis (Hellman and Pritchard, 1971: 870); other correlates include ruptured membranes and hydramnios (Niswander and Gordon, 1972; Taylor, 1976: 272). Face presentations are generally related to those factors that inhibit extension of the head, such as pelvic contraction, large infant size (Gordon, Rich, Deutschberger, and Green, 1973: 51–56; Hellman and Pritchard, 1971: 864–865), and a faulty uterine axis most common among multiparae (women who have given birth at least two times) with pendulosity of the abdomen (Taylor, 1976: 265). Associated difficulties and causes of fetal death with face presentation are attributed to trauma and hypoxia (a below normal level of oxygen), attempted maneuvers to correct the position of the head, and difficult forceps operations (Taylor, 1976: 539–543; Perlstein, 1966).

Delivery by cesarean section is suggested for some cases of brow and face presentation that appear to be troublesome (malpresentations). Although figures vary, cesarean sections in general have been reported for about 4 to 11 percent of all deliveries, depending on the time and types of patients and institutions observed (Taylor, 1976: 539).

Indications for cesarean sections also vary. In about one half of the cases, the main indication is a previous cesarean section scar that may rupture, expecially during labor (Hellman and Pritchard, 1971: 1165–1166). Indications for the second half of the cases range in the following descending order of frequency: cephalopelvic disproportion (contracted pelvis); uterine inertia (poor uterine contractions); toxemia (a term referring to metabolic disorders of pregnancy accompanied by hypertension and edema or excessive fluid retention); placentia previa; abruptio placentae; malpresentation; diabetes; elderly primipara (a woman over age 35 giving birth for the first time); fetal distress; large infant size; prolapse of the umbilical cord; pelvic tumor; or poor obstetrical history (e.g., previous fetal deaths) (Niswander and Gordon, 1972; Taylor, 1976: 539–543).

Historically, the cesarean section was nearly always fatal for the mother, although now it is relatively safe (Hellman and Pritchard, 1971: 1165). The primary dangers are hemorrhage, shock, peritonitis (inflamation of the abdominal walls), embolism (obstruction or occlusion of a vessel) (Taylor, 1976: 550–553), abnormal CNS function (Drorbaugh et al., 1975: 532), prematurity (Drillien, 1972: 563–574; Naeye, 1977: 228–229), or respiratory distress (Hardy et al., 1979: 155). The current maternal mortality rate of about 7 percent is mostly due to the indications for the cesarean section rather than the operation itself. Similarly, the relatively high fetal loss, 9 percent for a primary cesarean section and 2.9 percent for a repeat section, is linked to maternal and fetal complications rather than to the operation or method of delivery (Taylor, 1976: 550–553).

In contrast, the dangers related to version and extraction result mostly from the method of delivery rather than the reason for its use. For example, external version (manipulation through the abdominal wall) increases the risk of premature separation of the placenta, whereas internal version (manipulation with the whole hand in the uterus) frequently causes rupture of the uterus and subsequent infection (Greenhill, 1966: 1102–1108; Taylor, 1976: 553–537). For these reasons, cesarean section is often recommended instead.

b. Forceps marks at delivery

i. *absent*
   present
   Source: U.S. Department of Health, Education, and Welfare, Part IIIb, 1966: 5

ii. The obstetric forceps is an instrument, consisting of two blades fitted together, designed to extract the fetus from the mother without injury. Indications for forceps comprise the following: insufficient or subsided labor, (the reason for nearly three quarters of forceps use); arrest of the rotation of the head (malpresentation); complications such as toxemia, placenta previa, abruptio placentae, and prolapse of the cord; face and brow presentations, which require forceps more frequently than the vertex presentation; and contracted pelvis (Greenhill, 1966: 1124–1126).

Many different kinds of forceps instruments and procedures exist, each influencing the degree of the injury resulting from their use. For this reason, in the CPP presence or absence of "forceps marks," rather than only forceps use, was selected as a variable to indicate some evidence of tissue trauma about the head or face. Presumably, the other more serious consequences of forceps use would be apparent with signs of tissue damage.

iii. Dangers to the infant resulting from the use of forceps are: asphyxia, compression of the brain, fracture of the skull, rupture of cerebral sinuses, concussion of the brain, injury to the eyes, facial paralysis, deafness, and cephalhematoma (a blood cyst of the scalp) (Greenhill, 1966: 1152–1153). Other correlates of forceps use include delayed intelligence during preschool years (Broman, Nichols, and Kennedy, 1975; Friedman et al., 1977: 779–783), marked neurological abnormality (Nelson and Broman, 1977: 371–377), and neonatal brachial (relating to the arm) paralysis (Gordon et al., 1973). In most cases, little evidence exists of long-term neurological or intellectual injury resulting from forceps use or some of the more mild types of birth trauma in general (Gordon et al., 1973).

c. *Prolapsed cord*

i. *absent*   none
   present   occult
            cord through cervical os into vagina
            cord through vaginal introitus

Source: U.S. Department of Health, Education, and Welfare, Part III–A, 1966: 76

ii. Prolapse of the umbilical cord occurs when the cord lies alongside or below the presenting part of the fetus and the membranes are ruptured (Taylor, 1976: 296).

Three degrees of prolapse exist: (1) an occult form, where the cord is near the pelvis but cannot be reached with the fingers during an internal examination and thus is not suspected; (2) a forelying form, in which the cord can be felt through the external or cervical os (the opening in the lower part of the cervix that connects with the vagina) (Fluhmann, 1966: 188), but is in the intact bag of waters (the amniotic sac and contained anmiotic fluid); and (3) the prolapsed form, where the cord is prolapsed into the vagina or even outside the vulva (i.e., through the vaginal introitus or entrance) and the bag or waters is ruptured.

Prolapse of the cord has been reported for about .5 percent of a sample of deliveries. A cord may prolapse whenever the presenting part does not fit appropriately into the pelvis when the membranes rupture. Other predisposing conditions include an abnormally long cord, low implantation of the placenta, escaping amniotic fluid, malpresentations, and malpositions (Taylor, 1976: 296).

iii. Prolapse of the cord can result in the death of the fetus if the cord becomes compressed by the presenting part and is not soon relieved. A necessarily hastened delivery in such a case introduces risks for both the mother and fetus – nearly one third of the infants die – although perinatal mortality is substantially less with breech deliveries (the breech is softer and more protective than the vertex) (Taylor, 1976: 297–298).

According to Niswander and others (Niswander, Friedman, Hoover, Pietrowski, and Westphal, 1966: 853), the acute anoxia of cord prolapse does not appear to have long-term effects on those infants who do survive. However, other researchers note several cases where defects such as mental retardation and neurological disorders have been tied to cord prolapse and accompanying difficulties (e.g., prematurity) (Taylor, 1976: 299). Thus, the nature and severity of cord prolapse may depend in part on the entire pregnancy condition (Naeye, 1977; Werner, Simonian, Bierman, and French, 1967: 490–505).

d. Cord around the neck, tight

i. *absent* none
   present 1–6 times as given
             7 or more times
             around neck but number of times not specified
   Source: U.S. Department of Health, Education, and Welfare, Part III–A, 1966: 76

ii. Looping of the umbilical cord around the neck, trunk, or other part of a fetus has been reported for about 20 percent of all pregnancies and occurs most frequently with unusually long cords. Although loops are usually single, multiple loops also occur and, in rare instances, a fetus may have eight loops of cord around its neck (Taylor, 1976: 331).

iii. In most cases, loose loops around the neck are not harmful to the infant. However, loops may become tight enough to constrict blood vessels and induce a number or complications such as hypoxia, delay of the presenting part, premature separation of the placenta, fetal distress, and rupture of the cord (Hellman and Pritchard, 1971: 413). According to Naey, a tight umbilical cord around the neck was one of the 20 major causes of perinatal mortality in the nationwide CPP (Naeye, 1977). For these reasons, the cord must be severed and the child delivered immediately if the cord cannot be unwrapped.

e. Cord around the neck, loose

i. *absent*   none
   present   1–6 times as given
              7 or more times
              around neck but number of times not specified
   Source: U.S. Department of Health, Education, and Welfare, Part III–A, 1966: 76

ii. Loose loops of cord around the neck of a fetus are easier for an examiner to disentangle than tight loops. However, multiple looping may still produce a relative shortening of the cord, with consequences similar to those of a tight cord around the neck or a very short cord (Taylor, 1976: 331).

iii. The possible dangers and consequences of a loose cord around the neck are similar to those of a tight cord around the neck.

f. Cord complications

i. *absent*   none
   present   prolapsed cord
              cord around the neck, tight
              cord around the neck, loose

ii. "Cord complications" is a composite variable indicating the absence or presence of one or more of the three cord-related variables: (1) prolapsed cord, (2) cord around the neck, tight, or (3) cord around the neck, loose.

iii. The consequences of the three correlated variables are similar. In addition, one complication may lead to another so that their aggregation represents the possibility of a combination of effects.

g. Placenta previa

i. *absent*
   present
   Source: U.S. Department of Health, Education, and Welfare, Part III–A, 1966: 29, 77

ii. The placenta "may be considered as a two-layered membrane [in the uterus] which separates the maternal and fetal circulations but through which certain constituents pass" (Taylor, 1976: 54). These constituents include nourishment, nitrogen, glucose, and vitamins (Taylor, 1976: 54–71).

Placenta previa is the partial or total development of the placenta in the lower uterine segment (or internal os). It occurs in about 0.5 to 0.7 percent of all deliveries. The etiology of placenta previa is unknown, although it is considerably more frequent among multigravidas (Greenhill, 1966: 593–595). Symptoms include a "painless recurring uterine bleeding" in the last trimester of pregnancy, which is frequently followed by spontaneous abortion (Taylor, 1976: 465).

iii. Maternal death is relatively low with placenta previa, and perinatal deaths are dependent upon delivery conditions (Naeye, 1977). The primary danger is antepartum (before), intrapartum (during), or postpartum (after labor or delivery) hemorrhage, which increases the risk of anoxia (complete loss of oxygen), CNS disturbance, or intrauterine death of the fetus. Those infants who do survive are frequently premature or risk infection (Taylor, 1976: 467–470; Graham et al., 1962: 1–52).

Whether or not long-term physical growth and development are impaired is not entirely clear. Only a small number of neurologic abnormalities was found at age 4 in one sample of subjects who had survived placenta previa; children of mothers in another sample who experienced placenta previa, abruptio placentae, and prolapse of the umbilical cord were no different from normal children on intelligence scores or fine and gross motor tests at age 4 (Niswander, Gordon, and Drage, 1975: 892–899). The few studies conducted on this issue make definite conclusions unwarranted, however.

h. Abruptio placentae

i. *absent*
  present
  Source: U.S. Department of Health, Education, and Welfare, Part III–A, 1966: 29, 77

ii. Abruptio placentae is the premature separation of a normally implanted placenta or of a placenta previa that occurs between the twentieth week of pregnancy and the birth of the infant. Its incidence is similar to that of placenta previa, generally ranging from .5 to .7 percent within a sample of deliveries (Greenhill, 1966: 609).

Overall, the causes of abruptio placentae are unknown, although its frequent association with hypertension and albuminuria (the presence of protein in urine, usually indicating a disease or affliction) suggests it may be one outcome of toxemia. Abruptio placentae has also been linked less frequently to trauma such as a blow to the abdomen, short umbilical cord, or rupture of the membranes in hydramnios. Symptoms of abruptio placentae include "sudden, severe pain" near the uterus followed by a dull ache, at times nausea, and uterine hemorrhage. Systolic blood pressure falls with the extent of shock and blood loss (Greenhill, 1966: 612–614: Taylor, 1976: 472–475).

iii. Abruptio placentae is one of the most serious accidents that can occur in a pregnancy. Although prognosis can be good with mild or partial separation, maternal mortality is 1 percent and fetal mortality is nearly 100 percent with complete detachment. With all degrees of detachment, the perinatal mortality rate is 38 percent (Naeye, 1977; Niswander and Gordon, 1972; Taylor, 1976: 474).

Similar to placenta previa, the long-term effects of abruptio placentae are not clear. One study examining its effects along with other complications concluded that intrauterine hypoxia in general is "apparently not a major cause of neurologic dysfunction in the surviving child" (Niswander et al., 1975: 892). Once again, however, the limited amount of work conducted in this area hinders firm conclusions.

i.   Marginal sinus rupture

i. *absent*
   present
   Source: U.S. Department of Health, Education, and Welfare, Part III–A, 1966: 29

ii. A sinus is a passage for blood that does not have the coverage of ordinary vessels, e.g., passages in the gravida's (pregnant woman's) uterus. The marginal sinus of a placenta comprises thin-walled collections of blood located at the margin of the placenta (*Stedman's Medical Dictionary*, 1976).

According to one study, nearly one half of the cases of bleeding among patients during the third trimester is due to a ruptured marginal sinus, followed in frequency by placenta previa (one quarter of the cases), and then abruptio placentae, cervical tears, or unknown causes. The rupture of the marginal sinus, rather than placental separation, may produce the bleeding in placenta previa, particularly when the placenta is normally implanted. Whereas placenta previa tends to bleed more frequently before labor, the marginal sinus tends to bleed more frequently during labor (Friedman, 1966: 607–608).

ii. Relative to placenta previa and abruptio placentae, rupture of the marginal sinus has the lowest rate of fetal mortality and no maternal mortality. The incidence of toxemia, present in nearly two thirds of those cases with abruptio placentae, is nearly absent with placenta previa and rupture of the marginal sinus. In general, then, the effects and consequences of marginal sinus rupture are considerably milder than other causes of antenatal hemorrhage (Friedman, 1966: 608), although sinus rupture is among the 20 most prevalent causes of perinatal mortality (Naeye, 1977).

j. Placental bleeding

i. *absent*   none
  present   placenta previa
        abruptio placentae
        marginal sinus rupture

ii. Placental bleeding is a composite variable indicating the presence or absence of one or more of the three placenta-related variables: (1) placenta previa; (2) abruptio placentae; or (3) marginal sinus rupture.

iii. Placenta previa, abrupio placentae, and marginal sinus rupture are the three most important causes of antenatal hemorrhage of late pregnancy. (Fish, Bartholomen, Colvin, and Grimes, 1951). Although the etiology and consequences of these causes vary somewhat, a composite of the three does provide important information on whether or not the gravida experienced any major placental bleeding before or during labor.

k. Irregular fetal heart rate

i. *absent*
  present
  Source: U.S. Department of Health, Education, and Welfare, Part III–A, 1966: 63–64

ii. Fetal heart sounds are one of the best indicators of pregnancy. Studies of fetal heart rate with electronic monitoring, which was used in the CPP, show a gradual decrease in fetal heart rate and an increase in cardiac irregularity as a pregnancy progresses. Previously, these signs were routinely interpreted as fetal hypoxia or distress. Recent evidence suggests, however that such changes may also reflect physiologic development of the autonomic nervous system (Hon, 1966: 820).

In the CPP, an irregular fetal heart rate was one under 100 or above 160 beats per minute, regardless of the type of presentation. Heart rate measurements were conducted directly before delivery.

iii. Irregular fetal heart rate directly before or during delivery can be considered a sign of hypoxia or compromised fetal environment. The complete loss of heart sounds does not always indicate a fetal death; for example, heart rate loss may result from the prolongation of either the first or second stages of labor, or a combination of both (Eastman and Hellman, 1961: 863).

The long-term impact of abnormal heart rate seems quite clear, however. In examinations of the effects of prenatal and perinatal events in infancy and childhood, for example, fetal heart rate abnormalities were among the strongest discriminators of low birth weight among infants as well as CNS abnormalities in a sample of 7-year-old children (Drorbaugh et al., 1975: 532). Fetal distress, defined in terms of an irregular fetal heart or meconium staining, was also among those factors most strongly associated with neonatal brachial plexus paralysis, a mostly transient affliction linked to nerve damage in the neck during delivery (Gordon et al., 1973). Among the 60 prenatal factors tested to discriminate between children with serious motor and mental handicaps, fetal heart rate and use of midforceps were the most powerful predictors (Graham et al., 1962; Nelson and Broman, 1977).

l. Meconium during labor

i. *absent*
   present
   Source: U.S. Department of Health, Education, and Welfare, Part III–A, 1966: 64

ii. Meconium is a substance found in the intestines of the fetus about the middle of gestation. It comprises mucus, lanugo (fetal or embryonic hair), vernix caseosa (a fatty substance that covers the skin of the fetus), and bile pigments. Under normal conditions, meconium is discharged from the bowel at birth or soon after. However, in cases of intrauterine asphyxia, meconium may be expelled into the amniotic sac prior to delivery (Taylor, 1976: 75).

ii. The passage of meconium during labor or meconium-stained amniotic fluid are distinct signs of fetal distress unless an infant has a breech delivery. Further, dangers related to meconium aspiration exist. Meconium is both a severe irritant to the lungs and a cause of pneumothorax, the presence of air or gas in the surface of the lung cavity (Taylor, 1976: 566–567). The presence of meconium is also one of numerous correlates included in scales of birth distress or asphyxia (Graham et al., 1962; Werner et al., 1968).

m. Plurality of birth

i. *absent*   single birth
  present multiple birth
Source: U.S. Department of Health, Education, and Welfare, Part III–A, 1966: 68

ii. Twins occur once in every 89 births, triplets once in every 16,666 births. The incidence of the remaining numbers of multiple births is very low. Twinning increases with the age and parity of the mother, and is more frequent among blacks than among whites (Taylor, 1976: 301–302).

iii. Multiple pregnancy is considered pathological because it is abnormal for a female to bear more than one offspring at one time. Further, the incidence of perinatal mortality, toxemia, hydramnios, malpresentation, prolapse of the cord, and premature labor are all greater with multiple births. Presumably, the "crowding" evidenced in multiple births produces damaging effects due to competition between fetal blood vessels and the placental area (Taylor, 1976: 308–309). Thus, in may cases one twin, usually the firstborn, may be healthier or stronger than the other.

n. Use of oxytocic during labor

i. *absent*   none used
  present induction
          augmentation
          combination of induction and augmentation used
          (unknown if for induction or augmentation)
Source: U.S. Department of Health, Education, and Welfare, Part III–A, 1966: 70

ii. Oxytocic is an agent used for the induction or stimulation of labor at or near term. Oxytocin is a polypeptide (type of amino acid) hormone derived from the posterior lobe of the pituitary gland that stimulates contraction of the uterus (*Stedman's Medical Dictionary*, 1976). Oxytocic solutions, of which oxytocin is one, are applied in cases of uterine dysfunction.

iii. Oxytocin and related agents in the past have caused both maternal and fetal mortality through rupture of the uterus and overwhelming uterine contractions. However, the intravenous method, available at the time of the CPP, is safe and effective and reduces many of the hazards related to uterine dysfunction (e.g., infection and traumatic delivery). Accidents can still occur if the drug is applied incorrectly. Certain factors, such as high station of the fetal head or intrapartum fever, can seriously militate against the drug's success (Eastman and Hellman, 1961: 863–869).

In contrast to previous hypotheses, women who receive oxytocic during labor do not show a higher incidence of psychological difficulty adjusting to pregnancy in comparison to women who do not receive it, controlling for obstetrician and other relevant factors such as pregnancy complications. Thus, the hazards related to oxytocic use are not necessarily a result of a woman's psychologic state during pregnancy and labor (Brown, Manning, and Grodin, 1972: 119–127).

2. Dichotomous prenatal condition variables

a. Diabetic mother

i. *absent*
   present
   Source: U.S. Department of Health, Education, and Welfare, Part III–A, 1966: 28

ii. For the purposes of this study, two variables were selected to indicate the absence or presence of diabetes or glucose abnormality in the gravida: (1) insulin therapy or oral hypoglycemic analogue, and (2) abnormal glucose tolerance test. These variables sufficiently – and most accurately – incorporate the more than 15 indicators available in the CPP for metabolic disorders.

About 0.2 to 0.3 percent of all pregnancies are affected by diabetes. However, a diagnosis of diabetes is problematic during pregnancy because pregnancy itself is diabetogenic (diabetes causing) and is often the first time diabetes mellitus (a chronic disorder of carbohydrate metabolism) is manifested. About two thirds of diabetic patients require an increased amount of insulin during pregnancy, and a number of patients experience hypoglycemia during the early months of pregnancy (Taylor, 1976: 80).

iii. Maternal mortality from diabetes during pregnancy in the United States is 0.7 percent relative to the general mortality rate of 0.027 percent. Most deaths result from vascular (blood vessel) accidents, toxemia, diabetic coma, or anesthesia.

In general, diabetic patients experience a higher incidence of hypertensive albuminuria and perinatal loss due to hydramnios and maternal complications (e.g., toxemia). Infants of diabetic mothers have a higher incidence of congenital abnormalities, respiratory distress, and an abnormally large amount of bilirubin, a red bile pigment in the blood, which often results in jaundice (Chung and Myrianthopoulos, 1975: 1–38; Hardy et al., 1979: 274; Taylor, 1976: 80–83).

Macrosomia (high birth weights of 10 to 12 pounds) is also more frequent among such infants due in part to their rapid perinatal growth as well as to excessive deposits of fat and water retention. The most noted result of the pregnancies of diabetic women, however, has been a high fetal mortality rate, which has subsided somewhat over the years with advanced methods of treatment (Plotz and Davis, 1966: 753–754).

b. Use of sedatives

i. *absent*   none
   present   chloral hydrate, glutethemide methyprylon, phenobarbital, etchlorvynol, secobarbital, ethinamate, magnesium sulfate, barbital, barbiturate, n.o.s., amobarbital, tuinal, butabarbital

   Source: U.S. Department of Health, Education, and Welfare, Part III–A, 1966: 16

ii. For the purposes of this study, 13 different kinds of sedatives were selected from a list of over 1125 possible medications or drugs a CPP patient could have ingested at any time during her pregnancy. No gravida self-reported using drugs of a very serious nature, such as heroin, or psychoactive drugs of a presumably less serious nature, such as marijuana. The above list is restricted in part to those drugs that were self-reported by the Philadelphia CPP sample.

iii. Nearly all drugs or "systemic agents" permeate the placenta to some degree and in turn may affect the fetus. Thus, alcohol, ether, nicotine, barbiturates, and penicillin – as examples – all cross the placental barrier regardless of their method of administration (Friedman, 1966: 383).

The rate and mechanism of transfer of these substances through the placenta influence the extent and severity of harm to the fetus. In general, the higher the fat solubility of the substance the faster the rate of transfer. Fat-soluble nonionized drugs, such as analgesics, sedatives, and hypnotics, penetrate

> extremely rapidly, achieving prompt equilibrium between maternal and fetal blood levels.... It would appear reasonable, on the basis of similarities between the blood-brain and blood-placental barriers, to expect materials that act on the maternal brain centers to cross the placenta to the fetus and exert similar influences on the fetal brain. (Friedman, 1966: 384)

Recent research on some of the drugs selected for study demonstrates their potential harm on the fetus. For example, phenobarbital, taken early in pregnancy, has been linked to anencephaly (marked deficient development of the brain), congenital heart disease, intersex (possession of both male and female sex characteristics), cleft palate and lip, and other abnormalities. Taken late in pregnancy, phenobarbital has also been shown to cause bleeding in the neonate (Taylor, 1976: 103) The effect that the amount of sedatives used during pregnancy has upon the psychological state of the gravida (Brown et al., 1972) and on the development of her offspring (Brackbill and Broman, 1979) is less clear, however. With regard to intelligence, the topic remains controversial (Broman, Kolata, and Brackbill, 1979: 446–448).

c. Previous cesarean section

i. *absent*
present

Source: U.S. Department, of Health, Education, and Welfare, Part III–A, 1966: 75

ii. Cesarean sections often result in a weak uterine scar that is an indication for a cesarean section in subsequent pregnancies. In one survey, nearly one half of all cesarean sections were performed because the patient had experienced a previous one (Taylor, 1976: 542).

iii. The gravida risks a uterine rupture if she decides not to deliver once again by cesarean section. Regardless, delivery by cesarean section, although a very safe operation, is still prone to those risks discussed under "Type of delivery."

d. Venereal conditions of the mother

i. *absent*   no disease or condition
present   1–7: number of diseases or conditions as given
             8: 8 or more diseases or conditions
Source: U.S. Department of Health, Education, and Welfare, Part III–A, 1966: 28

ii. The number of venereal conditions of the mother is a composite CPP variable that can comprise one or more of the following disorders noted during pregnancy: (1) syphilis, (2) positive serology, (3) positive cerebrospinal fluid, (4) positive treponema immobilization test, (5) positive dark field, (6) gonorrhea, (7) positive culture, (8) positive smear, or (9) other.

iii. If not treated, syphilis and gonorrhea may affect the fetus. Untreated syphilis, for example, results in the death of a fetus or in a syphilitic infant in most (90 percent) deliveries. If syphilis occurs during the early months of pregnancy, early premature labor frequently results; the fetus may escape infection if syphilis is contracted in late months, however, because the placenta acts as a barrier (Greenhill, 1966: 636–637; Taylor, 1976: 86–87). Latent gonorrhea may also affect the fetus. If left untreated, gonorrhea usually manifests itself as a fever on the seventh to the tenth day postpartum (Taylor, 1976: 86–87).

e. Neurological and psychiatric conditions of the mother

i. *absent*   no disease or condition
present   1–7: number of diseases or conditions as given
             8: 8 or more diseases or conditions
Source: U.S. Department of Health, Education, and Welfare, Part III–A, 1966: 29

ii. The number of neurological and psychiatric conditions of the mother is a composite CPP variable that can comprise one or more of the following disorders noted during pregnancy: (1) convulsive disorder, (2) convulsions during pregnancy, (3) mental retardation, (4) organic brain disease, (5) psychosis and neurosis, (6) other neurologic or neuromuscular disease, (7) alcoholism, (8) drug habituation and addiction, and (9) other.

In the CPP, convulsive disorders during pregnancy were treated synonymously with a diagnosis of epilepsy. The diagnosis of mental retardation was based upon relatively subjective criteria, such as a physical examination, evaluation of school performance, and past and current behavior. Because psychological test measurements were not included, the frequency of mental retardation was most likely underestimated. Clinical judgments and self-reports by the gravida were also used to assess psychosis, neurosis, and neurologic disease, as well as alcoholism and drug addiction. Once again, the frequencies of these conditions are most likely underreported (Niswander and Gordon, 1972, 257–268).

iii. In the national CPP, maternal convulsive disorders showed some relationship with an increase in perinatal deaths, although the number of cases was small. Infants of retarded mothers were slightly lower in birth weight, but four times higher in the rate of neurologic abnormalities at one year, in comparison to infants of mothers who were not retarded. Mothers with psychosis or neurosis showed no increased risk of adverse fetal outcome over other mothers, whereas the increased risk of neurological abnormality was considerably higher among infants of mothers with neurologic or neuromuscular disease. Cases of mothers with alcoholism or drug addiction were too limited to analyze (Henderson, Butler, and Clark, 1971: 139–140; Niswander and Gordon, 1972: 257–268).

Nervous and mental diseases that may lead to coma, convulsions, or paralysis during pregnancy are oftentimes difficult to diagnose, particularly in comparison to disorders with related symptoms, such as eclampsia (convulsions and coma which occur in a gravida with hypertension or edema).

In general, convulsions due to eclampsia or other disorders place the fetus at high risk because of accompanying complications such as abruptio placentae, fluctuations in blood pressure, and anoxia for both the mother and fetus. With eclampsia in particular, the perinatal mortality rate is high (25 percent). In turn, the detrimental impact of alcoholism and drug addiction is well documented, particularly in terms of intrauterine growth retardation, low birth weight, and fetal addiction (Taylor, 1976: 412–417).

f. Infectious diseases during pregnancy

i. *absent*   no disease or condition
  present 1–7: number of diseases and conditions as given
          8: 8 or more diseases or conditions

Source: U.S. Department of Health, Education, and Welfare, Part III–A, 1966: 30)

ii. The number of infectious diseases of the mother during pregnancy is a composite CPP variable that can comprise one or more of the following disorders: (1) known or presumed viral, (2) known or presumed bacterial, (3) known or presumed parasitic, (4) known or presumed fungal, (5) type unknown, (6) attenuated live vaccine, (7) diseases and conditions not elsewhere specified.

iii. The possible effect an infectious disease may have on an infant varies according to the type of disease and its severity. If properly treated, such diseases as scarlet fever or diphtheria may have no detrimental effect on the fetus. However, other diseases such as lymphopathia (a disease of the lymph nodes), hepatitis, rubella (German measles), maternal mumps, smallpox, herpes, and chicken pox are linked to a variety of complications, including perinatal mortality, premature labor, congenital anomalies, ocular defects, deafness, and neurological disorders (Stott and Latchford, 1976: 161–191; Taylor, 1976: 86–90, 419–420; Werner et al., 1967).

g. *Anesthetic shock in pregnancy*

i. *absent*   condition not noted
   present   anesthetic shock in pregnancy
           other anesthetic accident
   Source: U.S. Department of Health, Education, and Welfare, Part III–A, 1966: 29)

ii. Anesthetic shock comprises two CPP variables: (1) anesthetic shock in pregnancy, and (2) other anesthetic accident.

For deliveries, two types of anesthesia are used: general anesthesia, causing complete unconsciousness, decreased muscular reaction, and absence of pain produced by the inhalation of gases and liquids or drug ingestion, or regional anesthesia, causing insensibility in the body through an effect on the sensory nerve in a particular region while complete consciousness and motor functions are retained.

Anesthesia in general is used to relieve pain during labor or to allay the mother's fears and anxieties. However, most anesthetic substances which are absorbed into the blood depress the fetus to the same extent that they depress the mother (Moore, 1966).

iii. Complications related to the use of anesthesia during pregnancy vary according to the type of substance used and, in part, the method of administration. Signs of hypoxia and heart rate changes in the fetus may arise with the signs and symptoms of hypotension (a fall in blood pressure) in the mother. In general, hypotension in the mother during parturition (labor or childbirth) may be attributable to one or more factors: hypovolemia (lowered blood volume due to severe hemorrhage), vascular hypotension (from severe dilation of the blood vessels), surgical manipulations, positional changes, the use of tranquilizers, or vascular accidents (pulmonary collapse or cardiac failure).

Shock may occur during the inhalation of anesthesia or at postpartum as a result of discontinuing oxygen, extreme hypotension, or related factors. In contrast, an extreme and serious hypertension may develop after the use of oxytocic drugs alone or in combination with a vasoconstrictor drug.

The primary cause of fetal death from the use of anesthesia and its related complications is hypoxia. All barbiturates, narcotics, and inhalation anesthetic agents, as well as maternal hypotension, depress the fetus. For these reasons, drug overdose should be avoided and hypotension corrected before and during labor and delivery (Moore, 1966: 386–392).

h. Fetal death of siblings: 20 weeks

i. absent   none
   present   1–7 as given
              8 or more
   Source: U.S. Department of Health, Education, and Welfare, Part III–C, 1966: 16–17

ii. An abortion is any pregnancy that terminates at less than 20 weeks gestation (Hardy et al., 1979: 327). Spontaneous abortions occur in about 12 percent of all pregnancies (Greenhill, 1966: 563–564).

iii. The etiology of spontaneous abortion is not clear, although suggested causes include abnormal uterine environment, trauma, fetal abnormality, chromosomal abnormalities, blighted ova (an ova without an embryo), advanced maternal age, acute infections, and incompetency of the cervix.

Any woman who aborts once is potentially a "habitual aborter," because multiple abortions in the same woman are usually attributable to the same factors. Considerable evidence also suggests that serious emotional factors can contribute to infertility. Habitual aborters have, in some cases, achieved successful births through the aid of psychological support alone (Greenhill, 1966: 569–584).

In general, however, if a gravida's last prior pregnancy terminated in a fetal or neonatal death, the risk of still birth (birth of a dead child), neonatal death, or low birth weight is greatly increased in her next pregnancy (Greenhill, 1966: 563; Niswandeŕ and Gordon, 1972: 185– 197).

i. *Fetal death of siblings:* ≥ *20 weeks*

i. absent   none
   present   1–7 as given
            8 or more
   Source: U.S. Department of Health, Education, and Welfare, Part III–C, 1966: 16–17

ii. A stillbirth is the death of any fetus of 20 or more weeks gestation. The stillbirth rate in a selected sample in the national CPP was about 23 percent (Hardy et al., 1979: 35).

iii. The etiological factors related to the stillbirth of an immature fetus are similar to those listed for the etiology of an abortion. The stillbirth of an immature fetus greatly increases the risk of future stillbirths (Niswander and Gordon, 1972: 185–197).

j. *Premature siblings*

i. absent   none
   present   1–7 as given
            8 or more
   Source: U.S. Department of Health, Education, and Welfare, Part III–C, 1966: 16–17

ii. In this study, infants born at less than 37 weeks of gestation were considered premature. The gestational age of an infant was measured from the first day of the last menstrual period, as is discussed in the section on gestational age. Traditionally, a premature infant has been defined as one that weighs 5.5 pounds or less at birth. Unfortunately, this definition fails to incorporate those factors other than gestational age that influence birth weight, for example, fetal disease, mother's nutrition, and socioeconomic status. Other objective measures of prematurity such as crown–heel length vary considerably and are often subject to greater measurement error than birth weight (Arey and Anderson, 1966: 982– 984).

Infant prematurity occurs in about 5 to 10 percent of all live births; however, two thirds of all neonatal deaths occur among premature infants. Mortality rates are highest among those premature infants who have the lowest birth weights (Arey and Anderson, 1966: 983).

iii. Prematurity alone is rarely the cause of neonatal death; rather, the premature infant is more vulnerable during the neonatal period because of a number of functional handicaps. For example, many premature infants have a reduced ability to oxygenate their blood, less effective respiratory movements, capillary fragility, hemorrhagic manifestations, and increased susceptibility to infections (Arey and Anderson, 1966: 983–991).

Prematurity in previous pregnancies enhances the risks of prematurity in later pregnancies because the complications evidenced earlier are frequently repeated. The risks for stillbirths and neonatal deaths are similarly increased (Niswander and Gordon, 1972: 185–197).

k. Neonatal death of siblings

i. *absent* none
present 1–7 as given
8 or more
Source: U.S. Department of Health, Education, and Welfare, Part III–C, 1966: 16–17

ii. A neonate is a newborn infant. The neonatal period begins immediately after birth and continues for the first month of life. Nearly three quarters of all deaths before age 1 occur during this time, with more than one half of all neonatal deaths taking place during the first 24 hours of life (Arey and Anderson, 1966: 982).

iii. Many factors are linked to neonatal death, although complications related to prematurity predominate. For example, pulmonary hyaline (transluscent) membranes, the primary cause of death among prematures, are present in up to half of all infants dying in the neonatal period. Fetal anoxia is directly associated with 10 to 20 percent of neonatal deaths that result, in part, from lesions of the placenta, abnormalities of the umbilical cord, or other complications of pregnancy and delivery. Thus, anoxia or hypoxia may commence during the prenatal period and extend into neonatal life. Hemorrhage within a ventricle or cavity of the brain is associated with about 10 percent of all neonatal deaths and occurs mostly among small and premature infants.

Other events related to neonatal death but that occur somewhat less frequently include intracranial trauma, fractures of the skull, fractures of the extremities or vertebrae, and spinal cord and brain stem injury (Arey and Anderson, 1966: 985–995). As mentioned, the occurrence of neonatal deaths increases the likelihood that they or related complications may recur in future pregnancies (Niswander and Gordon, 1972: 185–197).

l. Obstetrical history

i. *absent*   none
  present fetal death of sibling < 20 weeks
            fetal death of sibling > 20 weeks
            premature siblings
            neonatal death of siblings

ii. "Obstetrical history" is a composite variable indicating the absence or presence of one or more of the four variables related to complications with prior pregnancies: (1) fetal death of siblings < 20 weeks, (2) fetal death of siblings > 20 weeks, (3) premature siblings, and (4) neonatal death of siblings.

iii. Taken together, these four variables provide a composite indication of both previous perinatal mortality and the incidence of previous prematurity. All four variables constitute "high risk" factors relative to subsequent pregnancies (Taylor, 1976: 585–588).

m. Other uterine bleeding, first trimester

n. Other uterine bleeding, second trimester

o. Other uterine bleeding, third trimester

i. *absent*
  present
  Source: U.S. Department of Health, Education, and Welfare, Part III–A, 1966: 29

ii. "Other uterine bleeding" during the first, second, or third trimester of pregnancy includes vaginal bleeding of any kind aside from placenta previa, abruptio placentae, and marginal sinus rupture. "Other bleeding" variables also cover all trimesters of pregnancy.

iii. The etiology and hazards of all types of uterine bleeding have been discussed previously, although bleeding is often analyzed separately by trimester. For example, McNeil and associates (1970: 31) report somewhat more frequent bleeding during the last trimester and after delivery for behaviorally disturbed in comparison to control subjects. In contrast, Torrey, Hersh, and McCabe (1975: 287–297) show significantly more early and midtrimester bleeding among mothers of infants with early childhood psychosis, concluding that "probably as important as the incidence of bleeding in these mothers is its distribution by trimesters." Roberts (1971: 135–139), however, reports that antepartum bleeding and toxemia are not significantly related to lower development among infants at age 1; further, the increased frequency of neurological abnormalities among these infants may be due to other factors, such as gestational age at birth. More research is needed on the effects of bleeding during the different trimesters before definite conclusions can be made.

p.   Other uterine bleeding

i. *absent*   none
  present   other uterine bleeding, first trimester
             other uterine bleeding, second trimester
             other uterine bleeding, third trimester

ii. "Other uterine bleeding" is a composite variable indicating the presence or absence of one or more of the three variables related to other bleeding: (1) other uterine bleeding, first trimester, (2) other uterine bleeding, second trimester, and (3) other uterine bleeding, third trimester.

iii. Evidence in the preceding section suggested that uterine bleeding at different trimesters may have a differential effect on the fetus. However, as Greenhill (1966: 569) notes, uterine bleeding at any time during a pregnancy should be considered as a possible precursor to abortion.

q.   Anemia

i. *absent*   condition not noted
  present   during pregnancy only
             postpartum only
             during pregnancy and postpartum

  Source: U.S. Department of Health, Education, and Welfare, Part III–A, 1966: 28

ii. A mother was diagnosed as anemic in the CPP if a hemoglobin determination was less than 10 grams per 100 ml of blood or a hematocrit was less than 30 percent. Hemoglobin is an oxygen-transporting protein located in the red blood cells and is about one third the value of the hematocrit. The hematocrit is the percentage of red blood cells by volume in a sample of blood. At least two hematocrit determinations were made during the CPP prenatal examinations, the first at the initial examination and the second at 32 weeks of gestation. In the CPP, anemia was diagnosed in 9 percent of the white women and 34 percent of the black women, with the lower socioeconomic classes having the highest percentage of anemia (Broman et al., 1975: 88, 265). About 95 percent of pregnancy anemia is caused by an iron deficiency usually associated with factors existing prior to pregnancy, such as menstruation, a diet poor in iron, or previous pregnancies in which iron supplements were not taken. The body's increased demand for iron in pregnancy may itself produce anemia (Garn, Shaw, and McCabe, 1978: 557–65; Holly, 1966: 671).

iii. Some research has demonstrated that a high incidence of maternal anemia below 10 grams of hemoglobin per 100 ml of blood has been found among small-for-gestational-age infants born at or near term, but not among premature infants (Taylor, 1976: 101). In an examination of the CPP total study population, children whose mothers were anemic during pregnancy had significantly lower IQs at age 4, controlling for level of socioeconomic status (Broman et al., 1975: 88). Thus, the presence of anemia may possibly have long-range consequences on the subsequent health and development of children.

3. Continuous pregnancy and delivery variables

a. Duration of labor, stage one

i. *hours*   01–98
  minutes 01–59
  Source: U.S. Department of Health, Education, and Welfare, Part III–A, 1966: 68–69

ii. Duration of labor in the CPP was measured from onset based upon the time self-reported by the gravida, if labor occurred prior to admission to the hospital, or on the time observed in the hospital. Duration of the first stage of labor is defined as the time from onset of regular contractions to full dilation of the cervix (Niswander and Gordon, 1972: 292).

In the CPP, the average length of the first stage of labor was about 8 hours. Consistent with other findings, the first stage was substantially shorter for multiparae than for primiparae (first-time mothers) (Niswander and Gordon, 1972: 293). Other research has found that labors are also shorter for younger, more physically fit women, and for those whose fetus weighed less (Greenhill, 1966: 346).

iii. Prolonged first and second stage labors increase the risk of both fetal mortality and postpartum hemorrhage. Labor is also longer and more complicated when maternal factors such as hypertensive vascular disease, uterine leiomyomas (painful nodules of smooth muscle fibers), and overweight occur (Greenhill, 1966: 346–347). Prolonged or arrested progress of labor has been associated with adverse intellectual development (Friedman et al., 1977), abnormal fetal presentation (Friedman and Kroll, 1972), brachial plexus paralysis (Gordon et al., 1973), and serious mental and motor handicaps (Nedson and Broman, 1977).

b. Duration of labor, stage two

i. as given, in hours and minutes
   Source: U.S. Department of Health, Education, and Welfare, Part III–A, 1966: 68–69

ii. In the CPP, duration of the second stage of labor, which lasts an average of one-half hour, was defined as the period of time between the full dilation of the cervix and the completed delivery of the infant (the third stage of labor is the period between the complete delivery of the child and the delivery of the placenta, which, on the average, lasts about five minutes). (Niswander and Gordon, 1972: 314.)

iii. Greater fetal risk occurs when the duration of the second stage of labor is less than 30 minutes or more than 2 hours. A longer duration of the second stage of labor is associated with an increased mean birth weight (Niswander and Gordon, 1972: 314).

(Although a prolonged third stage of labor shares common antecedents with increased fetal risk, it has no direct effect on fetal outcome [Niswander and Gordon, 1972: 332]. For this reason, it was not included in present analyses.)

c. Apgar at one minute

d. Apgar at five minutes

i. 0–10 as given
   Source: U.S. Department of Health, Education, and Welfare, Part III–B, 1966: 3–4

ii. In 1953, Apgar (1953: 260–267) introduced a scoring system to evaluate an infant's physical condition at one and at five minutes after birth as well as to predict chances of survival during the first year of life. Subsequently, the Apgar score has been used to compare prenatal care across different hospitals, to evaluate the results of obstetrical practices (e.g., induction of labor), and to provide more information on the infant's development in the first five minutes of life. Since 1978, the one- and five-minute scores have also been included on the birth certificates of most states (National Center for Health Statistics, 1981: 1–15).

The scoring system incorporates the five most objective and easily identifiable signs of an infant's physical condition at birth and provides for each a possible score of 0, 1, or 2 (Chamberlain and Banks, 1974: 1225–1228). The five signs are: heart rate, respiratory effort, muscle tone, reflex irritability, and color. The Apgar score is the sum of the five values, with a range from 0 to 10. In general, a total score of 0 to 3 suggests that the infant is severely depressed and asphyxiated; a score of 4 to 6 indicates moderate depression, but usually no need for special resuscitative measures; a score of 7 to 10 demonstrates good to excellent infant health. The one-minute score is used to indicate the infant's condition at birth; the five-minute score is used to show condition at birth and improvement in the first five minutes of life, as well as to predict long-term health conditions and survival (National Center for Health Statistics, 1981: 1).

In the CPP study population, nearly 80 percent of both black and white infants had an Apgar score of 7 or above; less than 6 percent had a score of 3 or less. Five-minute scores were considerably higher: nearly 95 percent of the CPP infants scored above 7 (Hardy et al., 1979: 79–87).

iii. Infants in the national CPP with low Apgar scores had lower birth weights, a higher rate of neurological abnormalities during the first year, and a higher neonatal death rate, controlling for the effects of these variables upon one another (Hardy et al., 1979: 78–92). The 1978 Vital Statistics show that a higher incidence of mothers of infants with low Apgar scores are unmarried, are at either end of the extremes for childbearing ages, and have relatively fewer years of education (National Center for Health Statistics, 1981: 3–14). Additional studies point to significant relationships between low Apgar scores and neonatal plexus paralysis (Gordon et al., 1973), lower Bayley Mental and Motor scores at 8 months (Serunian and Broman, 1975: 696–700), developmental abnormality (Smith, Flick, Ferriss, and Sellmann, 1972: 495–507) and CNS dysfunction (Drorbaugh et al., 1975) at 7 years, and impaired WISC and

Bender Gestalt scores at 8 years (Schachter and Apgar, 1959: 1016–1025).

e. Gestational age

i. 1–50 weeks

Source: U.S. Department of Health, Education, and Welfare, Part III–A, 1966: 60

ii. In the CPP, gestational age was the time between the first day of the last menstrual period (LMP) reported by the gravida and the day of delivery. The shortcomings of this method of estimation are well documented; in particular, error may exist in the recall of a mestrual date or variations in menstruation or bleeding may occur.

For these reasons, a specially trained CPP interviewer recorded both the date of the LMP and the date of onset of the preceding period at the time of the prenatal registration. The hospital staff and the obstetrician independently collected additional information regarding the LMP, including an estimate of the duration of the pregnancy based on the gravida's physical changes and history. This estimate was reevaluated at each prenatal visit. Moreover, the primary obstetrician noted any inconsistencies found in the data when the pregnancy terminated (Hardy et al., 1979: 38–39). According to Cushner and Mellits (1971: 252–260), the LMP and gestational age data were found to be both valid and reliable in an analysis of the black, lower-, and lower-middle-class sample at Johns Hopkins University. Among the nationwide CPP samples, the Baltimore and Philadelphia samples are the most similar. Thus, considerable confidence can be placed on the reliability and validity of the CPP gestational age variable.

Among the national CPP sample, the mean gestational age was 38.8 weeks for blacks and 40.1 for whites, explaining, in part, the differences in birth weights found between the two races (see section f, below). However, the negligible difference found between males and females in gestational age cannot explain the sex differences that usually occur in birth weight (Hardy et al., 1979: 38–41).

iii. Short gestational age has been linked to numerous prenatal and perinatal complications as well as adverse outcome for the fetus. Premature delivery of an infant before term should be distinguished from low birth weight of an infant born at term. The standard classification of "premature" for infants who weigh less than 2,500 grams (5.5 pounds) at birth is not always accurate because infants born at term may be small for their gestational age (Fitzhardinge and Steven, 1972: 50). Indeed, the neonatal mortality rate among infants with birth weights of 1,600 to 2,500 grams is far greater for infants born before 36 weeks of gestation than for those born at 37 or more weeks of gestation (Behrman, Babson, and Lessel, 1971: 486–489; Taylor, 1976: 108). Because of this interaction, the complications related to gestational age are discussed in the following section with those related to birth weight.

f. Birth weight

i. as given in pounds and ounces

Source: U.S. Department of Health, Education, and Welfare, Part III–B, 1966: 7

ii. The birth weight of an infant was measured immediately upon delivery. In the CPP, the mean birth weight for white infants was 7.19 pounds compared to a mean of 6.68 pounds for black infants. Within each racial group, males weighed about one quarter of a pound more than females. The incidence of birth weight below 5.5 pounds ranged between 7 and 10 percent of the population. After 29 weeks, birth weight increases steadily with increasing gestational age until the 42nd week, when it levels off (Hardy et al., 1979: 46).

iii. Prematurity has been considered "the major obstetrical and pediatric problem in the country" (Taylor, 1976: 108; Behrman et al., 1971). Infants with both short gestational age and low birth weight are at a greater risk for neurological abnormalities during the first year (Hardy et al., 1979: 61–67), early brain damage due to hypoxia (Brand and Bignami, 1969: 233–254), and lower preschool intelligence (Broman et al., 1975). In general, cigarette smoking, low socioeconomic status, and maternal age (controlling for parity) have been found to be negative correlates of intrauterine growth as measured by gestational age and birth weight, with the degree of association varying by race (Penchaszadeh, Hardy, Mellits, Cohen, and McKusick, 1972a: 384–397; Penchaszadeh, Hardy, Mellits, Cohen, and McKusick, 1972b: 11–23).

In the national CPP, a relationship between low birth weight and gravida's smoking, weight gain, bleeding during pregnancy, placenta previa, abortion and stillbirth history, breech delivery, and parity was also found (Hardy et al., 1979; Niswander and Gordon, 1972). Numerous other factors associated with low birth weight and/or gestational age included mother's low educational level, poor diet, and chronic disease (Drillien, 1972; Taylor, 1976: 108), as well as infant's delayed physical growth, higher incidence of illness and visual defects, lower intelligence, academic achievement, and minimal brain dysfunction (Drillien, 1961: 452–464; Fitzhardinge and Steven, 1972: 405–420). Clearly, both gestational age and birth weight are strongly associated with early and long-term development.

g. Number of older siblings, liveborn

i. 1–28 as given

   Source: U.S. Department of Health, Education, and Welfare, Part III–C, 1966: 16–17

ii. In the CPP, parity was defined as the number of a mother's prior pregnancies excluding abortions (Niswander and Gordon, 1972: 154). For the purposes of the present study, parity is defined as the number of prior liveborn infants, because the number of prior stillbirths is provided in other variables. Both definitions of parity are widely used in the literature.

iii. Because maternal age and parity are closely interrelated, the correlates of parity are most easily distinguished within subgroups of maternal age. In the CPP, perinatal death rates for both black and white gravidas in each parity category increased with increasing age. For example, primiparae 30 years or older experienced substantially higher perinatal mortality rates than primiparae who were younger (Niswander and Gordon, 1972: 154). The considerably greater impact of maternal age on fetal development relative to parity has been substantiated elsewhere (Penchaszadeh et al., 1972a).

B. Birth events: theoretical context*

The preliminary selection of prenatal and perinatal variables for scale construction is based on an extensive literature, only briefly presented in the preceding review, that demonstrates links between birth-related events and subsequent trauma to the CNS. In general, about 30 percent of all lifetime brain damage occurs during the prenatal period, from the time of conception to the onset of labor; 60 percent occurs during the natal period, from the onset of labor through the first two weeks of life.

---

* The discussion in this section relies heavily on Perlstein, 1966.

Hypoxia, or lack of oxygen to the brain, is suggested as the primary correlate of prenatal brain damage, potentially producing multiple lesions in both cortical and subcortical structures. These lesions may or may not be reflected in later cognition or behavior.

Factors contributing to hypoxia are those that interfere with placental circulation: compression of the umbilical cord, abruptio placentae, a history of threatened abortion, decreased maternal blood pressure, maternal anemia, acute maternal shock, and drug ingestion. Secondary correlates of cerebral damage include cerebral hemorrhage in the fetus, which is often linked to fetal anoxia or maternal toxemia of pregnancy. Likewise, maternal infections such as rubella, mumps, and syphilis contribute to fetal encephalitis (inflammation of the brain), whereas metabolic disturbances, such as maternal diabetes, have been associated with early brain injury.

Natal factors, which contribute most to brain injury, are attributed primarily to anoxia or vascular damage and trauma. Anoxia may be related to mechanical blockage of the respiratory tract or fetal asphyxia, which is often associated with maternal use of narcotics or sedatives.

In some cases, the birth process itself can contribute to asphyxiation. For example, complications related to breech deliveries may delay exposure of the fetal head, creating a period of nearly total anoxia; a prolapse or wrapping of the umbilical cord may either strangle the fetus or interfere with fetal blood supply; and placenta previa, abruptio placentae, and placental infarcts, which create insufficient blood supply, also contribute to asphyxia. Premature infants, or those with very low or high birth weights, may be considerably more vulnerable to cerebral trauma of birth and delivery events. In addition to malpresentations or abnormal positions in delivery, high or midforceps may cause injury to the brain. The incorrect use of oxytocin induction may also be deleterious and has been linked directly to cerebral palsy.

In terms of vascular trauma, sudden pressure changes, such as the change from a high intrauterine to a lower atmospheric pressure in a cesarean section, may induce hemorrhagic damage to the brain. Such injury is potentially exacerbated when certain indications for cesarean section, such as fetal distress or toxemia, also occur.

The variables selected for the present study and the factors discussed in this review are not exhaustive. Moreover, many factors occur simultaneously in a number of the pregnancies. For example, a premature infant with anoxia may have low birth weight and a breech delivery, with complications related to all three conditions (such as prolapsed cord or placenta previa).

Unfortunately, as chapter 1 points out, much of the research conducted on birth related events is methodologically flawed. Many of the links between birth injury and later CNS development are also not clear-cut. The dearth of rigorous research using large sample sizes warrants further investigation of individual and aggregate effects.

The following section describes attempts to assess the reliability and interrelationships of the 38 CPP birth related items used in the analyses. Included is a discussion of the methods applied for aggregating variables.

C. Aggregation of birth-related variables

This section applies three methods of aggregating birth related events: (1) item analysis with coefficient alpha to assess reliability among the 31 dichotomous prenatal, pregnancy, and delivery variables, (2) principal components analysis to assess interrelationships among the 25 individual variables, and (3) principal components analysis to detect underlying constructs for the 7 continuous variables.

The combining of variables not only provides a single measure of birth injury but also reduces measurement error while enhancing reliability. Ideally, combined measures also represent single underlying constructs reflecting linear dependence among items.

1. Reliability assessment

The internal consistency method using Cronbach's alpha provides an excellent technique for assessing reliability of an empirical measure (Carmines and Zeller, 1979). In contrast to the retest method and the split-halves approach, coefficient alpha requires only a single test administration. Thus, error is avoided either in the multiple testing of like subjects or in the method by which test items are divided into halves.

According to Cronbach,

α estimates the proportion of the test variance due to all common factors among the items. That is, it reports how much the test score depends upon general and group, rather than item specific, factors. . . . What is required is that a large proportion of the variance be attributable to the principal factor running through the test. (1951: 320)

Cronbach's alpha reduces to the following expression when using a correlation matrix:

$$\alpha = N\bar{p}/[1 + \bar{p}(N - 1)] \tag{1}$$

where N is the number of items and $\bar{p}$ is the mean interitem correlation. The mean interitem correlation is calculated by summing the correlations for each item and then dividing by the total number of items (Carmines and Zeller, 1979: 44).

Alpha ranges between .00 and 1.00, expressing the average interitem correlations of zero and unity. The larger the alpha level (i.e., the closer to 1.0) for the selected items, the more internally consistent or homogeneous is the scale. It is difficult to specify a satisfactory level of reliability, although Carmines and Zeller (1979: 51) recommend that "reliabilities should not be below .80 for widely used scales." A very low alpha (e.g., $\alpha < .4$) indicates that there is little internal consistency between items and no homogeneous way of creating a sum score.

In the present analysis, the alpha coefficient is a generalization of the Kuder–Richardson 20 reliability coefficient (Kuder and Richardson, 1937: 151–160) because items are dichotomously scored. Items are dropped one at a time from each set to determine their contribution to the reliability of the measure.

a. Sample

The sample for aggregation analyses comprised 1,797 black males and females across all 7 CPP cohorts who met the necessary selection criteria outlined in chapter 2, aside from cohort and sibling exclusions. Subjects in all cohorts were used to enhance sample size. Frequency distributions of selected variables for subjects in all 7 cohorts were very similar to distributions for subjects in the first 4 cohorts, so that a cohort or sibling bias was not evident. Males and females were combined in analyses because their distributions on selected items were also very similar.

b. Item analysis – dichotomous variables

Tables A.1 through A.4 provide the following information for assessing item reliability: (1) the mean value for each item, (2) the item total correlation (which determines how the individual item correlates with the sum of the scores of the remaining items), and (3) the alpha level if the item is deleted. The lower the alpha drops with the deletion of a particular item, the stronger the item's association with the remaining variables.

Concerning individual and composite pregnancy and delivery complication, Table A.1 shows that distributions for each variable are comparable to those presented in the literature for live births. For example, with the

Table A.1. *Reliability assessment of pregnancy and delivery complications – composite and individual variables*

Variables	Mean	Item total correlation	Alpha if item is deleted
Type of delivery	.059	.025	.134
Forceps marks	.076	.026	.135
Cord complications[a]	.252	.046	.129
Placental bleeding[a]	.033	.066	.116
Irregular heart rate	.044	.159	.066
Meconium during labor	.258	.054	.119
Plurality of birth	.013	−.025	.149
Oxytocic during labor	.125	.060	.110

Notes: [a]composite variable; alpha = .135.

first variable, type of delivery, 94 percent of all deliveries occur with vertex or occiput presentation; 6 percent occur with a cesarean section, breech presentation, or version and extraction. In turn, forceps marks, cord complications, and placental bleeding constitute, respectively, 7.6, 25.2, and 3.3 percent of the deliveries in this sample.

Altogether, the eight individual and composite items have an alpha of .135, that is, only 13.5 percent of the variance in the total score is due to a common factor among the eight items. With regard to alpha levels if an item is deleted, irregular fetal heart rate, which occurs in 4.4 percent of the sample, explains a greater proportion of the variance relative to the other items. In turn, multiple birth, which occurs in 1.3 percent of the sample, contributes the least amount of variance to the alpha level.

When the five variables that constitute the two composites – cord complications and placental bleeding – are assessed individually, the total alpha level decreases slightly, as shown in Table A.2. Irregular fetal heart rate contributes the greater proportion of the variance in the alpha level; loose cord around the neck contributes the least proportion.

Low alphas in Tables A.3 and A.4 (.157 and .282 respectively) also appear in examinations of individual and composite prenatal variables. In Table A.3 the use of sedatives explains the most amount of variation; the occurrence of anemia explains the least. In Table A.4, prior fetal deaths at less than 20 weeks (prior abortions) contribute the most amount of variation and, once again, anemia contributes the least.

Concerning frequencies on individual variables, Tables A.3 and A.4 show that anemia occurs within 40.6 percent of the sample. In turn, 38.3 percent of the mothers have experienced a poor obstetrical history, com-

Table A.2. *Reliability assessment of pregnancy and delivery complications – individual variables*

Variables	Mean	Item total correlation	Alpha if item is deleted
Type of delivery	.059	.050	.114
Forceps marks	.076	.016	.132
Prolapsed cord[a]	.006	.023	.128
Cord neck, tight[a]	.066	−.013	.146
Cord neck, loose[a]	.182	−.014	.166
Placenta previa[b]	.014	.093	.103
Abruptio placentae[b]	.031	.051	.113
Marginal sinus rupture[b]	.026	.052	.114
Irregular heart rate	.044	.162	.067
Meconium during labor	.258	.050	.115
Plurality of birth	.013	−.023	.139
Oxytocic during labor	.125	.069	.099

Notes: [a] comprises cord complications; [b] comprises placental bleeding; alpha = .1296.

Table A.3. *Reliability assessment of prenatal conditions – individual and composite variables*

Variables	Mean	Item total correlation	Alpha if item is deleted
Diabetic mother	.011	.059	.150
Use of sedatives	.129	.117	.104
Previous cesarean section	.023	.066	.145
Veneral conditions	.101	.053	.144
Neurological and psychiatric conditions	.076	.098	.121
Infectious diseases	.047	.002	.164
Anesthetic shock	.010	−.039	.167
Obstetrical history[a]	.383	.090	.113
Other uterine bleeding[a]	.324	.078	.124
Anemia	.406	−.004	.198

Notes: [a]composite variable; alpha = .157.

prising a fairly high percentage of prior abortions and premature siblings (18.9 and 21.8 percent respectively); prior stillbirths and neonatal deaths occur with considerably less frequency. The composite proportion of other uterine bleeding, which occurs in 32.4 percent of the sample, indicates whether or not a gravida experienced uterine bleeding at any

Table A.4. *Reliability assessment of prenatal conditions –
individual variables*

Variable	Mean	Item total correlation	Alpha if item deleted
Diabetic mother	.011	.044	.280
Use of sedatives	.129	.129	.254
Previous cesarean section	.023	.046	.279
Venereal conditions	.101	.047	.281
Neurological and psychiatric conditions	.076	.085	.269
Infectious diseases	.047	.027	.282
Anesthetic shock	.010	−.035	.287
Fetal death < 20 weeks[a]	.189	.157	.241
Fetal death ≥ 20 weeks[a]	.066	.049	.278
Premature siblings[a]	.218	.113	.256
Neonatal death[a]	.049	.092	.269
Bleeding, 1st trimester[b]	.138	.158	.227
Bleeding, 2nd trimester[b]	.098	.157	.229
Bleeding, 3rd trimester[b]	.182	.120	.257
Anemia	.406	−.005	.306

Notes: [a]comprises obstetrical history; [b]comprises uterine bleeding; alpha = .282.

time during her pregnancy. "Other" uterine bleeding occurs most frequently in the third trimester (18.2 percent), followed by bleeding in the
first and second trimesters (which occurs in 13.8 and 9.8 percent of the
cases, respectively). Aside from the use of sedatives and the number of
venereal diseases, which occur in 12.9 and 10.1 percent of the sample, the
remaining variables are present with a frequency of less than 10 percent.

Overall, the very low alphas presented in the reliability analyses in
Tables A.1 through A.4 indicate little internal consistency and stability
among the birth injury items. This result is not surprising because it may
not be plausible to expect that all of these items are caused by the same
latent variable. Accordingly, item analysis does not appear to be a feasible method for scaling variables.

c. Principal components analysis – dichotomous variables

In order to assess interrelationships among the 25 individual birth related
variables, a principal components analysis was performed, as shown in
Table A.5. A 12-factor solution was varimax rotated; the 12 eigenvectors
with eigenvalues greater than 1.00 explained 56.5 percent of the variance.

Table A.5. *Principal components analysis on dichotomous prenatal and perinatal variables*

Variable	Factor 1	2	3	4	5	6	7	8	9	10	11	12	Communality (h²)
Type of delivery	-.056	-.021	.661	.213	.161	-.242	.007	-.052	.060	-.052	.137	.053	.602
Forceps marks	-.114	-.041	-.063	-.122	.014	.657	-.055	-.001	.112	.071	-.069	.073	.497
Prolapsed cord	.022	-.034	-.043	-.010	.683	-.127	.026	-.032	.054	.056	-.138	-.061	.517
Cord neck, tight	.022	.016	.001	-.021	.002	.100	.041	.719	.057	-.065	.085	-.109	.557
Cord neck, loose	.034	.004	-.017	-.006	.013	.086	.019	-.728	.064	-.091	.127	-.071	.574
Placenta previa	.066	.051	.512	-.038	-.284	-.048	.438	-.078	.048	.058	-.056	-.189	.595
Abruptio placentae	.096	.024	.616	-.092	-.004	.145	-.137	.088	-.104	.044	-.151	.056	.485
Marginal sinus rupture	.022	-.001	-.062	-.033	.117	.059	.798	.042	.003	-.000	-.053	.043	.666
Irregular heart rate	.001	.050	.297	-.122	.571	.181	.085	.082	.093	-.229	.399	.026	.656
Meconium during labor	-.044	.059	-.076	.118	.322	.121	.046	-.094	.496	.136	-.082	-.311	.523
Plurality of birth	.075	.117	.022	-.038	-.046	.027	.024	-.047	.044	.039	-.041	.773	.629
Oxytocic during labor	.135	.045	.031	.202	-.076	.620	.121	.021	-.098	-.955	.199	-.064	.530
Diabetic mother	-.162	-.031	.068	.731	-.079	.129	-.057	-.086	-.073	.006	-.058	-.081	.616
Veneral conditions	.063	-.121	-.010	.049	.025	-.007	-.016	.039	.061	.724	.143	.110	.585
Neurological and psychiatric conditions	.109	.082	-.027	.009	-.043	.110	-.162	-.032	.038	.109	.695	-.091	.566
Infectious diseases	.274	.157	.086	-.051	.078	.153	-.331	-.049	.149	-.079	-.495	-.146	.546
Anesthetic shock	-.097	-.059	.127	.262	.297	.205	.063	-.060	-.568	.173	-.166	.132	.633
Fetal death < 20 weeks	.245	.163	-.017	.466	.077	-.150	-.075	.054	.054	.187	.171	.005	.409
Fetal death ≥ 20 weeks	.270	-.041	-.064	.457	-.022	-.112	.191	.122	.192	-.348	-.013	.103	.521
Premature siblings	.721	-.015	.014	.028	.045	-.083	.004	.055	-.105	.156	.048	.063	.574
Neonatal death	.742	-.067	.049	-.013	-.041	.069	.022	-.072	.034	-.083	-.019	.006	.599
Bleeding, 1st trimester	.031	.733	-.112	.074	.055	-.084	-.000	-.026	-.012	-.079	.039	.203	.616
Bleeding, 2nd trimester	-.107	.721	.109	-.025	-.048	.064	-.024	.032	-.016	.001	.007	-.041	.554
Bleeding, 3rd trimester	.048	.380	.057	-.025	-.101	.002	.272	.007	.053	.455	-.078	-.245	.512
Anemia	-.111	-.098	.082	.078	-.015	.102	.016	.006	.641	.109	-.051	.340	.587
Percentage of variance	6.2	5.4	5.3	4.9	4.8	4.6	4.5	4.3	4.3	4.2	4.1	4.0	

Note: Sum variance = 56.5%.

Table A.6. *Principal components analysis on continuous prenatal and perinatal variables*

Variables	Mean	Factor			Communality (h^2)
		1	2	3	
Labor, stage one	8.43	−.134	.273	.582	.431
Labor, stage two	.33	−.018	.003	.663	.439
Apgar, one minute	7.88	.894	.017	−.058	.803
Apgar, five minute	9.07	.888	.083	−.000	.796
Gestational age	38.42	.025	.778	.077	.611
Birth weight	6.80	.081	.813	−.077	.674
Older siblings	2.15	−.071	.209	−.767	.637
Percentage of variance	24.2	19.7	18.8		

Note: Sum variance = 62.8%.

Clearly, there is no evidence of a single underlying construct that represents a substantial proportion of the explained variance. As shown, the first factor loaded most heavily on prior premature siblings and neonatal deaths, indicators of poor obstetrical history. The second factor loaded most heavily on uterine bleeding, the third on delivery and placental complications, and the fourth on poor obstetrical conditions (death and prior evidence of fetal deaths). The fifth factor loaded most heavily on poor delivery incidence (prolapsed cord and irregular fetal heart rate), as did the sixth, in terms of procedures used for delivery (forceps and oxytocic). The seventh factor was loaded predominantly on marginal sinus rupture, the eighth on cord complications, and the ninth on characteristics of the child (meconium and stress). The tenth factor loaded primarily on evidence of venereal conditions and the eleventh most heavily on evidence of a multiple birth.

Great caution should be taken in examining this principal components analysis of skewed, dichotomous variables. No clear, birth-event factors emerge from Table A.5. Moreover, the total variance explained for the number of factors is very low (56.5 percent). Generally, factor loadings are not favorable for aggregating these variables.

d. Principal components analysis – continuous variables

A principal components analysis was performed on the seven continuous birth related variables, as shown in Table A.6. A 3-factor solution was varimax rotated; the 3 eigenvectors with eigenvalues greater than 1.00 explained 62.8 percent of the variance.

As shown, the first factor loaded most heavily with the two variables specifying the infant's physical condition: Apgar measured at one and five minutes. The second factor loaded on those variables relating to the maturity of the infant: gestational age and birth weight. The third factor provides some indication of the mother's parity: length of labor and number of previous births. Overall, then, continuous variables reflect both the condition and development of the infant as well as the nature of the delivery process, although there is no strong evidence of a single underlying construct.

2. Summary

Two methods of aggregation – coefficient alpha and principal components analysis – were applied to various subgroups of the 38 prenatal, pregnancy, and delivery variables in order to create single summary measures for analyses, as well as to enhance reliability. In general, no evidence existed of a single underlying construct with either method of aggregation. Alternative methods for combining variables in terms of summary counts, along with other variables selected for analysis, are described in the next section.

Major dependent and independent variables

Variables selected for preliminary analyses included the 38 prenatal and pregnancy items discussed in the preceding section, other birth-related events, and psychological, achievement, familial, and socioeconomic factors. The following briefly outlines the primary dependent and independent variables as well as their reliability and validity, data distributions, and interrelationships for males and females. Variables range in time from prenatal and pregnancy events to intellectual and behavioral measures at 4, 7, 13–14, and 18 years.

Included is a brief description of those transformations implemented to normalize skewed distributions. Transformations were selected according to goodness-of-fit tests using one of the five available statistics (D statistic) based upon the empirical distribution function (EDF). (For a further description of the function of the D statistic for testing normality of data distributions, see Stephens, 1974: 730–737.)

1. Dependent variables

a. Four-year intelligence tests

i. Stanford–Binet Intelligence Scale

In the present study, the Standord–Binet Intelligence Scale assesses the intellectual development of children between the ages of 30 months, the upper age limit on the Bayley Scales of Mental and Motor Development, and 48 months, the lower age limit on the WISC, which was administered at 7 years. According to Sattler (1965: 173–179; see also Lezak, 1976: 225–226), the Stanford–Binet measures primarily visual–motor capabilities, nonverbal reasoning, social intelligence, and language functions between the ages of 2 and 5 years, and abstract reasoning and memory skills at older ages. The third revision of the Stanford–Binet, which was used in the CPP, is based on a standardized sample with rescaled intelligence scores normally distributed at a mean of 100 and a standard deviation of 16.

The CPP applied a short form of the Stanford–Binet. Silverstein (1969: 753–754) demonstrates that the short and long forms have comparable reliability. The high internal reliability of the short form has been shown (Broman et al., 1975) on the national CPP sample. The accepted validity of the Stanford–Binet as a measure of global intelligence has been discussed in depth (Cronbach, 1970; Friedes, 1972a), although in general it appears to reflect more strongly verbal relative to performance or spatial skills (Silverstein, 1970: 193–227).

ii. Graham–Ernhart Block Sort Test

Source: U.S. Department of Health, Education and Welfare, Part III–D, 1966: 73–84

The Graham–Ernhart Block Sort Test was used in the CPP to supplement the Stanford–Binet by assessing concept formation in children as well as by diagnosing brain damage. The test comprises tasks of increasing difficulty that range from matching like-shaped blocks to sorting blocks that are constant on one or two dimensions (U.S. Department of Health, Education, and Welfare, Part III-D, 1966: 73).

According to Graham and his colleagues (Ernhart, Graham, Eichman, Marshall, and Thurston, 1963: 17–33; Graham, Ernhart, Craft, and Berman, 1963: 1–16), the Block Sort has an acceptable test–retest reliability (.70) and discriminates significantly between normal and brain damaged children. For the purposes of the present study, scores on the Graham–

Ernhart, which range from 0 to 45, were arc sine transformed to normalize their positively skewed distribution.

b. Seven-year intelligence tests

i. *Wechsler Intelligence Scale for Children (WISC)*
   Source: U.S. Department of Health, Education, and Welfare, Part III–E, 1970: 37

According to Friedes (1972b), the WISC is "the best available test purported to measure intelligence in children." In contrast to the Stanford–Binet, the WISC examines both intellective and nonintellective factors rather than a unidimensional construct.

The WISC comprises 12 subtests divided into two summary scales of verbal (Verbal IQ) and nonverbal (Performance IQ) intelligence, and includes a total summary intelligence scale (Full Scale IQ). The raw scores for each subtest are converted into scaled scores with a mean of 10 and a standard deviation of 3. Verbal IQs, Performance IQs, and Full Scale IQs are summaries of the scaled scores of the appropriate subtests and have distributions with a mean of 100 and a standard deviation of 15.

In the CPP, a short form of the WISC was administered that comprised 4 of the verbal subtests and 3 of the performance subtests. Silverstein (1967: 635–636) has shown that the long and the short forms are functionally equivalent.

Briefly, the 3 summary scales and 12 subtests measure the following (Glasser and Zimmerman, 1967):

(1) *Full Scale IQ* – a general measure of intelligence based upon a composite of all 12 subtests.
(2) *Verbal IQ* – a summary measure of verbal ability based upon a composite of 4 subtests.
    Information assesses how much general information a child has obtained from the surrounding environment, requiring such skills as remote memory, ability to comprehend, and associative thinking, in addition to interests and reading background.
    Comprehension determines the level of a child's use of practical judgment in daily events in addition to the development of social acculturation and a maturing conscience or moral sense. Possession of practical information and the ability to use past experience in socially acceptable ways are important.
    Vocabulary most likely represents the best single measure of intellectual ability by indicating a child's learning ability, extent of information and ideas, quality of language, degree of abstract thinking, and development of thought processes. This test is influenced by a child's education and environment.

Digit span determines the child's ability to attend in a simple situation, measuring both immediate auditory recall or immediate auditory memory (attention) span.

(3) *Performance IQ* – a summary measure of performance (nonverbal or spatial) ability based upon a composite of three subtests.

Picture arrangement assesses such abilities as perception, visual comprehension, planning with sequential and causal events, and synthesis into intelligible wholes.

Block design measures perception, analysis, synthesis, visual–motor coordination, and reproduction of abstract designs, in addition to logic and reasoning applied to space relationships. Nonverbal concept formation along with implicit verbal manipulation is also required.

Coding evaluates in particular visual–motor dexterity with pencil manipulation, in addition to the ability, speed, and accuracy of absorbing new material presented in an associative context.

The WISC was standardized on a sample of over 2,000 white males and females at different age levels who were representative of geographic location, type of location (urban or rural), and parental occupation in the 1940 census statistics. The validity of the WISC as a measure of mental ability is described by Wechsler (1958) using multiple kinds of evidence; it has received substantial corroboration by others (e.g., Freides, 1972b). Wechsler (1958) and others (e.g., Aurand, 1978) have also demonstrated high split-half correlations and test–retest reliability with the WISC.

In current neuropsychological research, the WISC verbal and performance summary scales and subtests, respectively, are used as one of a number of possible indicators of left and right hemisphere functioning. In turn, a large discrepancy between verbal and performance IQ scores (computed by subtracting scores or taking an absolute value) is used as one of several indicators of organic brain damage (Klove, 1974). In the present study, this discrepancy is defined as the *Difference between Verbal and Performance WISC scores*.

ii. *Wide Range Achievement Test (WRAT)*

Source: U.S. Department of Health, Education, and Welfare, Part III–E, 1970: 49–55

The Wide Range Achievement Test (WRAT) attempts to measure "achievement" rather than "intelligence," although the two concepts are not entirely clear (Matarazzo, 1972: 14–18). The WRAT is particularly appropriate for the present study because it assesses very elementary reading, arithmetic, and spelling skills that can be more easily tested with disadvantaged populations who may lack a more formal education (Aurand, 1978).

The WRAT comprises three parts:

(1) *Spelling* – which consists of copying marks that resemble letters, writing one's name, and dictated words;
(2) *Reading* – which involves recognizing and naming letters and pronouncing words; and
(3) *Arithmetic* – which includes counting, reading number symbols, solving oral problems, and figuring written computations.

According to Lezak (1976), the WRAT, which was developed by Jastak (1953), is "carefully standardized with a full set of norms for each subtest." Reading and spelling constitute a large verbal component; arithmetic measures mostly motivation and arithmetic ability. Although some have criticized the validity of the WRAT (Courtney, 1949; Sims, 1949), the test is widely used and correlates at fairly high levels with the WISC and Stanford–Binet Mental Age; it correlates at a very high level with the California Achievement Test (CAT) (Washington and Teska, 1970: 291– 294). For the purposes of the present study, scores on the WRAT were square root transformed to normalize their positively skewed distribution.

iii. *Bender Gestalt Test, Koppitz scoring*

　　Source: U.S. Department of Health, Education, and Welfare, Part III–E, 1970: 31–36

iv. *Bender Gestalt, time in seconds*

The Bender Gestalt is a nonverbal measure of perceptual activity and motor response, along with a spatial component. Of all visuographic tests, it is the most widely applied, in part because of its diversity (Lezak, 1976: 310–311). The test can be used to evaluate intellectual capacity and functioning as well as emotional stability (Billingslea, 1963: 233). The Koppitz method of scoring was developed to assess abilities among children (Koppitz, 1960: 432–435).

The Bender test is a set of nine geometrical designs comprising dots, lines, angles, and curves, which children must reproduce. In the Koppitz method of scoring, 30 errors are possible in reproduction; thus, the higher the score (a maximum of 30 points), the poorer a child's performance.

Norms for Koppitz scoring were established on a sample of 1,055 children from diverse backgrounds with ages ranging from 5 to 10 years. The Bender discriminates among children with many different levels of visual–motor functioning up to age 8 years, beyond which time it distinguishes only inferior from average performance. According to Koppitz, very fast test performance is more often a sign of immaturity and impulsiveness rather than ability; very slow performance is either a sign of compulsiveness or visual–motor impairment (Koppitz, 1960).

The Bender's ability to discriminate between neurological and psychiatric patients as well as organically impaired and normal patients has been demonstrated (Billingslea, 1963; Lezak, 1976). The test's effectiveness may be due in part to its requirement of "a high level of integrative behavior that is not necessarily specific to visuopractic functions but tends to break down with cortical damage" (Lezak, 1976: 320). The Bender has also been found to be an effective measure of developmental changes among a sample of British children (Keogh, 1969: 15–22), although it was not an accurate test of neurological impairment among inner-city children (Welcher, Wessel, Mellits, and Hardy, 1974: 899–910).

Adequate test–retest reliability for the Bender, particularly for developmental errors, was reported for five different grades in one study (Goff and Parker, 1969: 407–409) whereas interjudge reliabilities of the Koppitz scoring method were found to be highly accurate in another study (Snyder and Kalil, 1968: 1351). Whether or not sex differences exist on the Bender is not clear and needs to be more thoroughly investigated (Dierks and Cushna, 1969: 19–22). For the purposes of the present study, Bender Gestalt Time in Seconds was logarithmically transformed to normalize its skewed distribution.

v. *Goodenough–Harris drawing test*

   Source: U.S. Department of Health, Education, and Welfare, Part III–E, 1970: 45

The Draw-A-Man Test, originally published in 1926 by Goodenough (for a description of the test, see Stewart, 1953), was extensively revised by Harris in 1963. The CPP used the revised form, which is described in detail in *Children's Drawings As Measures of Intellectual Maturity* (Harris, 1963).

Since its original publication, the Draw-A-Man Test has "enjoyed widespread popularity"; in 1961 it was among the ten most frequently used tests in clinical psychology, even though it can be applied only to children. The test requires only that a child "make a picture of a man," a task that is easy to administer and quick to complete. Harris's revision of the test redeveloped the Goodenough scoring criteria on a more "highly objective, empirical basis"; implemented a new standardization of the test; converted the IQ computation to the deviation IQ concept from the old mental age/chronological age ratio; and introduced a companion Draw-A-Woman Test (Dunn, 1972: 671–672).

Similar to the original test, the revision is intended to assess intellectual capacity (maturity) through the accuracy of a child's observation and level of conceptual thinking, rather than artistic ability (Anastasi, 1972: 669–671). Other research also suggests that performance on the Draw-A-Man may be related to a compulsivity-cautiousness cognitive style, possibly reflective of personality differences (Lewis and Livson, 1977: 237–242). The notion that personality may influence Goodenough–Harris scores was discouraged by Harris and others (Honzik, 1966: 28–30); however, in a review of studies focusing on delinquent children, Harris does suggest that "a Goodenough IQ markedly lower than that earned on the Binet may afford some indication of emotional or nervous instability "(Harris, 1963: 28). Whether or not the Draw-A-Man Test can be used as a projective technique remains an open issue, however.

Norms for the revised Goodenough–Harris test were generated on a new standardization sample in 1950 of nearly 3,000 children between the ages of 5 and 15 whose parents were representative of U.S. occupations as well as of four major geographic areas. In the new test, as in the earlier version, scoring reliabilities are over .90; split-half reliabilities are in the .70s and .80s, and retest reliabilities fall in the .60s and .70s. In general, correlations between the Goodenough–Harris and the Stanford–Binet, WISC, WAIS, and other tests are significant. Harris suggests that the drawings reflect conceptual maturity only up to the stage when a child ceases to use concrete concepts and relies more on higher order abstractions and verbal means of expression (Anastasi, 1972: 670).

vi. California Achievement Test (CAT)

The California Achievement Test (CAT), which was described briefly in chapter 2, is "designed for the measurement, evaluation, and analysis of school achievement. The emphasis is upon content and objectives in the basic curricular areas of reading, mathematics, and language" (Tiegs and Clark, 1970: 14).

The 1970 edition, which is used in the present study, is the latest of a number of revisions that have been available to schools for over 50 years. Nearly 300 state-approved reading, language, and mathematics texts as well as recommended subjects of study were referenced in revising the 1970 edition. Selection of the standardization sample involved a two-stage stratified random sampling from public schools with more than 300 students and from Catholic schools (Bryan, 1978: 35).

The public school population was stratified according to geographic region, average enrollment per grade, and community type; and the Catholic schools, according to enrollment, geographic region, and type of school (diocesan or private). The sampling technique provided for proportionate representation in the national norms of minority group students in the total school population. The final standardization sample contained 203,684 students from schools in 36 states. (Bryan, 1978: 35)

The CAT covers grades 1 through 12 with five overlapping levels of tests at grades 2, 4, 6, and 9. This overlap allows the test to be administered according to a student's attainment level rather than chronological age, if necessary. Overall, 11 test scores are available: a total battery score; 3 tests (reading, math, and language); their 6 respective subtests; and a total spelling score. Tests and corresponding subtests are as follows (Tiegs and Clark, 1970: 16–25):

(1)   *Total Reading* – intended to measure reading progress, comprehension, the interpretation of written material, and the criticism of its content.
     Vocabulary, in lower levels, assesses skills of auditory and visual discrimination, structural analysis, and pre-reading abilities; in upper levels, evaluates functional vocabulary and the ability to adapt meaning to context.
     Comprehension, in lower levels, evaluates the ability to demonstrate basic reading skills; in upper levels, measures the ability to read materials approximating school content areas effectively.
(2)   *Total Math* – intended to measure a student's level of achievement in a general mathematics program.
     Computation assesses a student's skill in the fundamental operations necessary in addition, subtraction, multiplication, and division of positive integers, fractions, and measurement quantities.
     Concepts and problems tests a student's ability to perform written single-step and multiple-step problems involving fundamental operations and the understanding of basic concepts.
(3)   *Total Language* – intended to assess basic communication skills.
     Mechanics determines a student's ability to recognize those words that need capitalization and to use punctuation marks.
     Usage and structure tests a student's ability to distinguish between standard and nonstandard English usage, to recognize possible sentence transformations, and to identify sentence elements, their functions, and total sentence structure and type.
(4)   *Spelling* – determines a student's ability to distinguish between correctly spelled and misspelled words.
(5)   *Total Battery* – reflects a student's standing in terms of total achievement level.

For the purposes of the present study, Level Four CAT tests for grades 7 and 8 were used for analyses. CAT scores, defined in terms of mean national percentile ranks, were square root transformed to normalize their positively skewed distributions.

A student's percentile rank is defined as the percentage of the students in the national norm group who had a lower score. Percentile ranks are recommended over other types of scores available for the CAT for determining the current status of a student's achievement. Their limitations in terms of unequal scale units should be recognized, however (Tiegs and Clark, 1970: 47–50).

Generally, alternate form reliabilities for the total battery and the 3 tests are high, ranging from .80 and .96; reliabilities for subtests are lower but still adequate. Evidence of content validity is derived mostly from data showing the appropriate placement of items in various levels and from subtest intercorrelations. More important is the content validity achieved (described earlier) of examining nationwide texts and course curricula (Womer, 1978: 37–38).

The language tests are open to more criticism than other items in the CAT battery primarily because they appear to be overly difficult at each grade level (Bryan, 1978: 36) and omit certain tests of important skills such as paragraph organization (Purves, 1970: 134–135). Overall, however, the language tests are considered to be "good state-of-the-art instruments" (Page, 1970: 134). Indeed, the CAT in general is highly praised in terms of its validity, comprehensive test and interpretive materials, reliability, and standardization procedure.

c. *Test score biases*

The nature and extent of biases in the testing of cognitive and intellectual abilities among children and adults have been widely discussed, but with no clear resolutions (Cole, 1981: 1067–1077; Haney, 1981: 1021–1033). Debates concern the possible influences of a wide range of biases, including racial, socioeconomic, and cultural factors (Brace, 1980: 333–334; Dorfman, 1980: 339–340; Garcia, 1981: 1172–1180; Jensen, 1979; Jensen, 1980: 325–333; Kline, 1980: 349–350; Olmedo, 1981: 1078–1085; Overall and Levin, 1978: 910–915); motivational and adjustment difficulties (Scarr, 1981: 1159–1166); limited test applicability, such as for selection and placement in employment and education (Bersoff, 1981: 1047–1056; Lambert, 1981: 937–952; Reschly, 1981: 1094–1102; Schmidt and Hunter, 1981: 1128–1137); coaching and developed test abilities (Anastasi, 1981: 1086–1093); and test examiner effects (Bradbury, Wright, Walker, and Ross, 1975: 51–55; Cronbach, 1970). In turn, attempts to develop tests that are more "culture free," such as the WISC-R (revised), introduce difficulties in interpretation and often show mixed results (Reynolds and Hartlage, 1979: 589–591; Sandoval, 1979: 919–927; Swerdlik, 1978: 110–125; Terrell, Taylor, and Terrell, 1978: 1538–1539; Vance and Gaynor, 1976: 171–172; Vance and Hankins, 1979: 815–819; Weiner and Kaufman, 1979: 100–105).

The racial and socioeconomic homogeneity of the sample examined in the present study eliminates many of the possible cultural and background biases discussed in the literature. Further, documented evaluations of the reliability of test administration in the CPP provide confidence in test score results. Other unknown or undetected biases may exist, however, and for this reason statistical procedures, described in the following sections, have been selected to control such errors. Regardless, results and conclusions must be interpreted with great caution, recognizing the chance that unknown factors may be influential.

d. Criminality

i. *Age at first arrest*

The age of a subject when he or she first experienced a police contact that resulted in an official arrest.

ii. *Age at first offense*

The age of a subject when he or she first experienced a police contact that resulted in an official arrest or a remedial disposition (a police contact that does not result in an official arrest). The importance of age in relation to crime is discussed in *Delinquency in a Birth Cohort* (Wolfgang et al., 1972).

iii. *Age at last offense*

The age of a subject when he or she last experienced a police contact that resulted in an official arrest or remedial disposition.

iv. *Total number of arrests*

The total number of arrests a subject experienced. Arrests were logarithmically transformed to normalize their skewed distribution. Zero was replaced by .5 as a representation of those individuals in the sample with no arrests because log 0 does not exist. On a logarithmic scale, the distance between .5 and 1 is the same as the distance between 1 and 2.

v. *Arrest record: arrest/no arrest*

    absent   no arrest
    present   1 or more arrests

A dummy variable indicating the absence or presence of an arrest record.

vi. *Total number of offenses*

The total number of offenses a subject experienced. Offenses were logarithmically transformed to normalize their skewed distribution. Once again, zero was replaced by .5

vii. *Offense record: offense/no offense*

    absent   no offense
    present   1 or more offenses

A dummy variable indicating the absence or presence of an offense record.

viii. *Total number of injury offenses*

The total number of offenses a subject experienced that involved inflicting injury on one or more persons (e.g., rape or aggravated assault). "Injury" is defined according to an offense gravity scale developed by Sellin and Wolfgang (1964), which has been widely applied in subsequent research (Wolfgang et al., 1972; Sellin Center for Studies in Criminology and Criminal Law, 1981).

ix. *Total number of theft offenses*

The total number of offenses a subject experienced that involved a theft of some sort (e.g., stealing an automobile), as defined originally by the Sellin–Wolfgang seriousness scale. (Sellin and Wolfgang, 1964; Sellin Center for Studies in Criminology and Criminal Law, 1981).

x. *Total number of damage offenses*

The total number of offenses a subject experienced that involved damage to an object (e.g., destroying public property), as defined originally by the Sellin–Wolfgang seriousness scale (Sellin and Wolfgang, 1964; Sellin Center for Studies in Criminology and Criminal Law, 1981).

xi. *Total number of nonindex offenses*

The total number of the less serious nonindex offenses a subject experienced, such as truancy or running away.

xii. *Total number of very violent offenses*

The total number of the more violent or serious offenses, specifically, murder, assault with intent to kill, aggravated assault, rape, and attempted rape. These offenses may or may not be included in the "injury offender" category.

xiii. *Total number of less violent offenses*

The total number of offenses in the "injury offender" category exclusive of the "very violent" offenses.

2. Independent variables

a. Prenatal maternal conditions

i. Number of prenatal examinations

The number of prenatal examinations a mother attended was constructed by counting the number of times a mother was present at an examination. In this case, a mother's attendance was determined by the presence of data from a total of 6 possible tests to measure fetal heart rate: (1) fetal heart, 1st prenat, (2) fetal heart, 3rd prenat, (3) fetal heart, 5th prenat (4) fetal heart, 7th prenat, (5) fetal heart, 9th prenat, and (6) fetal heart last prenat.

ii. Number of prenatal conditions

The number of prenatal conditions is a count of 8 dichotomous items, 5 of which were examined in a previous section. Cigarette smoking, marital status, and history of hypertension are the 3 additional items. A count technique was determined to be useful for combining these relatively infrequent factors because aggregation and scaling techniques were not appropriate.

The relationships between cigarette smoking during pregnancy, single marital status, hypertension, and subsequent complications among offspring have received substantial attention in the literature. Specifically, a mother's smoking during pregnancy is correlated with a higher incidence of perinatal mortality (Hardy et al., 1979: 27; Hardy and Mellits, 1972: 1332–1336) and a reduction in birth weight among offspring (Niswander and Gordon, 1972; Yerushalmy, 1965: 881–884), as well as deficits in later physical and mental development (Butler and Goldstein, 1973: 573–575). Women who are unmarried during their pregnancies demonstrate a higher incidence of pregnancy complications than married women (National Center for Health Statistics, 1980). Poor fetal prognosis related to hypertension during pregnancy has also been shown (Greenhill, 1966; Friedman and Neff, 1977 in Hardy et al., 1979).

In the following list of items, *heavy cigarette smoking* comprises the number of cigarettes smoked per day (U.S. Department of Health, Education, and Welfare, Part III-A, 1966: 12). Thirty or more cigarettes smoked daily was considered "heavy." The *mother's marital status* (U.S. Department of Health, Education, and Welfare, Part III-C, 1966: 4–5) was "single" if the mother reported being single, widowed, divorced, or separated at the time of registration; mothers reporting a married or common law status were considered not to be single. A mother was *hypertensive* (U.S. Department of Health, Education, and Welfare, Part II–A, 1966: 30) if she evidenced a history of hypertension when she was not pregnant or during a prior pregnancy.

Overall, a mother could have one or more of the following prenatal conditions:

Heavy smoker	(1 = ≥ 30 cigarettes per day)
Drug use	(1 = sedatives were used)
Marital status	(1 = single)
Diabetes	(1 = present)
Hypertension	(1 = hypertension)
Veneral conditions	(No. of venereal conditions)
Neurological status	(No. of neurological and psychiatric conditions)
Infectious diseases	(No. of infectious conditions)

iii. *Poor obstetrical history*

Poor obstetrical history is a count of the four items that constituted "obstetrical history" in the previous section:

Fetal deaths, early	(No. of fetal deaths < 20 weeks)
Fetal deaths, late	(No. of fetal deaths ≥ 20 weeks)
Premature siblings	(No. of premature siblings)
Neonatal siblings	(No. of neonatal deaths of siblings)

iv. *Mother's age*

Mother's age was reported at the time of registration into the CPP. The negative effect of maternal age, particularly 35 years or older, on fertility and fecundity, regardless of parity, is now fairly well documented (De-Cherney and Berkowitz, 1982: 424–426; Fédération CECOS, Schwartz, and Mayaux, 1982: 404–406). Significant relationships between maternal ages at either age extreme and subsequent pregnancy and delivery complications, have also been reported (Hardy et al., 1979). Maternal age was logarithmically transformed to normalize its positively skewed distribution.

b. Pregnancy and birth complications

i. *Pregnancy and delivery conditions*

Pregnancy and delivery conditions is a count of the 17 items related to pregnancy and delivery that were discussed in the previous section. "Anemia" was excluded because it deflated the correlation of "birth complications" with other events – such as Apgar – and was shown in the previous reliability assessment to have a low interitem correlation.

Initial analyses in the present sudy grouped the first 8 of the following variables to create an indicator of pregnancy complications, and grouped the last 9 variables to create an indicator of delivery complications. However, correlation coefficients showed that the aggregation of all 17 variables produced a stronger predictor of birth events:

Placenta previa
Abruptio placentae
Marginal sinus rupture
Uterine bleeding, first trimester
Uterine bleeding, second trimester
Uterine bleeding, third trimester
Anesthetic shock
Other anesthetic accident
Cesarean or breech delivery
Prolapsed cord
Irregular heart beat
Meconium during labor
Multiple birth
Use of oxytocic during labor
Cord around the neck, tight
Cord around the neck, loose
Forceps marks at delivery

ii. *Duration of labor*

Duration of labor, discussed previously, is the sum of labor stages 1 and 2 square root transformed to normalize its positively skewed distribution.

iii. *Apgar at one minute*

Apgar at one minute, discussed previously, was arc sine transformed to normalize its negatively skewed distribution.

iv. *Apgar at five minutes*

Apgar at five minutes, discussed previously, was arc sine transformed to normalize its negatively skewed distribution.

v. *Birth weight*

Birth weight was discussed in the previous section.

vi. *Gestational age*

Gestational age was discussed in the previous section.

c. *Parity and birth order*

Number of older siblings, discussed previously, provides information on both the mother's parity and a child's birth order in the family. The variable was square root transformed to normalize its positively skewed distribution.

1. Socioeconomic status at registration

i. Income

Income at registration into the CPP was designated either by the reported income rate at the onset of pregnancy or the income during the first three months of pregnancy (U.S. Department of Health, Education, and Welfare, Part III–C, 1966: 10, 11). Possible sources of income included finances from the mother and husband or father, relatives, family, and friends, or public and private assistance. Income was square root transformed to normalize its positively skewed distribution.

ii. Mother's education

> Source: U.S. Department of Health, Education, and Welfare, Part III–C, 1966: 2, 3

The mother's education was determined by the highest reported grade completed at the time of registration. The importance of mother's education in predicting the preschool intelligence of her offspring has been demonstrated (Broman et al., 1975). The variable was arc sine transformed to normalize its positively skewed distribution.

2. 7-year physical development

i. Blood pressure, systolic

> Source: U.S. Department of Health, Education, and Welfare, Part III–E, 1970

Blood pressure was measured from the right arm with the child at rest in a reclining position. Systolic pressure is defined as "the highest arterial blood pressure of a cardiac cycle occurring immediately after systole [contraction] of the left ventricle of the heart" (*Stedman's Medical Dictionary*, 1976).

ii. Blood pressure, diastolic

> Source: U.S. Department of Health, Education, and Welfare, Part III–E, 1970: 17

Diastolic pressure is defined as "the lowest arterial blood pressure of a cardiac cycle occurring during diastole [dilation] of the heart" (*Stedman's Medical Dictionary*, 1976).

iii. Weight

> Source: U.S. Department of Health Education, and Welfare, Part III–E, 1970: 17, and Part III–B, 1970: 77

Weight was measured to the nearest quarter of a pound.

iv. *Height*

Source: U.S. Department of Health, Education, and Welfare, Part III–B, 1970: 77

Height was measured to the nearest .5 centimeter. Height was logarithmically transformed to normalize its positively skewed distribution. The ponderal index, computed as weight/height^3, is used as a measure of body size (Voors, Foster, Frerichs, Webber, and Berenson, 1976: 319–327).

f. *7-year lateral preference*

i. *Hand preference*

Source: U.S. Department of Health, Education, and Welfare, Part III–E, 1970: 22–23

Handedness was treated as a dichotomous variable. Predominantly left-handed individuals constituted one group; predominantly right-handed individuals constituted the other group. The few remaining individuals with variable or ambidextrous handedness were excluded from analyses. Consistent with other research on laterality, the incidence of left- and right-handedness in the CPP was about 11 and 89 percent respectively for a selected sample across all 7 cohorts.

Hand preference in the CPP was observed by placing three differently colored pencils directly in front of the child, who was then asked to make an "X" on a piece of paper with each pencil (Coren, Porac, and Duncan, 1979: 55–64, report a high concordance between observed and behavioral measures of handedness). If the same hand was not used with each of the three pencils the test was repeated two more times. Any preference that occurred fewer than four out of five times was coded as "variable."

ii. *Eye preference*

Source: U.S. Department of Health, Education, and Welfare, Part III–E, 1970: 23

Eye preference was treated as a dichotomous variable. Predominantly left-eyed individuals constituted one group; predominantly right-eyed individuals constituted the other group. The incidence of left and right eye preference was about 56 and 44 percent respectively. Eye preference in the CPP was observed by asking a child to look through a kaleidoscope after picking it up with both hands. The test was repeated three times with both hands on the kaleidoscope; any preference less than perfect was coded as "variable."

ii. *Foot preference*

    Source: U.S. Department of Health, Education, and Welfare, Part III–E, 1970: 23

Foot preference was treated as a dichotomous variable. Predominantly left-footed individuals constituted one group; predominantly right-footed individuals constituted the other group. The incidence of left-, right-, and variable-footedness in the CPP was 10, 66, and 24 percent respectively.

"Variable" foot preference occurred more frequently than left foot preference. The decision to classify "variable" with right foot preference in a dichotomy was based on numerous previous analyses – with a selection of validating variables – that indicated a greater distinction between left and "variable" foot preference relative to right and "variable" foot preference.

Foot preference in the CPP was observed by asking a child to kick a 3- to 4-inch Wiffle ball placed about one foot in front of the child. A consistent foot preference was then noted by the experimenter during three trials. If two right and one left (or vice versa) responses were observed, two more trials were performed and any preference less than four out of five was coded as "variable."

g. *Family constellation*

i. *Family size*

Total family size comprised the number of the study child's younger and older siblings (U.S. Department of Health, Education, and Welfare, Part III–C, 1966: 16–17), the study child (one), and the parents (one or two). The total was square root transformed to normalize its positively skewed distribution.

ii. *Husband or father in the household*

    Source: U.S. Department of Health, Education, and Welfare, Part III–C, 1966: 5

Presence of the father was treated as a dichotomous variable. A husband or father was considered present if the male residing with the mother was her husband and also father of the child, the father of the child but not her husband, or her husband but not the father of the child. A husband or father was considered not present if there was no husband or father of the child residing with the mother at the time of the 7-year examination.

iii. *Foster, adoptive parents; guardian*

> *Source:* U.S. Department of Health, Education, and Welfare, Part III–E 1970: 5, 6

Foster parents was treated as a dichotomous variable indicating the ab sence or presence of a child in a foster home, orphanage, institution, o residence with a guardian.

iv. *Marital stability*

Marital stability was treated as a dichotomous variable indicating the absence or presence of a "negative" change in the mother's marital statu: from the time at registration into the CPP up to the 7-year examination It comprised two variables: marital status of the mother at registratior and marital status of the mother at the 7-year examination (U.S. Depart ment of Health, Education,and Welfare, Part III–E, 1970: 6, 7).

A marriage was "stable" if the mother was married or single at the time of registration and married at the 7-year examination; a marriage was "unstable" if any other combination occurred, such as married at the time of registration and separated or divorced at the 7-year examination

v. *Number of persons supported*

> *Source:* U.S. Department of Health, Education, and Welfare, Part III–E 1970: 8

Number of persons supported indicates the number of individuals in the household who were dependent upon the total family income. The vari able is used as the denominator in constructing per capita income; it was logarithmically transformed to normalize its positively skewed distribu tion.

h. Socioeconomic status at 7 years

i. *Income*

> *Source:* U.S. Department of Health, Education, and Welfare, Part III–E, 1970: 10, 11

Family income was translated into June 1970 dollars, the midpoint year of the 7-year examinations, using the consumer price index for Philadelphia in order to eliminate cohort differences due to inflation. Income was logarithmically transformed to normalize its positively skewed distribu tion. Per capita income was calculated by dividing the total family income (at the 7-year examination) by the total number of persons in a family supported by that income.

ii. *Education of the head of household*

 Source: U.S. Department of Health, Education, and Welfare, Part III–E, 1970: 8, 9

Education data at the 7-year examination, obtained from the mother and husband, represented the highest educational level of the head of the household. The "education score" was created by Myrianthopoulos and French (1968: 283–299) as part of a composite measure of SES comparing income, education, and occupation.

iii. *Occupation of the head of household*

 Source: U.S. Department of Health, Education, and Welfare, Part III–E, 1970: 8, 9

Occupation data at the 7-year examination represented the highest occupational level of the head of the household and was part of the composite SES score created by Myrianthopoulos and French (1968).

E. Means and standard deviations of selected variables

Means and standard deviations, with *t*-test results in Table A.7, show that the most highly significant sex differences are also among the indicators of cognitive functioning and delinquency, as well as among indicators of physical growth, such as height, weight, and blood pressure. Aside from birth weight and smoking, no significant sex differences appear among birth-related variables and no significant differences exist on socioeconomic and background variables.

In the present study, subjects were excluded from analyses if missing values were present in the 7-year intelligence tests; the sample of subjects for the 4-year tests is somewhat smaller because of attrition. Missing values for most of the variables designated in the previous section constituted less than 5 percent of the sample. Estimated values were based either on the sample mean or on the predicted values of highly correlated variables for which data were present (Beale and Little, 1975: 129–145; Dixon, 1977).

Table A.7. *Untransformed variable means and standard deviations, by sex*

Variables	Males Mean	(S.D.)	Females Mean	(S.D.)
Stanford–Binet Intelligence Scale*	90.12	(12.11)	91.91	(13.53)
Graham–Ernhart Block Sort, Total Score***	31.28	(8.65)	33.49	(8.08)
WISC Full Scale IQ	92.79	(10.95)	92.03	(11.07)
WISC Verbal IQ	92.55	(11.14)	91.26	(11.49)
Information	9.18	(2.37)	9.10	(2.43)
Comprehension**	8.65	(2.45)	8.14	(2.33)
Vocabulary***	8.22	(2.38)	7.61	(2.30)
Digit span*	9.14	(2.83)	9.51	(3.05)
WISC Performance IQ	94.39	(12.68)	94.33	(11.96)
Picture arrangement**	8.87	(2.74)	8.30	(2.60)
Block design*	9.09	(2.27)	8.73	(2.09)
Coding***	9.63	(2.82)	10.54	(2.80)
WISC PIQ-VIQ Difference IQ	1.84	(13.02)	3.07	(11.92)
WRAT Spelling, raw score, square root transformed*	22.81	(4.67)	23.50	(4.66)
WRAT Reading, raw score, square root transformed*	31.36	(7.56)	32.68	(8.29)
WRAT Arithmetic, raw score, square root transformed	20.12	(3.42)	20.43	(3.22)
Bender Gestalt Test, total score***	7.85	(3.36)	8.70	(3.60)
Bender Gestalt, time (seconds) Goodenough–Harris drawing test,	96.63	(13.62)	93.70	(11.73)
standard score***	411.03	(184.01)	400.03	(176.72)
CAT, Total Reading, square root transformed	30.32	(24.53)	33.35	(25.76)
Vocabulary, square root transformed	33.12	(26.43)	35.99	(28.91)
Comprehension, square root transformed**	29.64	(23.81)	33.02	(24.11)
CAT, Total Math, square root transformed*	22.79	(21.82)	26.95	(22.55)
Computation, square root transformed***	23.29	(21.77)	28.41	(23.32)
Concepts and problems, square root transformed*	24.87	(22.31)	27.61	(22.01)
CAT, Total Language, square root transformed***	27.00	(23.43)	36.80	(25.58)
Mechanics, square root transformed***	28.23	(24.12)	38.97	(26.73)
Usage and structure, square root transformed***	30.01	(21.78)	35.16	(23.07)
CAT, Spelling, square root transformed***	26.82	(23.74)	39.43	(28.04)
CAT, Total Battery, square root transformed***	23.68	(22.54)	30.67	(24.83)

Table A.7. *(cont.)*

Variables	Males Mean	(S.D.)	Females Mean	(S.D.)
Age at first arrest	15.39	(1.37)	15.31	(1.57)
Age at first offense	13.95	(2.26)	14.15	(1.97)
Age at last offense	15.44	(1.99)	15.04	(1.57)
Total number of arrests, log transformed, with 0 = .5***	0.58	(1.80)	0.13	(0.59)
Arrest record: arrests/no arrests (1 = one or more arrests)***	0.22	(0.41)	0.07	(0.30)
Total number of offenses, log transformed, with 0 = 0.5***	0.91	(2.44)	0.29	(1.11)
Offense record: offenses/no offenses (1 = one or more offenses)***	0.31	(0.46)	0.14	(0.34)
Total number of injury offenses***	0.11	(0.53)	0.01	(0.13)
Total number of theft offenses***	0.27	(1.03)	0.08	(0.45)
Total number of damage offenses***	0.13	(0.52)	0.01	(0.10)
Total number of nonindex offenses***	0.45	(1.15)	0.16	(0.76)
Total number of very violent offenses**	0.08	(0.38)	0.02	(0.17)
Total number of less violent offenses**	0.06	(0.34)	0.004	(0.06)
Number of prenatal examinations	4.52	(1.33)	4.50	(1.29)
Number of prenatal conditions	0.80	(0.84)	0.71	(0.91)
A count of 8 items:				
Heavy smoker (1 = ≥ 30 cigarettes per day)*	0.01	(0.12)	0.002	(0.04)
Drug use (1 = sedatives were used)	0.12	(0.32)	0.09	(0.29)
Marital status (1 = single)	0.32	(0.46)	0.29	(0.45)
Diabetes (1 = present)	0.01	(0.10)	0.01	(0.10)
Hypertension (1 = hypertension)	0.10	(0.31)	0.10	(0.30)
Venereal conditions (number of venereal conditions)	0.12	(0.45)	0.12	(0.45)
Neurological status (number of neurological and psychiatric conditions)	0.05	(0.23)	0.06	(0.27)
Infectious diseases (number of infectious conditions)	0.06	(0.23)	0.04	(0.21)
Poor obstetrical history	0.59	(1.02)	0.70	(1.30)
A count of 4 items:				
Fetal deaths, early (number of fetal deaths < 20 weeks)	0.24	(0.58)	0.25	(0.62)
Fetal deaths, late (number of fetal deaths ≥ 20 weeks)	0.06	(0.26)	0.06	(0.27)
Premature siblings (number of premature siblings)	0.24	(0.60)	0.33	(0.86)
Neonatal siblings (number of neonatal deaths of siblings)	0.04	(0.23)	0.06	(0.29)

Table A.7. *(cont.)*

Variables	Males Mean	(S.D.)	Females Mean	(S.D.)
Mother's age at registration, log transformed	24.18	(6.52)	24.56	(6.26)
Pregnancy and delivery conditions				
A count of 17 pregnancy and delivery complications	1.22	(1.08)	1.18	(1.13)
Cesarean or breech delivery	0.05	(0.23)	0.07	(0.26)
Forceps marks at delivery	0.07	(0.26)	0.06	(0.24)
Prolapsed cord	0.01	(0.11)	0.01	(0.08)
Cord around neck, tight	0.08	(0.32)	0.08	(0.33)
Cord around neck, loose	0.22	(0.48)	0.18	(0.44)
Placenta previa	0.01	(0.08)	0.01	(0.08)
Abruptio placentae	0.02	(0.13)	0.01	(0.12)
Marginal sinus rupture	0.01	(0.10)	0.01	(0.11)
Irregular fetal heart rate	0.03	(0.18)	0.03	(0.18)
Meconium during labor	0.24	(0.43)	0.22	(0.41)
Multiple birth	0.01	(0.09)	0.01	(0.08)
Use of oxytocic during labor	0.10	(0.30)	0.10	(0.30)
Anesthetic shock	0.02	(0.13)	0.03	(0.17)
Other anesthetic accident	–	–	0.002	(0.04)
Uterine bleeding, first trimester	0.10	(0.30)	0.10	(0.31)
Uterine bleeding, second trimester	0.10	(0.30)	0.11	(0.31)
Uterine bleeding, third trimester	0.17	(0.38)	0.19	(0.39)
Duration of labor – sum of stages 1 and 2, square root transformed	7.87	(5.46)	7.57	(5.74)
Apgar at one minute, arc sine transformed	7.69	(1.86)	7.82	(1.77)
Apgar at five minutes, arc sine transformed	8.88	(1.18)	8.90	(1.14)
Gestational age	38.33	(3.45)	38.22	(3.72)
Birth weight in pounds***	7.05	(1.20)	6.68	(1.11)
Parity and birth order – number of older siblings, square root transformed	2.16	(2.15)	2.44	(2.44)
Income at registration, square root transformed, adjusted to 1970 dollars	4130.48	(1942.31)	3991.96	(1883.1)
Mother's education, arc sine transformed	10.31	(1.94)	10.41	(1.81)
Blood pressure, systolic*	101.57	(9.72)	100.10	(9.64)
Blood pressure, diastolic*	61.79	(7.63)	60.62	(7.80)
Weight in lbs. at 7-year exam***	54.80	(10.06)	51.73	(9.11)
Height in cms. at 7-year exam, log transformed***	124.31	(5.64)	122.49	(5.56)
Ponderal index (weight/height^3)	0.00003	(0.00003)	0.00003	(0.00003)

Table A.7. *(cont.)*

Variables	Males Mean	(S.D.)	Females Mean	(S.D.)
Hand preference, 1 = left-handed	0.12	(0.32)	0.10	(0.30)
Eye preference, 1 = left-eyed	0.42	(0.49)	0.42	(0.50)
Foot preference, 1 = left-footed (vs. right and variable)	0.10	(0.30)	0.10	(0.30)
Foot preference, 1 = left or variable footed (vs. right)**	0.16	(0.37)	0.23	(0.42)
Family size (sum of older and younger siblings), square root transformed	5.88	(2.38)	6.05	(2.54)
Husband or father in the household (1 = father figure absent)	0.39	(0.49)	0.43	(0.50)
Foster parents (1 = a foster child)	0.03	(0.18)	0.02	(0.13)
Marital stability (1 = mother who is single or married at registration but not married at the 7-year exam)	0.55	(0.50)	0.54	(0.50)
Number of persons supported in the household	5.80	(2.14)	5.88	(2.04)
Income at the 7-year exam, log transformed, adjusted to 1970 dollars	6603.91	(3438.63)	6561.28	(3280.95)
Education of head of household	41.13	(20.86)	42.00	(20.30)
Occupation of head of household	30.31	(25.70)	32.08	(26.12)
Samples sizes	487		500	

Notes: *p <. 05; **p < .01; ***p < .001.

References

Adler, F. (1975). *Sisters in crime: The rise of the new female criminal*. New York: McGraw-Hill.

Allen, M. (1977). The role of vision in learning disorders. *Journal of Learning Disabilities* 10: 411–415.

Allen, M., and M. M. Wellman (1980). Hand position during writing, cerebral laterality and reading: age and sex differences. *Neuropsychologia* 18: 33–40.

American Psychiatric Association (1987). *Diagnostic and statistical manual of mental disorders* (DSM III) Washington, D.C.: American Psychiatric Association.

Amitai, Y., J. W. Graef, M. J. Brown, R. S. Gerstle, N. Kahn, and R. E. Cochrane (1987). Hazards of "deleading" homes of children with lead poisoning. *American Journal of Diseases of Children* 141: 758–760.

Anastasi, A. (1972). The Goodenough–Harris Draw-A-Man Test. In O. K. Buros (ed.), *The seventh mental measurements yearbook*. Highland Park, N.J.: Gryphon Press.

Anastasi, A. (1981). Coaching, test sophistication, and developed abilities. *American Psychologist* 36 (10): 1086–1093.

Anderson, J. W. (1969). Little community in the big city: Social organization and community culture in an urban neighborhood. Unpublished master's thesis University of Pennsylvania.

Andrew, J. M. (1976). Delinquency, sex and family variables. *Social Biology* 23 168–174.

Andrew, J. M. (1978). Laterality on the tapping test among legal offenders *Journal of Clinical Child Psychology* 7 (2): 149–150.

Andrew, J. M. (1979). Violence and poor reading. *Criminology* 7: 361–365.

Andrew, J. M. (1980). Are left-handers less violent? *Journal of Youth and Adolescence* 9 (1): 1–9.

Andrew, J. M. (1981a). Delinquency: Correlating variables. *Journal of Clinical Child Psychology* 10: 136–140.

Andrew, J. M. (1981b). Violence among delinquents by family intactness and size. *Social Biology* 25: 243–250.

Apgar, V. (1953). A proposal for a new method of evaluation of the newborn infant. *Current Researches in Anesthesia and Analgesia* 32: 260–267.

Arey, J. B., and G. W. Anderson (1966). Pathology of the newborn. In J. P Greenhill (ed.), *Obstetrics*. Philadelphia: Saunders.

188

Armstrong, D. F. (1980). Relationships between biological and mental development at adolescence. Ph.D. dissertation, University of Pennsylvania.

Aronfreed, J. (1974). Discussion: Developmental gains in moral judgement. *American Journal of Mental Deficiency* 79 (2): 113–154.

Aurand, S. K. (1987). Review of the major tests of intellectual functioning in the Collaborative Perinatal Project. Unpublished manuscript, University of Pennsylvania.

Austin, R. L. (1978). Race, father-absence, and female delinquency. *Criminology* 15 (4): 487–504.

Bach-y-Rita, G., J. R. Lion, C. E. Climent, and F. R. Ervin (1971). Episodic dyscontrol: a study of 130 violent patients. *American Journal of Psychiatry* 127 (11): 1473–1478.

Bakan, P., G. Dibb, and P. Reed (1973). Handedness and birth stress. *Neuropsychologia* 11: 363–366.

Barnes, J., and N. O'Gorman (1978). Some medical and social features of delinquent boys. *Journal of the Irish Medical Association* 71 (1): 19–22.

Bartol, C. R. (1980). *Criminal behavior: A psychosocial approach*. Englewood Cliffs, N.J.: Prentice-Hall.

Bayley, N., and E. S. Schaefer (1964). Correlations of maternal and child behaviors with the development of mental abilities: Data from the Berkeley Growth Study. *Monographs of the Society for Research in Child Development* 29 (6, serial No. 97).

Beale, E. M. L., and R. J. A. Little (1975). Missing values in multivariate analyses. *Journal of the Royal Statistical Society* Series B, 37: 129–145.

Behrman, R. E., G. S. Babson, and R. Lessel (1971). Fetal and neonatal mortality in white middle class infants: Mortality risks by gestational age and weight. *American Journal of Diseases of Children* 121: 486–489.

Benton, A. L. (1973). Minimal brain dysfunction from a neuropsychological point of view. *Annals of the New York Academy of Sciences* 205: 29–37.

Berkson, G. (1983). Repetitive stereotyped behaviors. *American Journal of Mental Deficiency* 88 (3): 239–246.

Bernstein, J. E., J. G. Page, and R. S. Janicki (1974). Some characteristics of children with minimal brain dysfunction. In C. K. Conners (ed.), *Clinical use of stimulant drugs in children*. Amsterdam: Excerpta Medica.

Bersoff, D. N. (1981). Testing and the law. *American Psychologist* 36 (10): 1047–1056.

Bever, T. G. (1980). Broca and Lashley were right: Cerebral dominance is an accident of growth. In D. Caplan (ed.), *Biological Studies of Mental Processes*. Cambridge: MIT Press.

Billingslea, F. Y. (1963). The Bender Gestalt: a review and a perspective. *Psychological Bulletin* 60 (3): 233–251.

Blanchard, J. B., and F. Mannarino (1978). Academic, perceptual, and visual levels of detained juveniles. In L. J. Hippchen (ed.), *Ecologic-biochemical approaches to treatment of delinquents and criminals*. New York: Van Nostrand Reinhold.

Block, R. (1979). Community, environment, and violent crime. *Criminology* 17: 46–57.

Boffey, P. M. (1988). After years of cleanup, lead poisoning persists as a threat to health. *The New York Times*, Sept. 1, B14, col. 1.

Bogen, J. E. (1969). The other side of the brain II: An appositional mind. *Bulletin of the Los Angeles Neurological Societies* 37: 49–61.

Bordua, D. J. (1958). Juvenile delinquency and "anomie". An attempt at replication. *Social Problems* 6: 230–238.

Bowker, L. H. (1978). Menstruation and female criminality: A new look at the data. Paper presented at the annual meeting of the American Society of Criminology, Dallas, Texas.

Brace, L. (1980). Social bias in mental testing (Open peer commentary/Jensen: Bias in mental testing). *The Behavioral and Brain Sciences* 3: 333–334.

Brackbill, Y., and S. H. Broman (1979). Obstetrical medication and development in the first year of life. Unpublished manuscript, National Institute of Neurological Diseases and Stroke. Washington, D.C.: National Institutes of Health.

Bradbury, P. J., S. D. Wright, C. E. Walker, and J. M. Ross (1975). Performance on the WISC as a function of sex of E, sex of S, and age of S. *The Journal of Psychology* 90: 51–55.

Brand, M. M., and A. Bignami (1969). The effects of chronic hypoxia on the neonatal and infantile brain. *Brain* 92: 233–254.

Broman, S. H., G. B. Kolata, and Y. Brackbill (1979). Obstetrical medication study. *Science* 205: 446–448.

Broman, S. H., P. L. Nichols, and W. A. Kennedy (1975). *Preschool IQ: Prenatal and early developmental correlates*. New York: Wiley.

Brown, W. A., T. Manning, and J. Grodin (1972). The relationship of antenatal and perinatal psychologic variables to the use of drugs in labor. *Psychosomatic Medicine* 34 (2): 119–127.

Brownfield, D. (1986). Social class and violent behavior. *Criminology* 24 (3): 421–38.

Bryan, M. M. (1978). California Achievement Tests. In O. K. Buros (ed.), *The eighth mental measurements yearbook*. Highland Park, N. J.: Gryphon Press.

Bryden, M. P. (1979). Evidence for sex-related differences in cerebral organization. In M. A. Wittig and A. C. Peterson (eds.), *Sex-related differences in cognitive functioning: developmental issues*. New York: Academic Press.

Burstein, B., L. Bank, and L. F. Jarvik (1980). Sex differences in cognitive functioning: Evidence, determinants, implications. *Human Development* 23: 289–313.

Butler, N. R., and H. Goldstein (1973). Smoking in pregnancy and subsequent child development. *British Medical Journal* 4: 573–575.

Cameron, J. R. (1978). Parental treatment, children's temperament, and the risk of childhood behavioral problems: 2. Initial attitudes, and the incidence and form of behavioral problems. *American Journal of Orthopsychiatry* 48 (1): 140–147.

Campagna, A. F., and S. Harter (1974). Moral judgments in sociopathic and normal children. *Journal of Personality and Social Psychology* 31 (2): 199–205.

Campion, E., and G. Tucker (1973). A note on twin studies, schizophrenia and neurological impairment. *Archives of General Psychiatry* 29: 460–464.

Caplan, A. L., ed. (1978). *The sociobiology debate*. New York: Harper and Row.

Carey, S., and R. Diamond (1980). Maturational determination of the developmental course of face encoding. In D. Caplan (ed.), *Biological Studies of Mental Processes*. Cambridge: MIT Press.

Carmines, E. G., and R. A. Zeller (1979). *Reliability and validity assessment*. Beverly Hills: Sage Publications.

Carter-Saltzman, L. (1979). Patterns of cognitive functioning in relation to handedness and sex-related differences. In M. A. Wittig and A. C. Petersen (eds.), *Sex-related differences in cognitive functioning: Developmental issues.* New York: Academic Press.

Cavan, R. S., and T. N. Ferdinand (1981). *Juvenile Delinquency* (fourth edition). New York: Harper and Row.

Centers for Disease Control (1985). Preventing lead poisoning in young children. Atlanta: U.S. Department of Health and Human Services.

Chamberlain, G., and J. Banks (1974). Assessment of the Apgar score. *The Lancet* 2: 1225–1228.

Chilton, R. (1964). Delinquency area research in Baltimore, Detroit, and Indianapolis. *American Sociological Review* 29: 71–83.

Chipman, S. S., A. M. Lilienfeld, B. G. Greenberg, and J. F. Donnelly, eds. (1966). *Research methodology and needs in perinatal sudies.* Springfield Ill.: Thomas.

Chung, C. S., and N. C. Myrianthopoulos (1975). Factors affecting risks of congenital malformations: I. Epidemiologic analysis; II. Effect of maternal diabetes. *Birth Defects*, Original Article Series, The National Foundation of March of Dimes. 11 (10): 1–38.

Clark, D. (n.d.). The urban ordeal: Reform and policy in Philadelphia. Unpublished manuscript, School of Public and Urban Policy, University of Pennsylvania.

Clark, J. P., and E. P. Wenninger (1972). Socioeconomic class and area as correlates of illegal behavior among juveniles. In R. Giallombardo (ed.), *Juvenile delinquency: A book of readings.* New York: Wiley.

Clements, S. D. (1966). *Minimal brain dysfunction in children: Terminology and identification.* U.S. Public Health Service Publication No. 1415. Washington, D.C.: U.S. Department of Health, Education, and Welfare.

Climent, C. E., F. R. Ervin, A. Rollins, R. Plutchik, and C. J. Batinelli (1977). Epidemiological studies of female prisoners. IV. Homosexual behavior. *The Journal of Nervous and Mental Disease* 164 (1): 25–29.

Climent, C. E., A. Rollins, F. R. Ervin, and R. Plutchik (1973). Epidemiological studies of women prisoners. I. Medical and psychiatric variables related to violent behavior. *American Journal of Psychiatry* 130: 985–990.

Cloninger, C. R., K. O. Christiansen, T. Reich, and I. I. Gottesman (1978). Implications of sex differences in the prevalences of antisocial personality, alcoholism, and criminality for familial transmission. *Archives of General Psychiatry* 35: 941–951.

Cloninger, C. R., T. Reich, and S. B. Guze (1975). The multifactorial model of disease transmission: II. Sex differences in the familial transmission of sociopathy (antisocial personality). *British Journal of Psychiatry* 127: 11–22.

Cloward, R. A., and L. E. Ohlin (1961). *Delinquency and opportunity.* New York: Free Press.

Cohen, A. (1955). *Delinquent boys: The culture of the gang.* New York: Free Press.

Cole, N. S. (1981). Bias in testing. *American Psychologist* 36 (10): 1067–1077.

Colligan, R. C. (1974). Psychometric deficits related to perinatal stress. *Journal of Learning Disabilities* 7: 154–160.

Committee on Environmental Hazards (1987). Statement on childhood lead poisoning. *Pediatrics* 79 (3): 457–465.

Coren, S., and C. Porac (1980). Birth factors and laterality: Effects of birth order, parental age, and birth stress on four indices of lateral preference. *Behavior Genetics* 10 (2): 123–137.

Coren, S., C. Porac, and P. Duncan (1979). A behaviorally validated self-report inventory to assess four types of lateral preference. *Journal of Clinical Neuropsychology* 1 (1): 55–64.

Cortés, J. B., and F. M. Gatti (1972). *Delinquency and crime: A biopsychosocial approach.* New York: Seminar Press.

Cott, A. (1978). The etiology of learning disabilities, drug abuse, and juvenile delinquency, In L. J. Hippchen (ed.), *Ecologic-biochemical approaches to the treatment of delinquents and criminals.* New York: Van Nostrand Reinhold.

Courtney, P. D. (1949). Review of the Wide Range Achievement Test. In O. K. Buros (ed.), *The third mental measurements yearbook.* New Brunswick, N.J.: Rutgers University Press.

Cowie, J., V. Cowie, and E. Slater (1968). *Delinquency in girls.* London: Heinemann.

Cronbach, L. J. (1951). Coefficient alpha and the internal structure of tests. *Psychometrika* 16 (3): 297–334.

Cronbach, L. J. (1970). *Essentials of psychological testing* (Third ed.). New York: Harper and Row.

Curman, H., and I. Nylander (1976). A 10-year prospective follow-up study of 2268 cases at the Child Guidance Clinics in Stockholm. *Acta Paediatrica Scandinavica* 260: 1–71.

Cushner, I. M., and E. D. Mellits (1971). The relationship between fetal outcome and the gestational age and birth weight of the fetus. *Johns Hopkins Medical Journal* 128: 252–260.

Danziger, S. (1976). Explaining urban crime rates. *Criminology* 14 (2): 291–295.

Darlington, R. B., J. M. Royce, A. S. Snipper, H. W. Murray, and I. Lazar (1980). Preschool programs and later school competence of children from low-income families. *Science* 208: 202–204.

Datesman, S. K., and F. R. Scarpitti, eds. (1980). *Women, crime, and justice.* New York: Oxford University Press.

Davie, R., N. Butler, and H. Goldstein (1972). *From birth to seven: With full statistical appendix.* London: Longman Group.

DeCherney, A. H., and G. S. Berkowitz (1982). Female fecundity and age. *The New England Journal of Medicine* 306 (7): 424–426.

de la Burde, B., and M. S. Choate (1975). Early asymptomatic lead exposure and development at school age. *Journal of Pediatrics* 87 (4): 638–642.

Denhoff, E. (1973). The natural life history of children with minimal brain dysfunction. *Annals of the New York Academy of Sciences* 205: 188–205.

Denhoff, E., P. Hainsworth, and M. Hainsworth (1972). The child at risk for learning disorder: Can he be identified during the first year of life? *Clinical Pediatrics* 11 (3): 164–170.

Denno, D. (1982). Sex differences in cognition and crime: Early developmental, biological, and sociological correlates. Unpublished doctoral dissertation. Philadelphia: University of Pennsylvania.

Denno, D. (1984). Neuropsychological and early environmental correlates of sex differences in crime. *International Journal of Neuroscience* 23: 199–214.

Denno, D. (1985). Sociological and human developmental explanations of crime: Conflict or consensus? *Criminology* 23 (4): 711–41.

Denno, D. (1986). Victim, offender, and situational characteristics of violent crime. *The Journal of Criminal Law and Criminology* 77 (4): 1142–1158.

Denno, D. (1988). Human biology and criminal responsibility: Free will or free ride? *University of Pennsylvania Law Review* 137 (2): 615–671.

Denno, D., and R. Schwarz (1985). *Biological, psychological, and environmental factors in delinquency and mental disorder: An interdisciplinary bibliography.* Westport, Conn.: Greenwood Press.

Department of Education, Commonwealth of Pennsylvania (1979). Standards for Special Education for School Aged Exceptional Persons in the Commonwealth. Pennsylvania Code (22), Chapter 341.1, Document #78–519.

Dierks, D., and B. Cushna (1969). Sex differences in the Bender Gestalt performance of children. *Perceptual and Motor Skills* 28: 19–22.

Dimond, S., and J. G. Beaumont, eds. (1974). *Hemisphere function in the human brain.* New York: Wiley.

Dixon, W. J. (1977). *BMDP: Biomedical computer programs.* P. Series. Berkeley: University of California Press.

Dorfman, D. D. (1980). Test bias: What did Yale, Harvard, Rolls-Royce, and a black have in common in 1917? (Open peer commentary/Jensen: Bias in mental testing). *The Behavioral and Brain Sciences* 3:339–340.

Drillien, C. M. (1961). The incidence of mental and physical handicaps in school-age children of very low birth weight. *Pediatrics* 27: 452–464.

Drillien, C. M. (1972). Aetiology and outcome in low-birthweight infants. *Developmental Medicine and Child Neurology* 14: 563–574.

Drorbaugh, J. E., D. M. Moore, and J. H. Warram (1975). Association between gestational and environmental events and central nervous system function in 7-year-old children. *Pediatrics* 56 (4): 529–537.

Dubey, D. R. (1976). Organic factors in hyperkinesis: A critical evaluation. *American Journal of Orthopsychiatry* 46 (2): 353–365.

Dunn, J. A. (1972). The Goodenough–Harris Draw-A-Man Test. In O. K. Buros (ed.), *The seventh mental measurements yearbook.* Highland Park, N.J.: Gryphon Press.

Eagle, D. B., and T. B. Brazelton (1977). The infant at risk: assessment and implications for intervention. In M. McMillan and S. Henao (eds.), *Child psychiatry: Treatment and research.* New York: Brunner/Mazel.

Eastman, N. J., and L. M. Hellman (1961). *Williams obstetrics* (12th ed.). New York: Appleton-Century-Crofts.

Elliott D. S. (1966). Delinquency, school attendance and dropout. *Social Problems* 13: 306–318.

Elliott, D. S., and S. S. Ageton (1980). Reconciling race and class differences in self-reported and official estimates of delinquency. *American Sociological Review* 45 (February): 95–110.

Elliott, F. A. (1978). Neurological aspects of antisocial behavior. In W. H. Reid (ed.), *The Psychopath.* New York: Bruner/Mazel.

Elliott, F. A. (1988). Neurological factors. In V. Van Hasselt, R. Morrison, E. Bellack, and M. Herson (eds.) *Handbook of family violence.* New York: Plenum.

Epstein, H. T. (1974). Phrenoblysis: Special brain and mind growth periods: I. Human brain and skull development; II. Human mental development. *Developmental Psychobiology* 7: 207–224.

Ernhart, C., F. K. Graham, P. L. Eichman, J. M. Marshall, and D. Thurston (1963). Brain injury in the preschool child: Some developmental considerations. II. Comparison of brain injured and normal children. *Psychological Monographs: General and Applied* 77 (11): 17–33.

Farrington, D. (1983). Offending from 10 to 25 years of age. In K. Van Dusen and S. Mednick (eds.), *Prospective Studies of Crime and Delinquency*. Boston: Kluwer-Nijhoff.

Fédération CECOS, D. Schwartz, and M. J. Mayaux (1982). Female fecundity as a function of age: Results of artificial insemination in 2193 nulliparous women with azoospermic husbands. *The New England Journal of Medicine* 306 (7): 404–406.

Fianu, S. (1976). Fetal mortality and morbidity following breech delivery. *Acta Obstetrica et Gynecologica* (supplement) 56: 1–85.

Firestone, P., S. Peters, and M. Rivier (1977). Minor physical anomalies in hyperactive, retarded and normal children and their families. *Journal of Child Psychology and Psychiatry and Allied Disciplines* 19: 155–160.

Fish, J. S., R. A. Bartholomew, E. D. Colvin, and W. H. Grimes (1951). The role of marginal sinus rupture in antenatal hemorrhage. *American Journal of Obstetrics and Gynecology* 61: 20.

FitzGerald, S. (1986). Poisoned. *Philadelphia Inquirer*, August 19: A1.

Fitzhardinge, P. M., and E. M. Steven (1972). The small-for-date infant: II. Neurological and intellectual sequelae. *Pediatrics* 50: 50–57.

Fitzhugh, K. B. (1973). Some neuropsychological features of delinquent subjects. *Perceptual and Motor Skills* 36: 494.

Flor-Henry, P. (1973). Psychiatric syndromes considered as manifestations of lateralized temporal-limbic dysfunction. In L. V. Latiner and K. E. Livingston (eds.), *Surgical approaches in psychiatry*. Lancaster, Eng.: Medical and Technical Publishing.

Flor-Henry, P., and L. T. Yeudall (1973). Lateralized cerebral dysfunction in depression and in aggressive criminal psychopathy: Further observations. *International Research Communications System* 2: 31.

Fluhmann, C. F. (1966). The cervix uteri during pregnancy. In J. P. Greenhill, *Obstetrics*. Philadelphia: Saunders.

Fogel, R. L. (1976). Gao presentation before the international conference of the association for children with learning disabilities on review of the relationship of learning problems to juvenile delinquency. Unpublished paper, Seattle, Wash.

Fonzi, G. (1960). Hard-core families a festering empire. *Greater Philadelphia Magazine* 51 (6): 17, 18, 50–55.

Freides, D. (1972a). Review of the Stanford–Binet Intelligence Scale. In O. K. Buros (ed.), *The seventh mental measurements yearbook*. Highland Park, N.J.: Gryphon Press.

Freides, D. (1972b). Review of the Wechsler Intelligence Scale for Children. In O. K. Buros (ed.), *The seventh mental measurements yearbook*. Highland Park, N.J.: Gryphon Press.

Friedman, E. A. (1966). Therapeutic abortion. In J. P. Greenhill. *Obstetrics*. Philadelphia: W. B. Saunders.

Friedman, E. A., and B. H. Kroll (1972). Computer analysis of labor progression: V. Effects of fetal presentation and position. *The Journal of Reproductive Medicine* 8 (3): 117–121.

Friedman, E. A., and R. K. Neff (1977). *Pregnancy hypertension*. Littleten, Mass.: Publishing Sciences Group. Mid.

Friedman, E. A., M. R. Sactleben, and P. A. Bresky (1977). Dysfunctional labor:

XII. Long-term effects on infant. *American Journal of Obstetrics and Gynecology* 127: 779–783.

Frisch, R. E., and R. Revelle (1971). The height and weight of girls and boys at the time of initiation of the adolescent growth spurt in height and weight and the relationship to menarche. *Human Biology* 43: 140–159.

Gabrielli, W. F. (1981). The interaction of family and biological factors in learning law-abiding behavior. Ph.D. dissertation, University of Southern California.

Gabrielli, W. F., and S. A. Mednick (1980). Sinistrality and delinquency. *Journal of Abnormal Psychology* 89 (5): 645–661.

Gannon, T. M. (1970). Religious control and delinquent behavior. In M. E. Wolfgang, L. Savitz, and N. Johnston (eds.), *Sociology of crime and delinquency*. New York: Wiley.

Garcia, J. (1981). The logic and limits of mental aptitude testing. *American Psychologist* 36 (10): 1172–1180.

Garmezy, N. (1977). Observations on research with children at risk for child and adult psychopathology. In M. McMillan and S. Henao (eds.), *Child psychology: Treatment and research*. New York: Brunner/Mazel.

Garn, S. M., H. A. Shaw, and K. D. McCabe (1978). Effect of maternal smoking on hemoglobins and hemocrits of the newborn. *The American Journal of Clinical Nutrition* 31: 557–565.

Glantz, F. B., and N. J. Delaney (1973). Changes in nonwhite residential patterns in large metropolitan areas, 1960 and 1970. *New England Economic Review* 4: 2–13.

Glasser, A. J., and I. L. Zimmerman (1967). Reliability of the Koppitz Scoring System for the Bender-Gestalt test. *Journal of Clinical Psychology* 25: 407–409.

Glueck, S., and E. Glueck (1970). Working mothers and delinquency. In M. E. Wolfgang, L. Savitz, and N. Johnston (eds.), *Sociology of crime and delinquency*. New York: Wiley.

Goff, A. F., and A. W. Parker (1969). Reliability of the Koppitz Scoring System for the Bender–Gestalt test. *Journal of Clinical Psychology* 25: 407–409.

Gold, M., and D. J. Reimer (1975). Changing patterns of delinquent behavior among Americans 13 to 16 years old: 1967–72. *Crime and Delinquency Literature* 7 (4): 483–517.

Goldberger, A. S. (1972). Structural equation models in the social sciences. *Econometrica* 40 (6): 979–1001.

Goldberger, A. S. (1973). Structural equation models: An overview. In A. S. Goldberger and O. D. Duncan (eds.), *Structural equation models in the social sciences*. New York: Seminar Press.

Gordon, R. (1976). Prevalence: The rare datum in delinquency measurement and its implications for the theory of delinquency. In M. W. Klein (ed.), *The juvenile justice system*. Beverly Hills: Sage Publications.

Gordon, M., H. Rich, J. Deutschberger, and M. Green (1973). The immediate and long-term outcome of obstetric birth trauma. *American Journal of Obstetrics and Gynecology* September: 51–56.

Graham, F. K., C. B. Ernhart, M. Craft, and P. W. Berman (1963). Brain injury in the preschool child: Some developmental considerations. Performance of normal children. *Psychological Monographs: General and Applied* 77 (10, Whole No. 573).

Graham, F. K., C. B. Ernhart, D. Thurston, and M. Craft (1962). Development three years after perinatal anoxia and other potentially damaging newborn experiences. *Psychological Monographs: General and Applied* 76 (3, Whole No. 522).

Greenhill, J. P. (1966). *Obstetrics*. Philadelphia: Saunders.

Hamburg, B. A. (1974). The psychobiology of sex differences: An evolutionary perspective. In R. C. Freidman, R. M. Richart, and R. L. Vande Wiele (eds.), *Sex differences in behavior*. New York: Wiley.

Hamparian, D., R. Schuster, S. Dinitz, and J. Conrad (1978). *The violent few: A study of dangerous juvenile offenders*. Lexington, Mass.: Lexington Books.

Handford, H. A. (1975). Brain hypoxia, minimal brain dysfunction, and schizophrenia. *American Journal of Psychiatry* 132 (2): 192–194.

Haney, W. (1981). Validity, vaudeville, and values: A short history of social concerns over standardized testing. *American Psychologist* 36 (10): 1021–1033.

Hardy, J. B., J. S. Drage, and E. C. Jackson (1979). *The first year of life*. Baltimore: Johns Hopkins University Press.

Hardy, J. B., and E. D. Mellits (1972). Does maternal smoking during pregnancy have a long-term effect on the child? *Lancet* 2: 1332–1336.

Harlap, S., A. M. Davies, N. B. Grover, and R. Prywes (1977). The Jerusalem Perinatal Study: The first decade, 1964–73. *Israel Journal of Medical Sciences* 13 (11): 1073–1091.

Harris, D. B. (1963). *Children's drawings as measures of intellectual maturity*. New York: Harcourt, Brace, and World.

Hellman, L. M., and J. A. Pritchard (1971). *Williams obstetrics* (14th ed.). New York: Appleton-Century-Crofts.

Henderson, A. S. (1969). The physiological maturity of adolescent psychiatric patients, juvenile delinquents and normal teenagers. *British Journal of Psychiatry* 115: 895–905.

Henderson, N. B., B. V. Butler, and W. M. Clark, Jr. (1971). Relationships between selected perinatal variables and seven year intelligence. *Proceedings of the Seventy-Ninth Annual Convention of the American Psychological Association:* 139–140.

Henning, J. J., and R. H. Levy (1967). Verbal-performance IQ differences of white and Negro delinquents on the WISC and the WAIS. *Journal of Clinical Psychology* 23: 164–168.

Hindelang, M. J., T. Hirshi, and J. G. Weis (1979). Correlates of delinquency: The illusion of discrepancy between self-report and official measures. *American Sociological Review* 44: 995–1014.

Hirschi, T. (1969). *Causes of delinquency*. Berkeley: University of California Press.

Hirshi, T., and M. J. Hindelang (1977). Intelligence and delinquency: A revisionist review. *American Sociological Review* 42 (4): 571–587.

Hogan, R. (1974). Dilalectical aspects of moral development. *Human Development* 17: 113.

Holly, R. G. (1966). Diseases of the blood and blood-forming organs in pregnancy. In J. P. Greenhill, *Obstetrics*. Philadelphia: Saunders.

Hon, E. H. (1966). Placental dysfunction. In J. P. Greenhill, *Obstetrics*. Philadelphia: Saunders.

Honzik, M. P. (1966). Drawings of mind (Review of *Children's drawings as measures of intellectual maturity* by D. B. Harris). *Contemporary Psychology* 11: 28–30.

Hood, R., and R. Sparks (1970). *Key issues in criminology.* New York: McGraw-Hill.

Hoyenga, K. B., and K. T. Hoyenga (1979). *The question of sex differences: Psychological, cultural, and biological issues.* Boston: Little, Brown.

Jastak, J. (1953). Wide Range Achievement Tests. In A. Weider (ed.), *Contributions toward medical psychology: Theory and psychodiagnostic methods,* Vol. 2. New York: Ronald Press.

Jeffery, C. R. (1955). The historical development of criminology. In H. Mannheim (ed.), *Pioneers in criminology.* Montclair, N.J.: Patterson–Smith.

Jencks, C., S. Bartlett, M. Corcoran, J. Crouse, D. Eaglesfield, G. Jackson, K. McClelland, P. Mueser, M. Olneck, J. Schwartz, S. Ward, and J. Williams (1979). *Who gets ahead? The determinants of economic success in America.* New York: Basic.

Jensen, A. R. (1979). *Bias in mental testing.* New York: Free Press.

Jensen, A. R. (1980). Précis of "Bias in Mental Testing." *The Behavioral and Brain Sciences* 3: 325–333.

Jensen, G. (1973). Inner containment and delinquency. *Journal of Criminology and Criminal Law* 64: 464–470.

Jensen, G. J., and R. Eve (1976). Sex differences in delinquency: An examination of popular sociological explanations. *Criminology* 13 (4): 427–448.

Jöreskog, K. G. (1973). A general method for estimating a linear structural equation system. In A. S. Goldberger and O. D. Duncan (eds.), *Structural equation models in the social sciences.* New York: Seminar Press.

Jöreskog, K. G., and D. Sörbom, eds. (1979). *Advances in factor analysis and structural equation models.* Cambridge, Mass.: Abt Books.

Kagan, J., and H. Moss (1962). *Birth to maturity: A study in psychological development.* New York: Wiley.

Katz, S., M. Hediger, J. Schall, E. Bowers, W. Barker, S. Aurand, P. Eveleth, A. Gruskin, and J. Parks (1980). Blood pressure, growth, and maturation from childhood through adolescence: Results of a mixed longitudinal study from the Philadelphia blood pressure project. *Hypertension* 2 (4): 155–169.

Kawi, A. A., and B. Pasamanick (1958). Association of factors of pregnancy with reading disorders in childhood. *Journal of the American Medical Association* 166: 1420–1423.

Keller, J. F., J. W. Croake, and E. Riesenman (1973). Relationship among handedness, intelligence, sex and reading achievement of school age children. *Perceptual and Motor Skills* 37: 159–162.

Keogh, B. K. (1969). The Bender–Gestalt with children: Research applications. *Journal of Special Education.* 3: 15–22.

Kinsbourne, M., and E. K. Warrington (1966). Developmental factors in reading and writing backwards. In J. Money (ed.), *The disabled reader.* Baltimore: Johns Hopkins University Press.

Kirkegaard-Sorenson, L., and S. A. Mednick (1977). A prospective study of predictors of criminality: 4. School behavior. In S. A. Mednick and K. O. Christiansen (eds.), *Biosocial bases of criminal behavior.* New York: Gardner Press.

Kitcher, P. (1985). *Vaulting ambitions: Sociobiology and the quest for human nature.* Boston: MIT Press.

Klein, D. (1980). The etiology of female crime: A review of the literature. In S. K. Datesman and F. R. Scarpitti (eds.), *Women, crime, and justice.* New York: Oxford University Press.

Kleinpeter, U. (1976). Social integration after brain trauma during childhood. *Acta Paedopsychiatrica* 42 (2): 68–75.

Kline, P. (1980). Test bias and problems in cross-cultural testing (Open peer commentary/Jensen: Bias in mental testing). *The Behavioral and Brain Sciences* 3: 349–350.

Klove, H. (1974). Validation studies in adult clinical neurospychology. In R. M. Reitan and L. A. Davison (eds.), *Clinical neuropsychology: Current status and applications.* New York: Wiley.

Kohlberg, L., and D. Elfenbein (1975). The development of moral judgment concerning capital punishment. *American Journal of Orthopsychiatry* 45 (4): 614–640.

Konopka, G. (1973). "Formation of values in the developing person." *American Journal of Orthopsychiatry* 43: 86–96.

Koppitz, E. M. (1960). The Bender–Gestalt test for children: A normative study. *Journal of Clinical Psychology* 16: 432–435.

Kornhauser, R. (1978). *Social sources of delinquency: An appraisal of analytic models.* Chicago: University of Chicago Press.

Kratcoski, P. C., and J. E. Kratcoski (1975). Changing patterns in the delinquent activities of boys and girls: A self-reported delinquency analysis. *Adolescence* 10: 83–91.

Kuder, G. F., and M. W. Richardson (1937). The theory of the estimation of test reliability. *Psychometrika* 2: 151–160.

Kvaraceus, W. C., and W. B. Miller (1975). Norm violating behavior and lower-class culture. In R. S. Cavan (ed.), *Readings in juvenile delinquency.* Philadelphia: Lippincott.

Lambert, N. M. (1981). Psychological evidence in *Larry P. v. Wilson Riles:* An evaluation by a witness for the defense. *American Psychologist* 36 (10): 937–952.

Lander, B. (1954). An ecological analysis of Baltimore. In B. Lander (ed.), *Towards an understanding of juvenile delinquency.* New York: Columbia University Press.

Landrigan, P. J., and J. W. Graef (1987). Pediatric lead poisoning in 1987: The silent epidemic continues. *Pediatrics* 79: 457–465.

Lasich, A., and F. Bassa (1985). Stereotyped movement disorder of rocking. *Journal of Nervous and Mental Disease* 173 (3): 187–189.

Levy, J., and M. Reid (1976). Variations in writing posture and cerebral dominance. *Science* 194: 337–339.

Lewis, D. O., and D. A. Balla (1976). *Delinquency and pathology.* New York: Grune and Stratton.

Lewis, D. O., and S. S. Shanok (1977). Medical histories of delinquent and nondelinquent children: An epidemiological study. *American Journal of Psychiatry* 134: 1020–1025.

Lewis, D. O., S. S. Shanok, and D. A. Balla (1979). Perinatal difficulties, head and face trauma, and child abuse in the medical histories of seriously delinquent children. *American Journal of Psychiatry* 136: 419–423.

Lewis, D. O., S. S. Shanok, J. H. Pincus, and G. Glaser (1979). Violent juvenile delinquents: Psychiatric, neurological, psychological, and abuse factors. *Journal of the American Academy of Child Psychiatry* 18 (2): 307–319.

Lewis, H. P., and N. Livson (1977). Personality correlates of IQ discrepancy: Stanford–Binet and Goodenough–Harris. *The Journal of Genetic Psychology* 131: 237–242.

Lewis, M., W. MacLean, W. Bryson-Brockmann, R. Arendt, B. Beck, P. Fidler, and A. Baumeister (1984). Time-series analysis of stereotyped movements: Relationship of body-rocking to cardiac activity. *American Journal of Mental Deficiency* 89 (3): 287–294.

Lezak, M. D. (1976). *Neuropsychological Assessment*. New York: Oxford University Press.

Litt, S. M. (1972). Perinatal complications and criminality. Ph.D. dissertation, New School for Social Research, New York.

Litt, S. M. (1974). A study of perinatal complications as a factor in criminal behavior. *Criminology* 12 (1): 125–126.

Littlemore, D., M. Metcalfe, and A. L. Johnsen (1974). Skeletal immaturity in psychiatrically disturbed adolescents. *Journal of Child Psychology and Psychiatry and Allied Disciplines* 15: 133–138.

Loeber, R., and T. Dishion (1983). Early predictors of male delinquency: A review. *Psychological Bulletin* 94: 68–99.

Lombroso, C. (1876). *L'Uomo delinquente*. Milan: Hoepli.

Lombroso, C. (1903). Left-handedness and left-sideness. *North American Review* 170: 440–444.

Lombroso, C. (1920) *The female offender* (translation). New York: Appleton (originally published in 1903).

Lombroso, C. (1968). *Crime: Its causes and remedies* (translation). Montclair, N.J.: Patterson Smith (originally published in 1912).

Loney, J., J. E. Langhorne, and C. E. Paternite (1978). An empirical basis for subgrouping the hyperkinetic/minimal brain dysfunction syndrome. *Journal of Abnormal Psychology* 87 (4): 431–441.

Luchterhand, E., and L. Weller (1986). Effects of class, race, sex, and educational status on patterns of aggression in lower class youth. *Journal of Youth and Adolescence* 5 (1): 59–71.

Lumsden, C. J., and E. O.Wilson (1981). *Genes, mind, and culture: The co-evolutionary process*. Cambridge: Harvard University Press.

McBurney, A. K., and H. G. Dunn (1976). Handedness, footedness, eyedness: A prospective study with special reference to the development of speech and language skills. In R. M. Knights and D. G. Bakkers (eds.), *The neuropsychology of learning disorders*. Baltimore: University Park Press.

Maccoby, E. E., C. H. Doering, C. N. Jacklin, and H. Kraemer (1979). Concentrations of sex hormones in umbilical-cord blood: Their relation to sex and birth order of infants. *Child Development* 50: 632–642.

Maccoby, E. E., and C. N. Jacklin (1974). *The psychology of sex differences*. Stanford: Stanford University Press.

McCord, J., and W. McCord (1975). The effects of parental role model on criminality. In R. S. Cavan (ed.), *Readings in juvenile delinquency*. Philadelphia: Lippincott.

McCord, W., and J. McCord (1964). *The psychopath: An essay on the criminal mind*. Princeton, N.J.: Van Nostrand.

McFalls, J. A. (1976). Social science and the Collaborative Perinatal Project: An opportunity for research. *Public Data Use* 4 (5): 37–47.

MacFarlane, J. W., L. Allen, and M. P. Honzik (1962). *A developmental study of the behavior problems of normal children between twenty-one months and fourteen years*. Berkeley: University of California Press.

McMahon, R. R. (1970). The individual and his needs as they relate to the treatment of delinquency. *Popular Government* 36: 7–11.

McNeil, T. F., R. Wiegerink, and J. E. Dozier (1970). Pregnancy and birth complications in the births of seriously, moderately, and mildly behaviorally disturbed children. *The Journal of Nervous and Mental Disease* 151 (1): 24–34.

McTamney, J. F. (1976). The effects of modes of discipline and communication styles on delinquency and character traits in adolescent boys and girls. Unpublished Ph.D. dissertation, Catholic University of America.

Magnusson, D., S. Stattin, and A. Duner (1983). Aggression and criminality in a longitudinal perspective. In S. A. Mednick and K. Van Dusen (eds.), *Prospective studies of crime and delinquency*. Boston: Kluwer–Nijhoff.

Marshall, W., A. K. Hess, and C. V. Lair (1978). The WISC–R and WRAT as indicators of arithmetic achievement in juvenile delinquents. *Perceptual and Motor Skills* 47: 408–410.

Matarazzo, J. D. (1972). *Wechsler's measurement and appraisal of adult intelligence* (5th ed.). Baltimore: Williams and Wilkins.

Mayers, K. S., B. D. Townes, and R. M. Reitan (1974). Adaptive Abilities Among Delinquent and Nondelinquent Boys. Unpublished paper of proposed research.

Meade, A. (1973). Seriousness of delinquency, the adjudicative decision and recidivism: A longitudinal configural analysis. *The Journal of Criminal Law and Criminology* 64 (4): 478–485.

Mednick, S. A. (1970). Breakdown in individuals at high risk for schizophrenia: Possible predispositional perinatal factors. *Mental Hygiene* 54 (1): 50–63.

Mednick, S. A., W. F. Gabrielli, and B. Hutchings (1984). Genetic influences in criminal convictions: Evidence from an adoption cohort. *Science* 224: 891–894.

Mednick, S. A., M. Harway, B. Mednick, and T. E. Moffitt (1981). Longitudinal research: North American data sets. In T. E. Jordan (ed.), *Child development, information and formation of public policy*. St. Louis: University of Missouri Press.

Mednick, S. A., T. E. Moffitt, and S. A. Stack (1987). *The causes of crime: New biological approaches*. New York: Cambridge University Press.

Mednick, S. A., E. Mura, F. Schulsinger, and B. Mednick (1971). Perinatal conditions and infant development in children with schizophrenic parents. *Social Biology* 18: 103.

Mednick, S. A., V. Pollock, J. Volavka, and W. F. Gabrielli, Jr. (1982). Biology and violence. In M. E. Wolfgang and N. A. Weiner (eds.), *Criminal violence*. Beverly Hills: Sage.

Menkes, M., J. S. Rowe, and J. H. Menkes (1967). A twenty-five year follow-up study on the hyperkinetic child with minimal brain dysfunction. *Pediatrics* 39: 393–399.

Merton, R. K. (1957). *Social theory and social structure*. New York: Free Press.

Miller, W. B. (1958). Lower class culture as a generating milieu of gang delinquency. *Journal of Social Issues* 14: 5–19.

Minde, K., G. Webb, and D. Sykes (1968). Studies on the hyperactive child: VI. Prenatal and paranatal factors associated with hyperactivity. *Developmental Medicine and Child Neurology* 10: 355–363.

Moffitt, T. E. (in press). The neuropsychology of delinquency: A critical review of theory and research. In N. Morris and M. Tonry (eds.), *Crime and justice: An annual review of research*. Chicago: University of Chicago Press.

Moffitt, T. E., W. F. Gabrielli, and S. A. Mednick (1981). Socioeconomic status, IQ, and delinquency. *Journal of Abnormal Psychology* 90 (2): 152–156.

Monahan, T. (1957). Family status and the delinquent child: A reappraisal and some new findings. *Social Forces* 35: 250–258.

Montagu, A., ed. (1980). *Sociobiology examined.* Oxford: Oxford University Press.

Moore, D. C. (1966). Anesthesia for vaginal delivery and cesarean section. In J. P. Greenhill (ed.), *Obstetrics.* Philadelphia: Saunders.

Moore, M. (1985). Causation and the excuses. *California Law Review* 73: 1091–1153.

Morgan, T. (1988). Learning disabilities and crime: Struggle to snap the link. *New York Times* (Oct. 31) B1, B3.

Morrison, J. R., and M. A. Stewart (1973). Evidence for polygenetic inheritance in the hyperactive child syndrome. *American Journal of Psychiatry* 130 (7): 791–792.

Moyer, K. E. (1974). Sex differences in aggression. In R. C. Friedman, R. M. Reichart, and R. L. Vande Wiele (eds.), *Sex differences in behavior.* New York: Wiley.

Moyer, K. E. (1987). *Violence and aggression: A physiological perspective.* New York: Paragon House.

Muller, P. O., K. C. Meyer, and R. Cybriwsky (1976). *Philadelphia: A study of conflicts and several cleavages.* Cambridge, Mass.: Ballinger.

Murray, C. A. (1976). The link between learning disabilities and juvenile delinquency. Manuscript prepared for the National Institute for Juvenile Justice and Delinquency Prevention. LEAA, Washington, D.C.: Office of Juvenile Justice and Delinquency Prevention.

Myrianthopoulos, N. C., and K. S. French (1968). An application of the U.S. Bureau of the Census socioeconomic index to a large, diversified, patient population. *Social Science and Medicine* 2: 283–299.

Nachshon, I., and D. Denno (1987a). Birth stress and lateral preferences. *Cortex* ·23: 45–58.

Nachshon, I., and D. Denno (1987b). Violent behavior and cerebral dysfunction. In S. A. Mednick, T. E. Moffitt, and S. Stack (eds.), *The causes of crime: New biological approaches.* New York: Cambridge University Press.

Naeye, R. L. (1977). Causes of perinatal mortality in the U.S. Collaborative Perinatal Project. *Journal of the American Medical Association* 238 (3): 228–229.

Naeye, R. L. (1978). Placenta previa: Predisposing factors and effects on the fetus and surviving infants. *The American College of Obstetricians and Gynecologists* 52 (5): 521–525.

National Center for Health Statistics (1980a). Factors associated with low birth weight: United States, 1976. Washington, D.C.: U.S. Department of Health, Education, and Welfare.

National Center for Health Statistics (1980b). Trends and differentials in births to unmarried women: United States, 1970–1976. Washington, D.C.: U.S. Department of Health, Education, and Welfare.

National Center for Health Statistics (1981). Apgar scores in the United States, 1978. *Monthly Vital Statistics Report* 30 (1): 1–15.

Needleman, H., I. Davidson, E. Sewall, and I. Shapiro (1974). Subclinical lead exposure in Philadelphia school children. *New England Journal of Medicine* 290: 245–248.

Needleman, H., C. Gunnoe, A. Leviton, R. Reed, H. Peresie, C. Maher, and P. Barrett (1979). Deficits in psychologic and classroom performance of children with elevated dentine lead levels. *New England Journal of Medicine* 300 (12): 689-695.

Nelson, K. B., and S. H. Broman (1977). Perinatal risk factors in children with serious motor and mental handicaps. *Annals of Neurology* 2: 371-377.

Nettler, G. (1984). *Explaining crime*. New York: McGraw-Hill.

"New proof offered on effects of lead in early childhood." *New York Times*, Aug. 25, 1988, B17.

Nichols, P. L., and T. Chen (1981). *Minimal brain dysfunction: A prospective study*. Hillsdale, N.J.: Erlbaum.

Nichols, P. L., T. Chen, and J. D. Pomeroy (1976). Minimal brain dysfunction: The association among symptoms. Paper presented at the eighty-fourth annual meeting of the American Psychological Association, Washington, D.C.

Nielsen, J., and T. Tsuboi (1970). Correlation between stature, character disorder and criminality. *British Journal of Psychiatry* 116: 145-150.

Niswander, K. R., E. A. Friedman, D. B. Hoover, H. Pietrowski, and M. Westphal (1966). Fetal morbidity following potentially anoxigenic obstetric conditions. *American Journal of Obstetrics and Gynecology* 95: 853.

Niswander, K. R., and M. Gordon (1972). *The women and their pregnancies*. Washington, D.C.: U.S. Department of Health, Education, and Welfare.

Niswander, K. R., M. Gordon, and J. S. Drage (1975). The effect of intrauterine hypoxia on the child surviving to 4 years. *American Journal of Obstetrics and Gynecology* 121 (7): 892-899.

Nottebohm, F. (1979). Origins and mechanisms in the establishment of cerebral dominance. In M. S. Gazzaniga (ed.), *Handbook of behavioral neurobiology. Vol. 2: Neuropsychology*. New York: Plenum.

Offer, D., R. C. Marohn, and E. Ostrov (1979). *The psychological world of the juvenile delinquent*. New York: Basic.

Olmedo, E. L. (1981). Testing linguistic minorities. *American Psychologist* 36 (10): 1078-1085.

The Ontario Department of Health (1967). *Supplement to the second report of the Perinatal Mortality Study in ten university teaching hospitals*. Ontario: Ontario Department of Health.

Overall, J. E., and H. S. Levin (1978). Correcting for cultural factors in evaluating intellectual deficit on the WAIS. *Journal of Clinical Psychology* 34 (4): 910-915.

Page, E. B. (1970). California Achievement Language Tests. In O. K. Buros (ed.), *The eighth mental measurements yearbook*. Highland Park, N.J.: Gryphon.

Parlee, M. R. (1973). The premenstrual syndrome. *Psychological Bulletin* 80: 454-465.

Pasamanick, B., and H. Knobloch (1966). Retrospective studies on the epidemiology of reproductive casualty: Old and new. *Merrill-Palmer Quarterly* 12: 1-26.

Paternoster, R., L. Saltzman, G. Waldo, and T. Chiricos (1983). Perceived risk and social control: Do sanctions really deter? *Law and Society Review* 17: 457-479.

Penchaszadeh, V. B., J. B. Hardy, E. D. Mellits, B. H. Cohen, and V. A. McKusick (1972a). Growth and development in an "inner city" population: An assessment of possible biological and environmental influences. I. Intrauterine growth. *Johns Hopkins Medical Journal* 131: 384-397.

Penchaszadeh, V. B., J. B. Hardy, E. D. Mellits, B. H. Cohen, and V. A.

McKusick (1972b). Growth and development in an "inner city" population: An assessment of possible biological and environmental influences. II. The effect of certain maternal characteristics on birth weight, gestational age and intra-uterine growth. *Johns Hopkins Medical Journal* 131: 11–23.

Perlstein, M. A. (1966). Perinatal brain injury with special reference to cerebral palsy. In J. P. Greenhill (ed.), *Obstetrics*. Philadelphia: Saunders.

Perry, L., E. Harburg, and J. E. Crowley (1978). Urban families and assault: A framework for research focused on black families. Paper presented at the Colloquium on the Correlates of Crime and Determinants of Criminal Behavior, Washington, D.C.

Pilavin, I. M., A. C. Vadum, and J. A. Hardyck (1969). Delinquency, personal costs and parental treatment: A test of a reward–cost model of juvenile criminality. *Journal of Criminal Law, Criminology and Police Science* 60 (2): 165–172.

Pollak, O. (1950). *The criminality of women*. Philadelphia: University of Pennsylvania Press.

Prahl-Anderson, B., C. J. Kowalski, and P. H. J. M. Heydendael (1979). *A mixed longitudinal interdisciplinary study of growth and development*. New York: Academic.

Prentice, N. M., and F. J. Kelly (1963). Intelligence and delinquency: A reconsideration. *Journal of Social Psychology* 60: 327–337.

Purves, A. C. (1970). California Achievement Language Tests. In O. K. Buros (ed.), *The eighth mental measurements yearbook*. Highland Park, N.J.: Gryphon.

Raspberry, W. (1980). Youth crime funds go to the whites. *The Philadelphia Inquirer*, April 1.

Reinisch, J. M., R. Gandelman, and F. S. Spiegel (1979). Prenatal influences on cognitive abilities: Data from experimental animals and human genetic and endocrine syndromes. In M. A. Wittig and A. C. Petersen (eds.), *Sex-related differences in cognitive functioning: developmental issues*. New York: Academic.

Reitan, R. M., and L. A. Davison (1974). *Clinical neuropsychology: Current status and applications*. New York: Wiley.

Report of the Interdisciplinary Group in Criminology (1978). Unpublished manuscript on file at the Sellin Center for Studies in Criminology and Criminal Law, University of Pennsylvania.

Reschly, D. L. (1981). Psychological testing in educational classification and placement. 36 (10): 1094–1102.

Reynolds, C. R., and L. Hartlage (1979). Comparisons of WISC and WISC–R regression lines for academic prediction with black and with white referred children. *Journal of Consulting and Clinical Psychology* 47 (3): 589–591.

Rie, H. E., and E. D. Rie (1980). *Handbook of minimal brain dysfunction*. New York: Wiley.

Roberts, C. J. (1971). Manifestations of cerebral dysfunction in infancy and their association with toxaemia and antepartum haemorrhage: A cohort study. *British Journal of Preventive and Social Medicine* 25: 135–139.

Robins, L. N. (1966). *Deviant children grown up: A sociological and psychiatric study of sociopathic personality*. Baltimore: Williams and Wilkins.

Rogers, M. E., A. M. Lilienfeld, and B. Pasamanick (1955). *Prenatal and paranatal factors in the development of childhood behavior disorders*. Copenhagen: Ejnar Munksgaard.

Rosenberg, H. (1978). Family planning, nutrition, and crime. In L. J. Hippchen (ed.), *Ecologic–biochemical approaches to treatment of delinquents and criminals.* New York: Van Nostrand Reinhold.

Rydberg, E. (1966). Mechanism of labor in cephalic presentation. In J. P. Greenhill (ed.), *Obstetrics.* Philadelphia: Saunders.

Sameroff, A. J. (1975). Early influences on development: Fact of fancy. *Merrill–Palmer Quarterly* 21 (4): 267–294.

Sandoval, J. (1979). The WISC–R and internal evidence of test bias with minority groups. *Journal of Consulting and Clinical Psychology* 47 (5): 919–927.

Satterfield, J. (1987). Childhood diagnostic and neurophysiological predictors of teenage arrest rates: An eight-year prospective study. In S. A. Mednick, T. E. Moffitt, and S. Stack (eds.), *The causes of crime: New biological approaches.* New York: Cambridge University Press.

Sattler, J. M. (1965). Analysis of functions of the 1960 Stanford–Binet Intelligence Scale, form L–M. *Journal of Clinical Psychology* 21: 173–179.

Scarr, S. (1981). Testing for children: Assessment and the many determinants of intellectual competence. *American Psychologist* 36 (10): 1159–1166.

Schachter, F. F., and V. Apgar (1959). Perinatal asphyxia and psychologic signs of brain damage in childhood. *Pediatrics* 24: 1016–1025.

Schafer, S. (1969). *Theories in criminology.* New York: Random House.

Schmidt, F. L., and J. E. Hunter (1981). Employment testing: Old theories and new research findings. *American Psychologist* 36 (10): 1128–1137.

School District of Philadelphia (1979). CSET: Child Study Evaluation Team. Pamphlet, Philadelphia: The School District of Philadelphia (Division of Special Education).

Schulsinger, F. (1977). Psychopathy and heredity. In S. A. Mednick and K. O. Christiansen (eds.), *Biosocial bases of criminal behavior.* New York: Gardner Press.

Schur, E. M. (1971). *Labeling deviant behavior.* New York: Harper and Row.

Schur, E. M. (1973). *Radical nonintervention.* Englewood Cliffs, N.J.: Prentice-Hall.

Schweinhart, L. J., and D. P. Weikart (1980). *Young children grow up: The effects of the Perry Preschool Program on youths through age 5.* Ypsilanti, Mich.: High/Scope Educational Research Foundation.

Sellin, T. (1938). *Culture, conflict and crime.* New York: Social Science Research Council.

Sellin, T., and M. E. Wolfgang (1964). *The measurement of delinquency.* New York: Wiley.

Sellin Center for Studies in Criminology and Criminal Law (1981). Collection and coding of offense data for the Biosocial Project. Unpublished manuscript, University of Pennsylvania.

Sellin Center for Studies in Criminology and Criminal Law (1987). Criminal behavior over the life span: The relationship of juvenile delinquency to adult crime. Unpublished manuscript, University of Pennsylvania.

Serunian, S. A., and S. H. Broman (1975). Relationship of Apgar scores and Bayley Mental and Motor scores. *Child Development* 46: 696–700.

Shah, S., and L. Roth (1974). Biological and psychophysiological factors in criminality. In D. Glaser (ed.), *Handbook in criminology.* Chicago: Rand-McNally.

Shanok, S. S., and D. O. Lewis (1981). Medical histories of female delinquents: Clinical and epidemiological findings. *Archives of General Psychiatry* 38: 211–213.

Shannon, L. (1978). A longitudinal study of delinquency and crime. In C. Wellford (ed.), *Quantitative studies in criminology*. Beverly Hills: Sage.

Shapiro, T., and R. Perry (1976). Latency revisited: The age 7 plus or minus 1. *Psychoanalytic Study of the Child* 31: 79–105.

Shaw, C. R., and H. D. McKay (1942). *Juvenile delinquency and urban areas*. Chicago: University of Chicago Press.

Siann, G. (1985). *Accounting for aggression: Perspectives on aggression and violence*. Boston: Allen and Unwin.

Silverstein, A. B. (1967). Validity of WISC short forms at three age levels. *Journal of Consulting Psychology* 31: 635–636.

Silverstein, A. B. (1969). The internal consistency of the Stanford–Binet. *American Journal of Mental Deficiency* 73: 753–754.

Silverstein, A. B. (1970). The measurement of intelligence. *International Review of Research in Mental Retardation* 4: 193–227.

Simon, R. J. (1975). *Women and crime*. Lexington, Ky.: Lexington Books.

Simpson, A. L. (1976). Comments: Rehabilitation as the justification for a separate juvenile justice system. *California Law Review* 64: 984–1017.

Sims, V. M. (1949). Review of the Wide Range Achievement Test. In O. K. Buros (ed.), *The third mental measurement yearbook*. New Brunswick, N. J.: Rutgers University Press.

Slone, D., S. Shapiro, O. P. Heinonen, R. R. Monson, S. C. Hartz, V. Siskind, L. Rosenberg, and A. A. Mitchell (1976). Maternal drug exposure and birth defects. In S. Kelly, E. B. Hook, D. T. Janerick, and I. H. Porter (eds.), *Birth defects: Risks and consequences*. New York: Academic.

Smart, C. (1976). *Women, crime and criminology: A feminist critique*. London: Routledge and Kegan Paul.

Smith, A. C., G. L. Flick, G. S. Ferriss, and A. H. Sellmann (1972). Prediction of developmental outcome at seven years from prenatal, perinatal, and postnatal events. *Child Development* 43: 495–507.

Smith, M., T. Delves, R. Lansdown, B. Clayton, and P. Graham (1983). The effects of lead exposure on urban children: The Institute of Child Health/ Southampton study. *Developmental Medicine and Child Neurology* 25 (47): 1–54.

Snyder, R. T., and J. Kalil (1968). Item analysis, inter-examiner reliability and scoring problems for Koppitz Scoring on the Bender Gestalt for six-year-olds. *Perceptual and Motor Skills* 27: 1351–1358.

Sorrells, J. M. (1977). Kids who kill. *Crime and Delinquency* 23 (3): 312–320.

Spellacy, F. (1978). Neuropsychological discrimination between violent and non-violent men. *Journal of Clinical Psychology* 34 (1): 49–52.

Spivak, G. (1983). High risk behaviors indicating vulnerability to delinquency in community and school: Final report. Unpublished manuscript, Hahnemann Medical School.

Stamm, J. S., and S. V. Kreder (1979). Minimal brain dysfunction: Psychological and neurophysiological disorders in hyperkinetic children. In M. S. Gazzaniga (ed.), *Handbook of behavioral neurobiology. Vol 2. Neuropsychology*. New York: Plenum.

Stedman's Medical Dictionary (1976). Baltimore: Williams and Wilkins.

Steelman, L. C., and J. A. Mercy (1980). Unconfounding the confluence model: A test of sibship size and birth-order effects on intelligence. *American Sociological Review* 45: 571–582.

Stephens, M. A. (1974). EDF statistics for goodness of fit and some comparisons. *Journal of the American Statistical Association* 69 (347): 730–737.

Stewart, N. (1953). Review of the Goodenough Draw-A-Man test. In O. K. Buros (ed.), *The Fourth Mental Measurements Yearbook*. Highland Park, N.J.: Gryphon Press.

Stott, D. H. (1966). *Studies of troublesome children*, London: Tavistock.

Stott, D. H. (1978). Epidemiological indicators of the origins of behavior disturbance as measured by the Bristol Social Adjustment Guides. *Genetic Psychology Monographs* 97: 127–159.

Stott, D. H., and S. A. Latchford (1976). Prenatal antecedents of child health, development, and behavior. An epidemiological report of incidence and association. *Journal of the American Academy of Child Psychiatry* 15: 161–191.

Stott, D. H., and D. M. Wilson (1977). The adult criminal as juvenile. *British Journal of Criminology* 17: 47–57.

Sutherland, E., and D. Cressey (1978). *Criminology* (10th ed.). Philadelphia: Lippincott.

Swerdlik, M. E. (1978). Comparison of WISC and WISC–R scores of referred black, white and Latino children. *Journal of School Psychology* 16 (2): 110–125.

Tait, C. D. and E. F. Hodges (1971). Follow-up study of predicted delinquents. *Crime and Delinquency* 17 (2): 202–212.

Taylor, E. S. (1976). *Beck's obstetrical practice and fetal medicine* (10th ed.). Baltimore: Williams and Wilkins.

Terrell, F., J. Taylor, and S. L. Terrell (1978). Effects of type of social reinforcement on the intelligence test performance of lower-class black children. *Journal of Consulting and Clinical Psychology* 46 (6): 1538–1539.

Thomas, W. I. (1923). *The unadjusted girl*. New York: Harper and Row.

Tiegs, E. W., and W. W. Clark (1970). *Examiner's manual and test coordinator's handbook: California Achievement Tests*. New York: McGraw-Hill.

Tittle, C. R., and W. J. Villemez (1977). Social class and criminality. *Social Forces* 56 (4): 474–502.

Tittle, C. R., W. J. Villemez, and D. A. Smith (1978). The myth of social class and criminality: An empirical assessment of the empirical evidence. *American Sociological Review* 43: 643–656.

Tomlinson-Keasey, C., and C. B. Keasey (1974). The mediating role of cognitive development in moral judgment. *Child Development* 45: 291–298.

Torrey, E. F., S. P. Hersh, and K. D. McCabe (1975). Early childhood psychosis and bleeding during pregnancy: A prospective study of gravid women and their offspring. *Journal of Autism and Childhood Schizophrenia* 5 (4): 287–297.

Towbin, A. (1971). Organic causes of minimal brain dysfunction: Perinatal origin of minimal cerebral lesions. *Journal of the American Medical Association* 217: 1207–1214.

Tracy, P., M. Wolfgang, and R. Figlio (1985). *Delinquency in two birth cohorts: Executive summary*. Washington, D.C.: U.S. Department of Justice.

U.S. Department of Health, Education, and Welfare (1966). *The collaborative study on cerebral palsy, mental retardation, and other neurological and sensory disorders of infancy and childhood*. Part III–A: Obstetrics; Part III–B: Pediatric-Neurology; Part III–C: Socioeconomics, Genetics, Virology, Pathology, General; Part III–D: Behavioral Examinations. Bethesda, Md.: National Institutes of Health.

U.S. Department of Health, Education, and Welfare (1970). *The collaborative study on cerebral palsy, mental retardation, and other neurological and sen-*

sory disorders of infancy and childhood. Part III–E: 7-Year and Final. Bethesda, Md.: National Institutes of Health.

U.S. Department of Justice (1985). FBI Uniform Crime Reports, 1984.

Vance, H. B., and P. E. Gaynor (1976). A note on cultural differences as reflected in the Wechsler intelligence scale for children. *The Journal of Genetic Psychology* 129: 171–172.

Vance, H. B., and N. Hankins (1979). Preliminary study of black and white differences on the revised Wechsler intelligence scale for children. *Journal of Clinical Psychology* 35 (4): 815–819.

Vandenberg, S. G. (1973). Possible hereditary factors in minimal brain dysfunction. *Annals of the New York Academy of Sciences* 205: 223–230.

Van Dusen, K., S. Mednick, W. Gabrielli, and B. Hutchings (1983). Social class and crime in an adoption cohort. *Journal of Criminal Law and Criminology* 74: 249–269.

Vedder, C., and D. Somerville (1970). *The delinquent girl.* Springfield, Ill.: Thomas.

Virkkunen, M., and P. Luukkonen (1977). WAIS (Wechsler Adult Intelligence Scale) performances in antisocial personality (disorder). *Acta Psychiatrica Scandinavica* 55: 220–224.

Vold, G. B. (1979). *Theoretical criminology* (2nd ed.). New York: Oxford University Press.

Voors, A. W., T. A. Foster, R. R. Frerichs, L. S. Webber, and G. S. Berenson (1976). Studies of blood pressure in children, ages 5–14 years, in a total biracial community: The Bogalusa Heart Study. *Circulation* 54 (2): 319–327.

Waber, D. P. (1976). Sex differences in cognition: A function of maturation rate? *Science* 192: 572–574.

Waber, D. P. (1977). Sex differences in mental abilities, hemispheric lateralization, and rate of physical growth at adolescence. *Developmental Psychology.* 13 (1): 29–38.

Waber, D. P. (1980). Maturation: Thoughts on renewing an old acquaintance. In D. Caplan (ed.), *Biological studies of mental processes.* Cambridge: MIT Press.

Ward, D. A., M. Jackson, and R. E. Ward (1980). Crimes of violence by women. In S. K. Datesman and F. R. Scarpitti (eds.), *Women, crime, and justice.* New York: Oxford University Press.

Washington, E. D., and J. A. Teska (1970). Correlations between the Wide Range Achievement Test, the California Achievement Tests, the Stanford–Binet, and the Illinois Test of Psycholinguistic Abilities. *Psychological Reports* 26: 291–294.

Wechsler, D. (1939). *Measurement and appraisal of adult intelligence.* Baltimore: Williams and Wilkins.

Wechsler, D. (1958). *Measurement and appraisal of adult intelligence* (4th ed.). Baltimore: Williams and Wilkins.

Weiler, C. (1974). *Philadelphia: Neighborhood, authority, and the urban crisis.* New York: Praeger.

Weiner, S. G., and A. S. Kaufman (1979). WISC–R versus WISC for black children suspected of learning or behavioral disorders. *Journal of Learning Disabilities* 12 (2): 100–105.

Welcher, D. W., D. W. Wessel, E. D. Mellitts, and J. B. Hardy (1974). The Bender Gestalt as an indicator of neurological impairment in young inner-city children. *Perceptual and Motor Skills* 38: 899–910.

Wender, P. H. (1971). *Minimal brain dysfunction in children.* New York: Wiley.

Werner, E., J. M. Bierman, F. E. French, K. Simonian, A. Connor, R. S. Smith, and M. Campbell (1968). Reproductive and environmental casualties: A report on the 10-year follow-up of the children of the Kauai pregnancy study. *Pediatrics* 42 (1): 112–127.

Werner, E., K. Simonian, J. M. Bierman, and F. E. French (1967). Cumulative effect of perinatal complications and deprived environment on physical, intellectual, and social development of preschool children. *Pediatrics* 39 (4): 490–505.

West, D. J., and D. P. Farrington (1973). *Who becomes delinquent?* London: Heinemann.

Williams, J. R., and M. Gold (1972). From delinquent behavior to official delinquency. *Social Problems* 20: 209–229.

Wilson, E. O. (1975). *Sociobiology: The new synthesis.* Cambridge: Harvard University Press.

Wilson, E. O. (1977). Biology and the social sciences. *Daedalus* 106: 127–140.

Wilson, J., and R. Herrnstein (1985). *Crime and human nature.* New York: Simon and Schuster.

Witelson, S. F. (1980). Neuroanatomical asymmetry in left-handers: A review and implications for functional asymmetry. In J. Herron (ed.), *Neuropsychology of left-handedness.* New York: Academic.

Witelson, S. F., and W. Pallie (1973). Left hemisphere specialization for language in the newborn. *Brain* 96: 641–646.

Wolfe, K. (1979). The impact of parental resources on childhood IQ. Ph.D. dissertation, University of Pennsylvania.

Wolfgang, M. E. (1955). Cesare Lombroso: 1835–1909. In H. Mannheim (ed.), *Pioneers in criminology.* Montclair, N.J.: Patterson Smith.

Wolfgang, M. E. (1958). *Patterns in Criminal Homicide.* Philadelphia: University of Philadelphia Press.

Wolfgang, M. E., and B. Cohen (1970). *Crime and Race.* New York: Institute of Human Relations.

Wolfgang, M. E., and F. Ferracuti (1982). *The subculture of violence.* Beverly Hills: Sage.

Wolfgang, M. E., R. M. Figlio, and T. Sellin (1972). *Delinquency in a birth cohort.* Chicago: University of Chicago Press.

Wolfgang, M. E., R. M. Figlio, P. E. Tracy, and S. I. Singer (1985). The National Survey of Crime Severity. Washington, D.C.: U.S. Department of Justice.

Wolfgang, M. E., T. P. Thornberry, and R. M. Figlio, eds. (1987a). *From boy to man, from delinquency to crime.* Chicago: University of Chicago Press.

Wolfgang, M. E., T. P. Thornberry, and R. M. Figlio (1987b). Juvenile and adult criminal careers. In M. E. Wolfgang, T. P. Thornberry, and R. M. Figlio (eds.), *From boy to man, from delinquency to crime.* Chicago: University of Chicago Press.

Womer, F. B. (1978). California Achievement Tests. In O. K. Buros (ed.), *The eighth mental measurements yearbook.* Highland Park, N.J.: Gryphon Press.

Yerushalmy, J. (1965). Cigarette smoking and infant survival. *American Journal of Obstetrics and Gynecology* 91: 881–884.

Yeudall, L. T. (1980). A neuropsychosocial perspective of persistent juvenile delinquency and criminal behavior. *Annals of the New York Academy of Sciences* 347: 349–355.

Yochelson, S., and S. E. Samenow (1976). *The criminal personality. Vol. I: A profile for change.* New York: Jason Aronson.

Zajonc, R. B., and J. Bargh (1980). Birth order, family size, and decline of SAT scores. *American Psychologist* 35 (7): 662–668.

Zajonc, R. B., and G. B. Markus (1975). Birth order and intellectual development. *Psychological Review* 82 (1): 74–88.

Zellermayer, J. (1976). Selected remarks on morality and will in adolescent development. *Annals of Psychiatry and Related Disciplines* 14: 98–110.

Zimring, F. (1979). American youth violence: Issues and trends. In N. Morris and T. Tonry (eds.), *Crime and justice: An annual review of research.* Chicago: University of Chicago Press.

Author index

211

Subject index

abnormal movements (females), 87, 92, 93

abortion, 155, 161; spontaneous, 146; uterine bleeding as precursor of, 150

abruptio placentae, 135–6, 137, 157

academic achievement, 125; Biosocial Project on, 31–2, 37, 38; case study on, 116; predictors and, 10, 12, 71–6, 85, 88, 93, 94

academic impairment, 8

achievement levels, 123–4

achievement test levels, 109, 118

adolescence, 25; CNS dysfunction recurrence in, 8, 10

adoptive parents, 182; *see also* parents

age: birth weight and maternal, 155; criminality variable and, 174; intelligence and moral development and, 49; mother's (as variable in study), 177; number of siblings and maternal, 156; offender group differences in intelligence and, 50, 52–9*t*; of offenders, 44–5; research and, 24; test score differences and, 71; test scores and, 64

aggregation of birth-related variables, 158–65

alcoholism, 143, 144

ambitions and aspirations (socially conforming), 37

analysis of variance (ANOVA), 50

anemia, 84, 114, 160; as prenatal condition variable, 150–1

anesthetic shock, 145–6

anoxia, 133, 135, 148, 157

Apgar score, 65, 152–4, 165, 178

arrest histories, 32–3; criminality variable analysis and, 174–5; female offenders', 117, 119, 121;

gender and, 97; male offenders', 109, 114–15; violent and chronic males and, 102

asphyxiation, 157

attachment (social control analysis), 21–2

attention-deficit disorder (ADD), 9; Biosocial Project and, 37, 38; case study (criminal male) and, 110; as predictor, 15–16; predictor analysis, 76, 89, 93

autistic children, 105

bacterial infections, 145

bed wetting, 105

behavioral problems, 32

behavior theory, 4

belief (social control analysis), 22

Bender Gestalt Test, 15, 38, 62, 119, 169–170

bioenvironmental predictors, *see* biological and environmental predictors

bioenvironmental theory of behavior, 4

biological and environmental predictors: ADD and, 15–16; biological theories and, 7–8; Biosocial Project and, 3–4, 5–6, 31, 34–6, 121–2; cerebral lateralization and, 12–15; controversy and, 2, 4, 5, 6; female offenders and strong, 86–9; gender (sex) and, 17–18; hyperactivity and, 15–16; integration with sociological theory and, 24–8; intellectual functioning and, 10–12; interaction between, 19; male offenders and strong, 84–6; mean group differences among adult offender groups and, 71–7; physical growth, 16–17; policy